Border Policing Technologies

MW01518708

This book is a unique and original examination of borders and bordering practices in the Western Balkans prior to, during, and after the migrant "crisis" of the 2010s. Based on extensive, mixed-method, exploratory research in Serbia, Croatia, FYR Macedonia, and Kosovo, the book charts technological and human interventions deployed in this region that simultaneously enable and hinder the mobility projects of border crossers.

Within the rich historical context of the Balkan Wars and subsequent displacement of many people from the region and beyond, this book discusses the types and locations of borders as well as their development, transformation, and impact on people on the move. These border crossers fall into three distinct categories: people from the Middle East, Africa, and Asia transiting the region; citizens of the Western Balkans seeking asylum and access to labour markets in the EU; and women border crossers. This book also maps border struggles that follow these processes, analyses the creation of labour "reserves" in the region, and examines the role that technology – in particular smartphones and social media – play in regulating mobility and creating social change. This volume also explores the role of the EU in, and the impact of the aforementioned processes on nation-states of the Western Balkans, their European future, and mobility in the region.

Whilst the book focusses on a particular region in Southeast Europe, its findings can be easily applied to other social contexts and settings. It will be particularly useful to academics and postgraduate students studying social sciences such as criminology, sociology, legal studies, law, international relations, political science, and gender studies. It will also be useful for legal practitioners, NGO activists, and government officials.

Sanja Milivojevic is a Senior Lecturer in Criminology at La Trobe, Melbourne, Australia. Sanja's research interests are borders and mobility, security technologies, surveillance and crime, gender and victimisation, and international criminal justice and human rights. She is Associate Director of Border Criminologies at Oxford University and editorial board member for the journal *Temida* (Serbia). Sanja publishes in English and Serbian. Her latest book, co-authored with Marie Segrave and Sharon Pickering, is *Sex Trafficking and Modern Slavery: The Absence of Evidence* (Routledge 2017).

Routledge Studies in Criminal Justice, Borders and Citizenship

Edited by
Mary Bosworth, University of Oxford
Katja Franko, University of Oslo
Sharon Pickering, Monash University

Globalizing forces have had a profound impact on the nature of contemporary criminal justice and law more generally. This is evident in the increasing salience of borders and mobility in the production of illegality and social exclusion. *Routledge Studies in Criminal Justice, Borders and Citizenship* showcases contemporary studies that connect criminological scholarship to migration studies and explore the intellectual resonances between the two. It provides an opportunity to reflect on the theoretical and methodological challenges posed by mass mobility and its control. By doing that, it charts an intellectual space and establishes a theoretical tradition within criminology to house scholars of immigration control, race, and citizenship including those who traditionally publish *either* in general criminological *or* in anthropological, sociological, refugee studies, human rights and other publications.

Nordic Nationalism and Penal Order
Walling the Welfare State
Vanessa Barker

Criminal Justice Research in an Era of Mass Mobility
Edited by Andriani Fili, Synnøve Jahnsen and Rebecca Powell

Women, Mobility and Incarceration
Love and Recasting of Self across the Bangladesh-India Border
Rimple Mehta

Border Policing and Security Technologies
Mobility and Proliferation of Borders in the Western Balkans
Sanja Milivojevic

For more information about this series, please visit: https://www.routledge.com/criminology/series/CJBC

Border Policing and Security Technologies

Mobility and Proliferation of Borders in the Western Balkans

Sanja Milivojevic

Routledge
Taylor & Francis Group

LONDON AND NEW YORK

First published 2019
by Routledge
2 Park Square, Milton Park, Abingdon, Oxon OX14 4RN

and by Routledge
605 Third Avenue, New York, NY 10017

First issued in paperback 2021

Routledge is an imprint of the Taylor & Francis Group, an informa business

British Library Cataloguing-in-Publication Data
A catalogue record for this book is available from the British Library

Library of Congress Cataloging-in-Publication Data
Names: Milivojevic, Sanja, 1972– author.
Title: Border policing and security technologies : mobility and proliferation of borders in the western Balkans / Sanja Milivojevic.
Description: Abingdon, Oxon ; New York, NY : Routledge, 2019. | Includes bibliographical references and index.
Identifiers: LCCN 2018059300| ISBN 9781138858930 (hardback) | ISBN 9781315717630 (ebk)
Subjects: LCSH: Border security—Balkan Peninsula. | Border security—Technological innovations—Balkan Peninsula. | Migration, Internal—Balkan Peninsula. | Balkan Peninsula—Boundaries. | Balkan Peninsula—Emigration and immigration.
Classification: LCC JV8295 .M55 2019 | DDC 363.28/509496—dc23
LC record available at https://lccn.loc.gov/2018059300

ISBN 13: 978-0-3677-8661-8 (pbk)
ISBN 13: 978-1-138-85893-0 (hbk)

Typeset in Bembo
by codeMantra

To Dad, in memory of the many borders he had to cross.

Contents

List of figures

List of table

Preface and acknowledgements

Border Policing and Security Technologies is before you against the odds. While I believed this book would see the light of day eventually, the volume in front of you is an artefact of a long, and at times a very difficult, journey, one I (somewhat hastily) commenced in early 2013. I was at the University of New South Wales in Sydney, looking for my next big adventure in the Western Balkans. At the dawn of what will later be called the "European migrant crisis", it was clear to me that the time was ripe to do a project on migration regulation strategies in this part of the world. I remember thinking and hoping that, almost a decade after I left Serbia to take on academic opportunities in Australia in 2004, I would still be considered an insider when I returned to research migration and mobility in the region. I thought that my Serbian passport and prior academic credentials and connections would enable access to research sites, such as border crossings and refugee camps, and government officials and movers and shakers behind the scenes. I remember wishing that things would had changed for the better in my Northern Hemisphere home and that gatekeepers would recognise that a genuine care for this troubled region drives my research agenda. I was, and still am, as passionate about the state of affairs in the Western Balkans as I was in the mid-1990s, when I graduated from Belgrade's Law School. After the war and NATO bombing of Serbia in 1999 I embraced academic opportunities in New York City, and later Australia. As I commenced a PhD programme at Monash University in Melbourne in 2004, a desire to return to the region was constantly there, steering my research agenda towards this part of the world. I remained in close touch with scholars, activists, policy-makers, and professionals working in the field of borders and mobility in Serbia, Croatia, and the rest of the region. I kept contributing to the criminological literature with the Western Balkans firmly in focus, hoping it would assist my colleagues in the region in unpacking many complexities pertinent to crime, criminal justice, and victimisation in this part of the world.

Yet this project has been plagued with difficulties from day one. I know I am not alone in thinking that the Western Balkans is a quite arduous place for social science researchers. Indeed, while mobility from the Global South has been the focus of inquiry for many years now in border criminologies, this region has largely been excluded from such quests. Scarcity of literature will be apparent to the reader when I attempt to review existing research on the topic in Chapter 1. The interest in the Western Balkans, however, rose significantly during the migrant "crisis". In 2016, Frontex (European Border and Coast Guard Agency) identified the Western Balkans migration route as the second largest corridor for irregular border crossers in Europe. The expansion of the European Union (EU) to Southeast Europe, liberalisation of visa regimes, and global developments such as wars in Syria, Afghanistan, and Iraq have had a major impact on mobility in the region, both for people transiting through Former Yugoslav Republic of Macedonia (FYR Macedonia), Serbia, and, to a lesser extent, Kosovo and Croatia, and those from the region seeking asylum or labour opportunities in the West. Nevertheless, researchers have been somewhat reluctant to investigate these important processes. The language barrier is a key obstacle for outsiders: to do research in the Balkans requires a good command of either the Serbian or the Croatian language, at the very minimum. A common issue is also access as obtaining the necessary permits to research mobility and migration in the region is almost impossible for non-citizens. On the other hand, researchers from the Western Balkans have been facing a multitude of difficulties too, such as limited funding, scarce (if any) opportunities to publish in English-language academic journals, minimal support for research from government research bodies, and lack of opportunities for cooperation and exchange of ideas – to name just a few. As both an insider and an outsider my position was rather unique and resulted in the range of (un)expected bumps I experienced along the way. I will return to some of these issues at the end of Chapter 1. Importantly, the timing of this research, while opportune, brought further complications: as I witnessed many times before, a "crisis" in the region is usually followed by a lack of transparency when it comes to government agencies and their general uncooperativeness and reluctance to participate in independent research. This is the main reason why it took me almost six years to finish this book. I am, however, forever grateful to all the people in Serbia, Croatia, FYR Macedonia, and Kosovo who took time to talk to me in either an official or an unofficial capacity: this book would never have happened without them. I am also thankful to my young and talented research team in Kosovo and FYR Macedonia – Qëndresa and Martin.

Border Policing and Security Technologies has been shaped, developed, re-thought, and re-written through a series of seminars, discussions, and conferences over a number of years. This book builds on the vast expertise and influence of many scholars, in particular my dear colleagues and friends Marie Segrave and Sharon Pickering from Monash University. I am deeply indebted to you both; you keep sharpening my mind and broadening my horizons year after year, and for this I am forever grateful. I am even more thankful for your friendship and the pervasive influence you have on me as a scholar and as a person. A special thanks goes to Mary Bosworth, an inspirational academic force from Oxford University's think-tank Border Criminologies, and Katja Franko from University of Oslo (editors of the series in which this book has been published, reviewers of this manuscript, and my academic hosts during the final stages of writing). I am grateful for your time and suggestions, and I am also convinced this book would be even further postponed if I had not secured fellowships at Oxford and Oslo in 2017 and 2018. The Centre for Criminology at Oxford was, along with the British Library, a sanctuary where this book was carved; my gratitude goes to PhD and MPhil students and staff at Oxford for creating such an inspiring and lively environment. I would also like to thank the participants at the Race, Migration and Criminal Justice workshop in Oxford in 2016, where I tested some of the ideas for this volume, particularly key arguments presented in Chapter 6.

This book would also not have been possible without the help of the people I worked with during the years of research and writing: colleagues from the University of New South Wales, La Trobe University, the University of Belgrade, the University of Zagreb, the Victimology Society of Serbia, Women's Room Zagreb, and the Institute for Criminology in Ljubljana. Last but certainly not least, I would like to extend my gratitude to the scholars at Border Criminologies (Oxford) and Border Observatory (Monash), in particular Nancy Wonders, Leanne Weber, Alpa Parmar, Ana Aliverti, Vanessa Barker, and my "academic soulmate" Maertje Van der Woude. I thank you for years of inspiration that made me dig deeper into the fascinating world of border criminologies. A special thanks also goes to Thomas Sutton and Hannah Catterall from Routledge for being so patient with me in all these years of drafting and re-drafting the book.

Finally, the biggest thank you goes to my Serbian family: Lenka, Borka, Tanja, Filip; an amazing research associate and driver extraordinaire Duško (Baćko) Cerovina; my adopted London family – Nicola, Anke, Max, Ulla, Laurence; Australian family and friends; and in particular my pocket rocket co-pilot Son. It is done. At last.

List of abbreviations/acronyms

CARDS	Community Assistance for Reconstruction, Development and Stabilisation
GA	Government agency
GAMM	Global Approach to Migration and Mobility
EU	European Union
eu-LISA	The EU Agency for the Operational Management of large-scale IT Systems in the area of Freedom, Security and Justice
EURODAC	European Dactyloscopy
EUROSUR	European Borders Surveillance System
Frontex	European Border and Coast Guard Agency
FYR Macedonia	Former Yugoslav Republic of Macedonia
IBM	Integrated Border Management
INGO	International non-governmental organisation
IPA	Instruments for Pre-accession Assistance
IO	International organisation
IOM	International Organization for Migration
ISPA	The Instrument for Structural Policies for Pre-Accession
NATO	The North Atlantic Treaty Organization
NGO	Non-governmental organisation
OSCE	Organisation for Security and Co-operation in Europe
PHARE	Poland and Hungary Assistance for the Restructuring of the Economy
SIS	Schengen Information System
UAV	Unmanned aerial vehicle
UK	United Kingdom
UN	United Nations
UNHCR	United Nations High Commissioner for Refugees
UNODC	United Nations Office on Drugs and Crime
US	United States
VIS	Visa Information System

Chapter 1

Introduction

Transnational mobility and multiplicity of borders

Can you see borders on Google Earth? No, you can't. From [space], we are all equal. God made us that way. But when you zoom in, you see borders. We created them. If you mix in colours it looks nice, doesn't it? ("Amooz" from Afghanistan, field notes from Bogovađa centre for asylum seekers, Serbia, 10 October 2013)

Introduction

Borders as geographic boundaries of political identities, nations, and legal jurisdictions are the product of human endeavours. As "Amooz", an asylum seeker from Afghanistan who I met in the Bogovađa centre for asylum seekers in Serbia poignantly remind us, nature does not warrant the formation of such borders. Human-made borders sometimes follow natural borders; often, however, they are entirely arbitrary. Borders fascinate and excite us. For many, crossing borders means an adventure, a holiday, and a journey of new discoveries. Borders can also be confronting: think, for example, of visual representations of border guards, often dressed in black or dark navy uniforms, equipped with military-style paraphernalia and weaponry, and an attitude that suggests impoliteness is essentially a job requirement. Or one could reflect on ever-expanding barbwire fences and concrete walls that separate states in North America, Europe, Africa, and the Middle East. There are more international borders in the world today than ever before. The proliferation of borders has been followed by their volatility; many of us in our lifetime experienced radical changes in border regimes, following the demise of states of which we were citizens. The year was 1995. I still remember a feeling of utter despair when I found myself at a border crossing in Višegrad, dividing Serbia and Republic of Srpska (a Serbian entity of a newly formed state of Bosnia and Herzegovina) after the disintegration of the Socialist Yugoslavia. The river Drina that I had crossed with my parents many times before on our way to the Adriatic coast was not just a river anymore. It was now a border that parted people, families, friends, and co-workers who spoke the same language. In the distance I could see the Mehmed Paša Sokolović

Bridge, which had been connecting communities in this part of the world for centuries, the very bridge that was the main character of Ivo Andrić's novel that landed him a Nobel Prize in literature in 1961. Bridges were no longer hinges but barriers that were increasingly difficult to clear. More than 5,000 km of international borders that popped up seemingly overnight in the Western Balkans[1] (Hills 2004) after the breakup of Yugoslavia, converted a symbolic demise of my homeland into a palpable reality.

One of the key features of borders is a function they play for sovereign states: they are a formal representation of state power and its ability to enforce social, economic, political, and cultural inclusion and exclusion within its territory by deciding what and whom is in – what and who belongs – and what and who is out. Yet borders are no longer simply the lines that separate nations; they are political, philosophical, socio-legal constructs, fluid, flexible, and often erratic. Borders, as Popescu (2011, pp. 10–11) reminds us, 'play central role in peoples' lives irrespective of their geographical location'. They are anything but static; borders penetrate deeply into the territory of sovereign nations and extend to digital spaces. Thus, borders and bordering practices as a complex assortment of socio-political processes associated with borders (Cooper and Perkins 2014) ebb and flow to and from countries of origin, transit and destination, through a range of border security technologies. Importantly, we experience borders differently, subject to our citizenship, race, nationality, gender, religion, and social status. It comes as no surprise, then, that border scholarship has been one of the fastest growing multidisciplinary areas of academic inquiry (for an extensive literature review and the development of border studies see Wilson and Donnan 2012; Pickering et al. 2014; Vaughan-Williams 2015). Scholars from a range of disciplines – criminology, international relations, political science, legal studies, law, sociology, anthropology, geography, ethnography, and many others – have been drawn to studying borders; their nature, character, and location; connections to global and local processes and actors; border struggles; and the impact of bordering practices on people in both the Global North and the Global South. Yet, while borders have been in the focus of academic inquiry for quite some time, a unified theory of borders and bordering remains elusive.

Border Policing and Security Technologies builds on this burgeoning scholarship, some of which I will introduce later in this chapter. The book aims to shed (however partial) light on this under-researched part of Europe, in which political instability, powerful gatekeepers, limited access, language restrictions, lack of funding opportunities, and other obstacles have kept researchers at bay for a long time (see Milivojevic 2018a). This theoretical and empirical study examines a myriad of techno-social installations and interventions, deployed to identify and govern mobile populations; it sketches and analyses the migration machine installed in the region prior, during, and after the migrant "crisis"[2] of the 2010s. In the book I focus on redesigned borders of the Western Balkans that simultaneously enable and hinder the passage of three categories of border crossers: non-citizens transiting the region, citizens of the Western Balkans seeking asylum and access to labour markets in the EU (often referred to as "bogus" asylum seekers), and women border crossers.

The crux of this book is in four key points of inquiry. I investigate the **nature and formation** of borders (processes of proliferation, heterogenisation, and externalisation of borders) and the **location** of physical, internal, and digital borders in the region. I also analyse **performance** of borders: a development of what Bigo (2014) called "solid", "liquid", and "gaseous" (or, as I call them, "cloudy") borders in this part of Europe that restrain or enable mobility. Finally, I look at the **impact** of borders and bordering practices on people on the move as they are classified as "green-", "grey-", and "black"-listers of transnational mobility (Broeders and Hampshire 2013). I map border struggles that follow these processes; analyse the creation of labour "reserves" in the region; and examine the role that technology plays in restraining and enabling mobility, and creating social change through the development of what I call counter-security technologies.

Border performativity is a good starting point from which I will outline the central contributions of this volume. Over a decade ago, Nancy Wonders suggested that border performativity

> takes as its theoretical starting point the idea that borders are not only geographically constituted, but are socially constructed via the performance of various state actors in an elaborate dance with ordinary people who seek freedom of movement and identification. (2006, p. 64)

As such, borders are performed through a range of measures and interventions by various actors that simultaneously include and exclude citizens and non-citizens. Drawing on Didier Bigo's work, in *Border Policing and Security Technologies* I map three types of borders that play this important function in the Western Balkans: "solid", "liquid", and "cloudy" borders.

"Solid" borders are those conceptualised as a line of demarcation. They are borders in the most traditional sense, often located at physical borders as walls of segregation that have to be defended by the use of force. They aim to stop and prevent the dangerous "Other" from entering the territory of sovereign states. In the following chapters I outline the development of solid borders as a complex array of fences, military-style pushbacks, and violence that immobilised and restrained people along physical, internal, and digital borders in the Western Balkans. Importantly, solid borders are complemented with "liquid" borders. Resembling "rivers full of locks" (Bigo 2014, p. 213), they regulate and filter human mobility. Contemporary states, Bigo argues, are more concerned with the development and management of liquid borders than with defending solid borders. As Mezzadra and Neilson (2013, p. 3) eloquently put it, contemporary borders, 'far from serving simply to block or obstruct global flows, have become essential devices for their articulation'. In the book, I map external and internal pressures that resulted in the development and expansion of liquid borders in the region, and their impact on peoples' mobility projects. Finally, I also look into the development of "gaseous", or, as I call them, "cloudy", borders. These borders are located and defended in the digital sphere, in computer systems, databases and servers, and within the satellite and drone surveillance systems of the Global South. The endeavour to map the location and performance, and the overall process of the proliferation and externalisation of borders in the Western Balkans, is the key contribution of this volume.

In the following chapters I argue that the EU has been impacting significantly on the region's legal and political systems of mobility management. In doing so, the West has commenced a peculiar process of converting the states of the Western Balkans from the "bad boys" of Europe to the wardens of the EU border regime (De Genova 2017a). Serbia, Croatia, FYR Macedonia, and Kosovo's role in reconciling a free flow of capital, money, goods, and services, while at the same time ensuring that mobility is properly governed, is at the core of this volume. I analyse the development of bordering practices installed along the redesigned physical borders of the Western Balkans, within states' territory, and in the digital realm, and their role in governing mobility. I look at the impact of such processes and argue that, through a range of states' interventions, transiting non-citizens, citizens of the Western Balkans, and women have been labelled as black-, grey-, or green-listers of transnational mobility. Black-listing, as Broeders and Hampshire (2013) note, follows a security logic by excluding known threats (wanted criminals, terror suspects, immigration offenders). Green-listing aims to facilitate mobility through biometrics and automated border controls, while grey-listing sorts out suspicious travellers through the collection of data and risk profiling but also, as I argue in the book, an assessment of their suitability for labour markets and/or asylum systems in countries of destination. As people move on through countries of origin or transit, they are constantly assessed and re-assessed through a range of bordering interventions. Through externalisation of bordering practices, the Global North creates "labour reserves" (Cross 2013): buffer zones where such assessment, as well as border struggles, takes place. Countries of origin and transit are also spaces where mobile bodies reclaim technology in order to enhance their migratory projects, record abusive bordering practices, and create a counter-narrative of migration, one that can potentially deconstruct the idea of migrants as a collective dangerous force (Huysmans 2006, p. 56).

This chapter commences our journey with an overview of contemporary border scholarship pertinent to this inquiry. The literature in what is now called border studies is 'so vast and diverse that covering it all would be futile' (Popescu 2011, p. 12), if not impossible. Instead, in this chapter I introduce some of the works that represent the foundation on which this volume is built, while a more extensive review of relevant literature is interwoven throughout the book. This chapter also maps the recent development of borders and bordering practices in the developed world, in particular the EU. It outlines how, under the rubric of co-operation with non-EU and/or potential and candidate countries, the Union 'essentially externalize[d] traditional tools of domestic EU migration control' (Boswell 2003, p. 619). Recognising that there has been little critical engagement with such practices in the Global South, the chapter sketches an ongoing process of "offshoring" (Pickering 2011) of borders, "Europeanisation" (Zimmerman and Jakir 2015) of the Western Balkan, and their impact on border crossers. Key terminology and methodology are also canvassed, as well as some issues pertinent to access to data and gatekeepers in researching migration and mobility. Finally, the chapter ends with the overall structure of this book.

Border accounts: from border theory to everyday borders

We live in times of the border paradox. It has never been easier, or more difficult, to cross borders, depending on one's identity, citizenship, race, and gender, but also the nature and location of borders. Borders, it seems, have never been more complex in terms of their location and character. On the one hand, they are more than just physical edges of states or transnational unions. As Wonders (2006) reminds us, borders exist wherever border control is performed. They are complex social institutions, 'marked by tensions between practices of border reinforcement and border crossing' (Mezzadra and Neilson 2013, p. 3). Contemporary borders are commonly defined as borderlands, border zones, borderscapes (see Donnan and Wilson 1999; Mezzadra and Neilson 2013; Hess and Kasparek 2017), or even deathscapes (De Genova 2017a). They are described as 'mobile, bio-political and virtual apparatuses of control' (Basham and Vaughan-Williams 2013, p. 509), and sophisticated systems through which people, goods, capital, and money are inspected, classified, filtered, or (temporarily or permanently) immobilised. Borders are also, as Bigo (2014, p. 217) argues, 'series of disconnected geographical points, linked through speed of information and data sharing'. Similar to our understanding of the nature of borders, the importance of borders as boundaries of social segregation, exclusion and inclusion, division and stratification, is also changing. As Walker (2006, p. 57) points out, '[a]lmost all the hard questions of our time … converge on the status of borders'.

Against the backdrop of globalisation in which processes of debordering and re-bordering are simultaneous (Popescu 2011), instead of the predicted weakening of states in a seemingly ever-smaller world (see Wilson and Donnan 2012) we are witnessing an ever-growing debate on borders – where are they, how secure are they, and how can we make them more secure. Underpinned by populist narratives of porous, weak, penetrable borders, border debates have arguably reached their pinnacle in the 21st century. It is hard if not impossible to remember a single election in Europe, the United States, or Australia in the last few decades that has not been fought, and won, on a border security platform. Whether it is building or maintaining walls to stop migration (the infamous 2016 US presidential elections; the 2018 Hungarian elections) or stopping immigration "floods" through border control measures (personified in the "Breaking Point" poster by the UK Independence Party in the 2016 Brexit campaign), clamping down on the "immigration problem" has been *the platform* for conservative, right-wing politics across the Global North. As Hungary's foreign affairs and trade minister told the media in June 2018, '[i]t's obvious that migration became the key factor of deciding the outcome of national parliamentary elections' (Turak 2018). Contemporary borders are, thus, seen as crucial in delineating between 'inside and outside, us and them, safe and dangerous, known and unknown' (Amoore et al. 2008, p. 96).

The regulatory nature of borders has been extensively documented in border scholarship (Mau et al. 2012; Mezzadra and Neilson 2013; Cooper and Perkins 2015; for a literature review see Pickering et al. 2014; Andersson 2016; Newell et al. 2016). Transnational mobility is undoubtedly 'an intensely stratified phenomenon' (Aas 2007, p. 31) as people are constantly assessed against the global hierarchy of mobility (Bauman 1998). Indeed, as Katja Franko (Aas 2007, p. 98) observed over a decade ago, '[r]ather than creating "citizens of the world", the globalising process seems to be dividing the world; creating and even deepening the "us" and "them" mentality – the national from the foreign'. In the world where the freedom of movement is bound to national boundaries, and where the right to leave refers to one's own country (Article 13 of the Universal Declaration of Human Rights; see also Weber 2015b) but not to a right to mobility (Milivojevic et al. 2017), the social sorting of the mobile population – classification of people that leads to their differential treatment (Lyon 2007a) – is largely based on their risk assessment and desirability in globalised labour markets. Risk associated with migration and mobility refers not only to national security but also to "the fabric of the nation" in cultural, social, and economic contexts (see Sassen 1999; Cornelisse 2015; Vasilev 2015). In what is commonly called a "world in motion", the limited mobility of those who need it most is a commonplace. Those from the least "desirable" nations and races, who have little social or economic capital, have been barred or discouraged from pursuing mobility (Bauman 1998; Kaufmann 2002; Adey 2009) and constructed as 'scapegoats for globalization-induced fears' (Popescu 2011, p. 84). The excluded encompass a broad category of "Other": from members of organized crime networks, potential terrorists, and paedophiles to illegalised non-citizens, refugees, asylum seekers, unskilled migrants, and migrant sex workers. A crisis over boundaries (Berman 2003) underpinned by an ever-growing catalogue of "threats" and perceived inability of nation-states to regulate mobile populations is just one of the many anxieties that characterise the globalised world; importantly, this anxiety has significant policy, legal, and social outcomes in the Global North and the Global South.

The developed world is firmly set on a path of strengthening immigration laws and its borders. Separating what Adey (2006) calls kinetic elites from the kinetic underclass has been formalised through a series of legislative and policy interventions in the area of border management, including pre-emptive and retroactive measures at geographical borders, in countries of origin and transit. As Leanne Weber (2013, p. 1) puts it, '[s]o important has the idea of border security become that in most developed countries, immigration control measures have spread to numerous "sites of enforcement", other than the physical border'. As such, a range of interventions that seek to regulate prospective border crossers target people long before they reach physical borders. Cataloguing green- and black-listers of transnational mobility in countries of origin and transit is now a centrepiece of states' migration and mobility control policies. Equal capital is invested in accelerating mobility of desired populations and preventing or removing undesired populations from a state's territory. At the same time, those assessed as suspicious (grey-listers) are subjected to additional risk analysis and profiling (Broeders and Hampshire 2013). Like a sieve, borders categorise and re-categorise men, women, and children, from the point of departure to long after they arrive in their country of destination. New frontlines in border policing include schools, hospitals, airspace, international waters, offshore processing centres, embassies, the Internet, and social media. Re-bordering is performed through a range of security technologies (Neal 2009; Milivojevic 2013) – technology-human interconnections developed to strengthen the flanks of the Empire and regulate mobility flows. Surveillance of mobile populations is emerging as a preferred method for strengthening risky borderlands. Across the Global South drones are increasingly deployed to identify undocumented migrants prior to border crossing (Hayes and Vermeulen 2012). They now patrol not only the maritime borders of the EU, the UK, Australia, and the deadly US–Mexico border but also the green borders of Turkey, Ukraine, Chile, and Serbia (Stein 2013; *ABC News*, 12 September 2014; *Press Online*, 19 October 2011; Cupolo 2013).

Many contemporary bordering strategies can be characterised as practices of crimmigration (Stumpf 2007; Aas 2011; Aliverti 2013), in which immigration and criminal justice processes come together within the context of the securitisation of migration. Security is one of the oldest and most basic functions of borders (Popescu 2011, p. 81), yet it has a whole new meaning in the era of globalisation. Security function of the border has been redesigned to protect national security against the threat that comes from across the border. Through the process of securitisation, the "normal politics" of migration have transformed into "emergency politics". Border policing, wherever it might be deployed, is arguably becoming more violent and deadly (see Weber and Pickering 2011; Bauböck 2015). As "regular" avenues diminish, transnational mobility remains achievable via undocumented means and irregular routes. Notwithstanding the graphic images of toddlers washing up on the shores of the Mediterranean or haunting videos of vessels smashing against the rocks at the shore of Christmas Island, the "collateral damage" of border control is increasingly accepted, if not normalised, in the public discourse of the West. The necessity of border protection, and the ultimate and common good that is at stake warrants, if not justifies, such tragedies. Borders are 'willing to tolerate casualties' (Inda, cited in Khosravi 2010, p. 29; see also Weber and Pickering 2011; Vaughan-Williams 2015).

Yet borders are never completely shut for grey-listers of transnational mobility. Neoliberal economies and demand for cheap labour drive a need for a constant supply of exploitable, low skilled workforce in countries of destination. While 'high levels of migration have caused governments to identify immigration as a potential threat to national identity and state security', as Zedner (2009, p. 59) argues, 'it is arguable that this conceals deeper concerns about ... maintaining control over labour markets'. Indeed, the demand for and control of labour reserves have for quite some time been a backbone of nation-states' mobility governance. As Vaughan-Williams (2015, p. 17) notes, neoliberal flexible migration policies respond quickly to the likely future demands of labour markets. In that sense, 'even the most physically intimidating of these new walls serves to regulate rather than exclude legal and illegal migrant labor' (Brown, cited in Mezzadra and Neilson 2013, p. 8). In fact, border control always involves economic motivations (De Genova 2010; Barker 2015) as borders continue to 'play a key role in producing the times and spaces of global capitalism' (Mezzadra and Neilson 2013, p. 4). I will revisit this important point later in the book. In the following section I look at the proliferation of borders in the EU – a 'new border laboratory' (Hess and Kasparek 2017, p. 60).

Border multiplication and externalisation in the EU: from regulating migration to governing mobility

The development of borders as a regulatory mechanism to strengthen its liberalised economies and political systems has been a constitutional part of European history. The core of what is going to be the future EU emerged in the 1970s, with a range of measures set to manage migratory flows (Boswell 2003). The 1980s brought further developments, such as the Single European Act, which saw the implementation of the Single European Market Initiative with free movement of goods, services, capital, and labour (Staab 2011). A purportedly borderless Union emerged in the 1990s as a product of global debordering, an artefact of globalisation and growing neoliberal capitalism that followed the end of the Cold War. As 'the most developed example of a post-sovereign society and normative power' (Csernatoni 2018, p. 178), the EU provided its citizens with unlimited freedom of movement within its borders. With the demise of internal borders, however, many others began to emerge to address "new threats", such as drugs and human trafficking, organised crime, and increased migratory pressures from the East. The external borders of the EU have ever since been hardened and supplemented by the emergence of new regions, such as the Western Balkans, Central/Eastern Europe, the Nordic region, and the like (see Scott 2012). The EU experiment, thus, represents 'a particularly salient example of how the functions, significance and symbolism of state borders have shifted' (Scott 2012, p. 84).

Following the fall of the Iron Curtain, the *Maastricht Treaty* (signed 1992; effective 1 November 1993) and the *Schengen Agreement* (signed 1985; effective 26 March 1995) set security, mobility, and borders on a central stage in the European political arena. Removing internal physical borders between member states was followed by the fortification of external ones. Political parties sought to gain electoral support by calling to regulate and curb migration (Boswell 2003, p. 621), amidst a growing concern that member states would not be able to cope with (often exaggerated) migratory inflow. There are two key phases of post-Schengen mobility management in the EU: the first phase (1999–2005) saw the harmonisation of legal frameworks with the *acquis communitaire*[3] (in further text the *acquis*), while in the second phase (2005–2010) conditions for legal migration were aligned, and areas for co-operation in combating irregular migration were established. The two phases amalgamated in 2010 (for more on this see Vaughan-Williams 2015).

The *Maastricht Treaty* positioned migration and asylum within Justice and Home Affairs (Pillar III of the EU). This was significant as member states had the power to initiate legislation changes on Pillar III issues, while the European Council that comprises national ministers had to verify such changes in order for a regulation to pass. However, the *Treaty of Amsterdam* (signed 1997; effective 1 May 1999) shifted portfolios of immigration and asylum to Pillar I of the EU, within its newly formed Area of Freedom, Security, and Justice. As such, migration and mobility have now been linked to police and judicial matters, and only the European Commission was permitted to submit legislative proposals to the European Council and the European Parliament, thereby strengthening the role of the EU in migration and mobility management (for more details see Feldman 2012; also Staab 2011). "Unauthorised mobility" has remained a security concern ever since, only to peak in the context of EU enlargement in the 2000s and 2010s. Framed as both a national and a supra-national security issue, migration and mobility have merged with critical security issues such as terrorism, transnational and organised crime, and Islamic fundamentalism (Popescu 2011; Michalowski 2015; De Genova 2017a). In fact, mobility itself became a security concern and a threat to the socioeconomic and cultural fabric of the Global North (such as unemployment, national identity, and the like – see Boswell 2003). To address those concerns, border security has been further transferred from the jurisdiction of member states to the administration in Brussels. As a result of the *Treaty of Lisbon Amending the Treaty of European Union* (signed 2007; effective 1 December 2009) the decision-making pertinent to border management transferred almost entirely to the portfolio of the EU (Boer and Goudappel 2007, p. 73). At the same time, the development of the *acquis* kept broadening member states and prospective and candidate states' duties in securing the external borders of the EU.

Accompanying these processes was the launch of the European border agency Frontex and the *Global Approach to Migration* in 2005 (renamed the *Global Approach to Migration and Mobility* – the *GAMM* in 2011). In this new and comprehensive overarching framework of the EU's external migration policy, the Commission acknowledged that '[m]igration is now firmly at the top of the European Union's political agenda' (European Commission 2011, p. 2). The *GAMM*'s four objectives have been defined as

> better organising legal migration, and fostering well-managed mobility; preventing and combating irregular migration, and eradicating trafficking in human beings; maximising the development impact on migration and mobility; and promoting international protection, and enhancing the external dimension of asylum. (European Commission 2018b)

Regulating mobility of third country nationals was, thus, singled out as a topic of strategic importance for the EU. Broadening the migration framework to include mobile populations was justified by the need for documented, lawful migration and mobility. As stated in the *GAMM*, '[w]ithout well-functioning border controls, lower levels of irregular migration and an effective return policy, it will not be possible for the EU to offer more opportunities for legal migration and mobility' (European Commission 2011, p. 5). Regulating migration through visa policies and border control mechanisms was, therefore, complemented by policing and monitoring of the mobile population (such as short-term visitors, tourists, students, researchers, business people, and visiting family members – European Commission 2011). A helping hand from a "ring of friends" (then President of the European Commission Romano Prodi, cited in Cadier 2013; see also Aas 2005) outside of the EU was sought as the Union's ability to monitor and regulate mobility was increasingly questioned in public discourse (Boswell 2003; Broeders 2007; Collett 2007).

The European Commission has 'long indicated the importance of cooperating with third (non-EU) countries on migration, in order for the [EU] to achieve its migration policy objectives' (Reslow 2012, p. 393). Temporal changes in border control that focus on conducting checks prior to border crossings have been accompanied by spatial changes (see Mitsilegas 2015), in which border control interventions occur in countries of origin and transit. The Union embraced border externalisation as 'the systematic enlistment of third countries in preventing migrants, including asylum seekers, from entering destination states' (Frelick et al. 2016, p. 194), which recently became a key pillar of EU mobility management (Casas-Cortes et al. 2016, p. 231). This process of "contracting out" of bordering practices (Pickering 2011) developed to counterbalance the perceived vulnerability of the EU after the abolishment of internal borders (Boswell 2003; Collantes-Celador and Juncos 2012) occurs through three key streams: the intensification of visa regimes and compliance-before-travel exercises for regular travellers, the deportation of "illegal" non-citizens, and the deployment of military-industrial assemblage for surveillance and governance in countries of origin and transit. In the following chapters I focus mostly on the third stream of border externalisation. Through this process, the EU has been exporting bordering practices to non-EU states, effectively moving its border outwards (McNamara 2013). Indeed, the external dimension of border control mobilises third countries, especially potential and candidate states, to "do border" for the Union and its member states. This transfer of bordering responsibilities was further consolidated by the launch of the Integrated Border Management (IBM), first applied in the Western Balkans in the period 2002–2006, and European Neighbourhood Policy in 2004 (see Popescu 2011; Scott 2012; Hess and Kasparek 2017). I will elaborate on these developments, in particular the IBM, in Chapter 3.

The central premise of these developments, according to Freedman (2007, p. 136), was to 'keep as many asylum seekers as possible away from external European borders, and to reduce the numbers to whom refugee status is granted'. In essence, the external dimension of EU co-operation in Justice and Home Affairs exports traditional tools of domestic and EU migration control to non-EU states in order to manage migration flows (Boswell 2003, p. 619). Countries of origin and transit emerged as principal sites for the detection, surveillance, and classification of people on the move, particularly men, women, and children undocumented border crossers. A new line of defence was created to 'check individuals as far from [the nation-state] as possible and through each part of their journey' (UK Cabinet Office, cited in Vaughan-Williams 2010, p. 1073). This pre-frontier system of management had a clear aim: to compensate for the perceived vulnerability of Europe (and the Global North more broadly) by assessing mobile bodies *before* they reach the physical border (see Gil-Bazo 2006 for the context of the Mediterranean states). As such, UK border checks are now routinely performed in Paris, Brussels, Calais, and Dunkerque, while travellers going to the US via Abu Dhabi or Dubai are submitted to border control prior to boarding the plane, thousands of kilometres away from the US Customs and Border control checkpoints in New York and Los Angeles. Yet such "cooperation" by countries of origin and transit is simply a rule exporting practice, not a collaborative process between partners (Renner and Trauner 2009; see also Aas 2005; Reslow 2012).

Border externalisation is a bifurcated process: the first segment focusses on regulating migrants through traditional border control measures exported from the EU (such as tough border control strategies, changing national legislation, capacity building, anti-smuggling and counter-trafficking measures, and strict and cohesive asylum policies). As I will discuss later in the book, potential and candidate states have been *instructed* to apply the EU standards of migration control as *conditio sine qua non* of the accession process. Importantly, 'the third countries concerned [have] not [been] involved in the production of the action plans [of the EU]. Instead, the action plans [have been] "brought to the attention" of their governments' (Reslow 2012, p. 394). The second segment focusses on the return of asylum seekers and illegalised migrants through readmission agreements. This segment of the externalisation of bordering practices is beyond the scope of this volume.

New migratory pressures in the 2010s generated by conflicts in Afghanistan, Iraq, Syria, and Sudan elevated mobility and migration to the very top of the security agenda in Europe and furthered what Mitsilegas (2015, p. 18) calls the 'transfer of security consideration of crime control onto the field of migration'. The European migrant "crisis," as it is now known (or, as Kasparek and Speer (2015) call it, a "long Summer of Migration"), brought a temporary collapse of the border regime of the EU and its member states. The process of re-bordering that commenced in mid-2015 has been particularly salient in countries of origin and transit, following the new *European Agenda on Migration* launched by the European Commission in 2015 and its novel "hot spot" approach to mobility management. The pressure by the EU to would-be EU members impacted significantly on states' legal and political systems, in particular in the Western Balkans. As I demonstrate in the following chapters, the outcome was a shift that transformed the region from the backdoor of Europe to the wardens of the EU border regime (De Genova 2017a) and – importantly – custodians of "a labour reserve" (Cross 2013) of the EU. The Western Balkans' role in the EU's "control dilemma" (Lahav and Guiraudon 2000), which aims to reconcile a free flow of capital, money, goods, and services while at the same time enabling the *right number* of the *right people* to cross borders, is explored in detail in this book.

Europeanisation, migrant "crisis", and beyond: the toolbox for mapping borders and bordering practices in the Western Balkans

It is not my intention at this point to reflect on a detailed history of migration and mobility in the Western Balkans and recent proliferation of borders and bordering practices in the region. This will be done in Chapter 3, when I look at mobility of non-citizens transiting through the region. I would, however, like to outline some important concepts that will be relevant later in the book, in particular issues pertinent to terminology, methodology, and challenges in researching mobility in the region.

Themes and terminology

The use of language and terminology is critical in mapping the complexity of migration and mobility in the 21st century. Take, for example, *the Western Balkans*. This geo-political phrase was coined by the EU officials as part of the post-conflict mediation in the late 1990s (Buzan and Wæver 2003, p. 379; Ejdus 2018) and included (at the time) non-EU members of the region: Croatia, Serbia, Montenegro, FYR Macedonia, Bosnia and Herzegovina, Albania, and Kosovo★.[4] As such, "the Western Balkans" does not correspond to physical borders of the Balkan region; it is a political creation of the administration in Brussels. While I offer a brief history of recent socio-political developments in the region at the beginning of Chapter 3, throughout the book I demonstrate that the EU's influence (exhibited by its power to create arbitrary borders in this "new region") extends much further, to mobility management and bordering practices. In order to further emphasise the heavy political connotations of issues pertinent to migration and mobility, throughout the book I frequently refer to *EUrope*. I borrow this phrase from Nick Vaughan-Williams (2015), who used it to emphasise that the spatial, legal, and policy boundaries of the EU are not equivalent with those of Europe. In this book, I use EUrope to accentuate the neo-colonial impact of the Union and its member states in mobility management in the region.

Another linguistically and theoretically important theme is *balkanisation*, commonly used to describe the formation of thousands of kilometres of new territorial borders in the region after the breakup of the Socialist Federative Republic of Yugoslavia. This term also has pejorative meaning, implying a savage nature of the region, marked by civil wars and war crimes; the region that is 'yet to be (re)admitted into the self-anointed circle of genuine and proper Europe-ness' (De Genova 2017a, p. 20). One of the key opportunities to achieve such readmission is the area of migration and border control. As I elaborate in the following chapters, this standpoint is critical in explaining the proliferation and multiplication of borders, and the escalation of bordering practices in the region. Indeed, "doing borders" on behalf of EUrope has been seen as a lifeline for the transformation of the Western Balkans: a critical point that can reverse the process of balkanisation, get much sought-after EU membership, and ensure a return of the region to authentic Europe-ness. The *Europeanisation* of the region, as 'an incremental process reorienting the direction and shape of politics in the way that political and economic dynamics of the EU become part of the organisational logic of national politics and policy making' (Zimmerman and Jakir 2015, p. 14), is another important theme in this volume.

The next key point is the language I use to describe **undocumented border crossers**. While a range of preferences has been outlined in policy and literature, such as "migrant", "irregular migrant", "illegal migrant", "undocumented migrant", and "illegalised migrant", the debate on the appropriate language is ongoing (see, for example, Pasplanova 2008). The International Organisation for Migration (IOM) defines "migrant" as 'someone living outside their country of origin either regularly or irregularly for a period of 12 months or more' (IOM 2008, p. 2). This definition is obviously flawed as migration flows, both documented and undocumented, fall short of the 12 months timeframe (Boswell and Geddes 2011). However, the definition stresses the importance of a more permanent character of migration. Mobility, on the other hand, refers to 'the simple crossing into and out of a national sovereign territory' (Milivojevic et al. 2017, p. 292). It is 'the complement of permanent migration: that is, as any form of territorial movement which does not represent a permanent, or lasting, change of usual residence' (Bell and Ward 2000). Thus, mobility is more temporary and can be a less successful process of movement of individuals within or across borders. In this book migration and mobility is considered in the context of international migration – or, more specifically, as the (permanent or semi-permanent) movement of people from the Global South to the Global North. A 'byproduct of national policies to restrict the legal entry of certain types of immigrants' (Boswell and Geddes 2011, p. 33), combating irregular mobility is now the key component of EU migration policy. This book focusses on mobility of border crossers that is considered to be irregular.[5] According to the IOM, irregular migration encompasses '[m]ovement that takes place outside the regulatory norms of the sending, transit and receiving countries' (IOM 2016). In the following chapters I investigate irregular mobility projects of non-citizens and citizens of the Western Balkans; other forms of irregularity, such as visa over-stayers, loss of status because of the non-renewal of a permit, and the like (see Morehouse and Blomfield 2011), are beyond the scope of the book.

Against this backdrop, the use of the term "migrant" to represent permanent, semi-permanent, or temporary border crossers has been contested in border literature as it implies an economic nature of international mobility. Similarly, the use of "illegal migrant" to describe undocumented border crossers has been discarded as it implies the moral or other unworthiness of certain categories of people (see Dauvergne 2004; Pasplanova 2008; Aas 2013). In this book, while I do refer to **irregular migration** to conform with national and international policies and practices, I refrain from using the term "irregular migrants" as irregularity is ultimately a social construct. Instead, I refer to non-citizens on the move as **illegalised migrants or non-citizens** – to underline the process of producing illegality by state and state agencies through its bordering processes.

Another critical point is the language around the so-called **migrant "crisis"** in Europe. Prior to the most recent migrant influx in Europe, bordering practices in the region were haphazard. During the 2010s, the region was one of the main pathways for illegalized migrants *en route* to Western Europe. Faced with some 764,000 people who transited through the region in 2015 alone (Frontex 2017a), and after being (not so gently) nudged by the EU member states to regain control over people coming from conflict regions in the Middle East (for the context of Croatia see Jakesevic and Tatalovic 2016), nation-states on the Western Balkans migration route suddenly found themselves at the epicentre of the emergency. The pressure was firmly on EU members (Slovenia in 2004 and Croatia in 2013) and potential and candidate states (primarily Serbia and FYR Macedonia, given their central position on the Western Balkan route, and, to lesser extent, Montenegro, Bosnia and Herzegovina, and Kosovo). A range of bordering practices were hastily developed, including fences along physical borders[6] in order to regulate non-citizens' transit through the region (see Frontex 2018d for recent statistics). As I demonstrate in the book, such physical barriers and other state-led initiatives gradually transformed the border regime in Serbia and FYR Macedonia. Borders, which had been permeable during the first couple of years of the crisis, became semi-permeable (Wonders 2006): for several months in 2015 passage was allowed only for citizens of Syria, Afghanistan. and Iraq considered to be "genuine" refugees. However, in March 2016 EU officials announced a complete closure of borders for all illegalized migrants (Jakesevic and Tatalovic 2016; Greider 2017; Milivojevic 2018a). Border securitisation in the Western Balkans resulted in a provisional immobilisation of people, with thousands still stranded in Serbia and Croatia, and, to a lesser extent, FYR Macedonia and Slovenia (Greider 2017). The region turned into a 'parking lot' for people 'no one else in Europe want to see' (Serbian President Aleksandar Vučić, cited in Beznec et al. 2016, p. 57). At the same time, states on the Western Balkans migration route have been commended by the EU for their role in the "crisis" (Teokarević 2016, p. 14). I consider the recent influx of people in Europe a crisis of border regimes (one that does not have a clear beginning or a clear end; Hess and Kasparek 2017) rather than a migrant crisis. As such, I will use the term "crisis" in inverted commas to emphasise the fictitious nature of this phenomenon that has been commonly used for political purposes.

The final theme I would like to elaborate on here is **security technology**. Aas et al. (2009, p. 4) define technology as 'a broad social matrix of action which enables humans to modulate their environments'. As I elaborate in Chapter 2, in this book I focus on the information and communication technology (in further text – technology) segment of security technologies, commonly defined as products that store, retrieve, manipulate, transmit, or receive information electronically in a digital form. Its components are software, hardware, data, transactions, communications technology, Internet, cloud computing, and the like. Technology, however, can by no means be reduced simply to hardware and software: machines, computers, smartphones, social media, databases, cable networks, robots, drones, or nodes. It is not socially neutral; on the contrary, technology in late modernity has to be considered in terms of "techno-social" fusions. While we should not debate technology from the perspective of determinism, technological advancements increasingly shape the world we live in, for better or for worse, and vice versa. As David Kaplan (2003, pp. 167–168; my emphasis) elegantly puts it,

> [t]echnologies are best seen as systems that combine technique and activities with implements and artifacts, within a social context of organization in which the technologies are developed, employed, and administered. They alter patterns of human activity and institutions by making worlds that shape our culture and our environment. If *technology consists of not only tools, implements, and artifacts, but also whole networks of social relations that structure, limit, and enable social life, then we can say that a circle exists between humanity and technology, each shaping and affecting the other.* Technologies are fashioned to reflect and extend human interests, activities, and social arrangements, which are, in turn, conditioned, structured, and transformed by technological systems.

Thus, it is these techno-social fusions in border control that I focus on in this book. As I explain in more detail in Chapter 2, security technologies, as defined in this book, encompass a myriad of technology-human interactions, intersections, installations, and interventions deployed to locate, track, screen, monitor, immobilise, filter, and govern objects of interest in order to identify threats, hazards, and risks. Its aim, to put it simply, is to segregate desired from undesired mobility – a topic that has been the focus of academic inquiry in border criminologies and social sciences more broadly for some time now (Milivojevic 2016). In this book, however, I focus also on counter-security technology as technology-human intersections that enable mobility, have the potential to create social change and alter the way we think about migration and mobility.

Methodology

This book is a product of a research project that looked at mobility and border control in the Western Balkans in the context of EU enlargement (2013–2015). As this research was the first of its kind in the region, I considered it to be exploratory and decided not to be 'crippled by methodology' (Ferrell 2009, p. 1). Indeed, I hoped that this research might be the first of what Pat Carlen called 'an uncharted voyage into an unofficial future' (2017, p. 19). The aim of the research was to document and analyse key debates and processes pertinent to the proliferation of borders and bordering practices in the Western Balkans. More specifically, the research aimed to map the process of border externalisation to the EU candidate and potential candidate states, and capture the impact of these processes on mobility of non-citizens in transit and citizens originating from the Western Balkans. Thus, the most appropriate methodological approach was qualitative as 'the collection and interpretation of the meaning of textual, verbal, or real-world observational data to inform about the causes, nature, and consequences of, as well as responses to, crime' (Miller et al. 2015, p. 3) or – in this case –borders and bordering practices. I decided to apply traditional mixed methods but to focus primarily on interviews with principal stakeholders in Serbia, Croatia, Kosovo, and FYR Macedonia as key states on the Western Balkans route. As this research was not representative, I opted for non-probability purposive sampling that aimed to include main government agencies (GA), non-governmental organisations (NGO), international organisations (IO), and academics working on issues of mobility and asylum in the region. The broader questions driving the research at the early stages of the project were:

- What is the impact of the EU membership and integration process on bordering practices and policies in the EU member states and candidate and potential candidate countries? What are the EU requirements for these countries in relation to border management?
- What is the nature /role of security technologies in border control, crime prevention, and policing of trafficking and people smuggling? What is the role of the EU in developing and deploying such technologies in the region?
- What is the impact of framing (agenda-setting) of the political and social debate on these processes and how they link to broader themes of national identity, post-conflict society, existential threat, and the survival of a nation?
- What is the impact of gender on border control policies and strategies used in border policing?

As I was about to commence fieldwork the situation in the region changed, following what would later be known as the migrant "crisis". Even before I set up the first set of interviews it was clear that a big change was looming in the background and that getting information, especially from government agencies, might prove to be difficult. This influenced my sampling, stirring the research towards a convenience and snowballing method, which I describe below. As the context changed, and the number of transiting non-citizens grew, some queries I intended to pursue were (deliberately or accidentally) omitted, while others were captured – often by chance rather than design. My key research questions also altered to encompass new developments:

- Where are borders located in times of increased mobility? What changes in border regimes, if any, shadow the process of the EU enlargement?

- How is border externalisation materialised in the Western Balkans? What are the EU requirements for candidate and potential candidate countries in relation to border management in times of increased mobility?
- What bordering practices have been deployed in the region, and how are they initiated?
- What security technologies have been designed, developed, and installed in the Western Balkans, and with what purpose? What is the role of EU in developing and deploying such technologies in the region?
- What are the implications of these processes on non-citizens, citizens, and women border crossers? What strategies do they use to resist such processes?

I opted for an open-ended approach to data collection, given the instability in the region at the time of the research. In doing so, I used my existing contacts to set up the first set of interviews with professionals working in the field of migration and mobility. I contacted key government agencies on the Western Balkans route as well as NGOs and international organisations working in the region. As access to some government agencies proved to be challenging (particularly law enforcement in Serbia and Croatia) and time-consuming, I applied a convenience and snowballing sampling approach in order to capture additional relevant participants (government ministries, specialised government agencies, and the like). Certainly, such a change in research design led to some important limitations of this study. I reflect on these issues in the next section of this chapter.

The research comprised of 47 semi-structured interviews in FYR Macedonia, Kosovo, Serbia, and Croatia as well as in Hungary and France.[7] Participants were employed in a range of national and international agencies,[8] NGOs,[9] and academia. Interviews were semi-structured and to some extent tailored to participants (depending on their experience and vocation). I conducted and transcribed all the interviews in Serbia and Croatia, while the rest was done by my Kosovo/FYR Macedonia research team. Most interviews covered the broad topics of an overview of the professional experience of the interviewee; an outline of their organisation and their workday and common tasks; their views on the process of EU enlargement; views and experience on working with people on the move; opinions and practices pertinent to the use of security technologies in mobility management, and their effectiveness; and views and experiences of the nature, structure, and dynamics of mobility of non-citizens and citizens of the Western Balkans seeking asylum abroad. A limited number of semi-structured interviews with women asylum seekers (n = 4) in the centre for asylum seekers in Bogovađa were also conducted. The research included over 50 hours of fieldwork observation in Bogovađa and in the city of Subotica near the Serbia-Hungary border. Observations included the monitoring of a daily routine and informal conversation with residents in Bogovađa, and observing the locations and activities of border crossers near the Serbian–Hungarian border. I have also received two written submissions from governmental agencies in the region (Serbian Directorate for Border Police and Croatian Police Directorate) as a substitute to formal face-to-face interviews. I attended, recorded, and analysed two round tables in Lajkovac, near Bogovada, at the beginning of the "crisis" (all from 2013). Finally, a media analysis of Croatian, Serbian, Macedonian, and Kosovar newspapers was also conducted, covering the period from January 2013 to December 2016.[10]

Drawing on the outlined research questions and primary research data, I identified four broad thematic areas that guided my analysis against the backdrop of increased migration and mobility in the region:

- Nature and formation of borders;
- Positionality and location of borders;
- Performance and function of borders; and
- Impact of bordering practices and border struggles.

Yet, as I outline next, this project was far from straightforward.

Challenges in researching migration and mobility in the Western Balkans

The Western Balkans has always been 'a polygon for geopolitical games, played in the neighbouring countries or in the countries of the region' (Simurdić 2016, p. 3). This part of Europe has long been one of the main routes for men, women, and children on the move, yet what we know about this part of the world is limited. While doing research in the Western Balkans I was constantly reminded why this is the case. Researchers in this region face well-documented tensions with gatekeepers, as we do in the developed world (see, for example, Fitz-Gibbon 2017). However, in researching mobility in the Global South there is a staggering lack of transparency when it comes to bordering practices. Access to information and oversight are arbitrary at best, while the gatekeepers' explanation for denying access are often absent. Certainly, this happened to me too. Almost every attempt to get border police in Serbia (and, to a lesser extent, other states on the Western Balkan migration route) on board was unsuccessful. Serbian police initially explicitly refused to provide access to relevant border agencies, nominate potential participants for interviews, or provide any data about border management. It was only after I requested access to information under the *Law on Free Access to Information of Public Importance* that border police responded to selected questions on the topic. This is disheartening, especially given my previous academic credentials and projects I've done with Serbian police. When asked about lack of access, my contacts in the force explained that the topic was 'too politically sensitive'. As such, they did not want to expose the agency to any scrutiny, especially given the instability in the region, a looming "crisis", and the pressure put on them by the EU. Such lack of engagement has resulted in an incomplete representation of the state of affairs in this part of the world, given that Serbian police is one of the key agencies in mobility management in the region.[11]

Furthermore, a significant number of participants in my research expressed a concern about a lack of access to physical border and border crossings, such as airports. Border monitoring practices that currently exist in Hungary (where NGOs have full access to crossings, airports, and detention centres, and have the right to interview border crossers – participant 10, NGO, Hungary) are a remote possibility in the Western Balkans. NGOs in the region have been mostly unsuccessful in pursuing projects that would enable border monitoring activities. As one participant from Serbia testified, their Belgrade-based NGO tried in vain multiple times to reach an agreement with the Serbian Ministry of Interior in order to gain access to border crossings (participant 4, NGO, Serbia). Needless to say, this lack of transparency begs a question about pushbacks, violence, mistreatment, and other human rights violations, such as violations of the right to seek asylum:

> We are uncertain whether the people who express intention to seek asylum actually get a paper that proves [such intention]. The airport is completely out of bounds. We have no access, ... we simply can't go there. We've been there once and took [an asylum seeker] with us. After that a chief of police called us and said: 'you'll never set foot in my airport ever again'. (participant 2, NGO, Serbia)

> We have no idea what is going on at the airport, no idea how many people seek asylum there. We simply have no clue what is going on. ... There is no explanation for this ban. ... What happens when people seek asylum at the airport? I reckon they are simply told - go back [to where you came from]. (participant 1, NGO, Serbia)

Similar lack of transparency has been registered in FYR Macedonia, Kosovo, and Croatia. In Croatia, NGOs suggested that access has occasionally been given to some civil society agencies, especially after Croatia joined the EU (participant 15, NGO, Croatia). Nevertheless, they still stress that government agencies continue to operate under conditions of non-transparency (participant 11, academic, Croatia; participant 14, NGO, Croatia). In FYR Macedonia, a local NGO unsuccessfully pursued reports of torture in a state-run asylum centre:

> A Syrian refugee reported a torture in [name of the centre]. He gave us the names of eight migrants who also complained of torture. We requested a permission [from the Ministry of Interior] to visit the centre

and verify their allegations. We got the permission, but two days before we were due to visit they were moved to [name of another centre]. That is suspicious. We requested to visit this centre too but didn't get a reply. (participant 36, NGO, Macedonia)

As researchers, we have to be concerned about such practices and call them out. While it is not my intention here to name and shame government agencies or individuals that participate in such shoddy practices, I believe that records of state but also IO and NGOs' engagement with non-citizens in transit, citizens leaving the country to seek asylum elsewhere, and women border crossers have to be the utmost priority and available to all interested parties, in particular independent researchers and human rights organisations. In the absence of such records we can only speculate why the gates are shut and what lies beneath. Alternatively, as I demonstrate in Chapter 6, we can use accounts of those who bear the brunt of such policies as a starting point in dismantling official truth-telling narratives, often obscured by a fog of non-engagement. Countries of origin and transit are spaces where migrants reclaim technology in order to enhance their migratory project, record abusive bordering practices, and potentially create a counter-narrative of migration, one that can deconstruct the idea of migrants as a collective dangerous force (Huysmans 2006, p. 56). They can assist us in getting the full picture of what is really going on, not just in the Western Balkans. I will get to this important point at the end of this volume.

Outline of the book

Within the rich historical context of the Balkan Wars and displacement that I outline in Chapter 3, *Border Policing and Security Technologies* maps borders and changes in bordering practices in the region, and highlights the impact of such processes on border crossers. The book maps for the first time the location of borders and bordering practices in this part of the world as well as their performance and impact on border crossers. It focusses on the development of security technologies in the Western Balkans, strategies to filter or (temporarily or permanently) immobilise people on the move, and interventions that specifically target women border crossers. It also focusses on counter-security technologies – tactics to re-appropriate mobility by people crossing borders in the region through the use of smartphone technology and social media. As bordering practices lack 'serious evaluation of their reversals, unintended consequences and limits' (Ceyhan 2008, p. 120), the aim of this book was to commence such evaluation. By answering the aforementioned questions, I hoped to contribute to our understanding of non-EU states' responses to the ever-expanding demands of Fortress Europe, their role as border custodians of EUrope, and the impact of compliance/non-compliance on their European future and mobility in the region.

This book, notwithstanding its limitations, is an important contribution to border criminologies. It charts a range of border performativities in the Western Balkans, in which state agencies and border crossers "perform" or "do" border in complementing and juxtaposing ways. Some of these processes occur predominantly at physical borders, as I will demonstrate in the case of citizens of the region that aim to seek asylum in Western Europe (Chapter 5). Others, however, occur simultaneously at physical and internal borders – as witnessed in the case study of women border crossers filtered through the migration machine in the region via counter-trafficking strategies (Chapter 6). Finally, some also occur in digital spaces, as I demonstrate in the case study of non-citizens transiting the Western Balkans, elaborated in Chapter 4. A holistic approach that captures border struggles and strategies to re-appropriate mobility by people crossing borders in the region is also novel. Importantly, I hope that this volume generates future research that will further investigate mobility and migration machine in the region, which has, for too long, been almost completely uncharted and whose importance in mobility management is unlikely to diminish in the near future.

The outline of the book is as follows. Chapter 2 examines developments in security technologies in the Global North. In it, I theorise security technologies, surveillance, and risk in regulating mobility, and detail the development of "solid", "liquid", and "cloudy" borders in the developed world. In particular, I chart EUropean border security "assemblage", a de-territorialised techno-social system for recording, stratifying, and managing mobility. In Chapter 3 I look at social sorting of non-citizens in the Western Balkans. I map both socio-political and the history of mobility and migration in the region as well as recent changes in border regimes prior to and during the migrant "crisis". I then outline the nature, location, development, and performance of borders and bordering practices along the Western Balkan route, and their impact on people transiting the region. In Chapter 4 I sketch the process of social sorting of citizens of Serbia, FYR Macedonia, and Kosovo that intended to seek asylum in the West. The chapter outlines the construction of a "bogus" asylum seekers narrative and the impact of intersections of racism and accounts of "illegality" on their migratory patterns. The chapter also looks at the role of the EU in the development and performance of these novel bordering practices, and their overall impact on the human rights of citizens of the countries in question. Chapter 5 provides an exploratory picture of intersections of (im)mobility and anti trafficking initiatives, and outlines how trafficking in people has been used to further restrict women's mobility. In Chapter 6 I theorise strategies that migrants in the region use to reclaim technology in order to further their migratory projects, create social memory of abusive bordering practices, and alter predominant narratives on irregular migration. The Conclusion brings together key points raised in the book and reflects on the importance of studying the nature, location, and performance of borders and bordering processes in this region and the Global South more broadly, as well as their impact on mobility and human rights of people they target. This chapter also maps future directions for researchers, activists, and policy-makers in the region and beyond.

Notes

1 For the purposes of this book, the Western Balkans is defined as comprising Albania, Bosnia and Herzegovina, Serbia, FYR Macedonia, Montenegro, Kosovo, and Croatia.
2 As I elaborate later in the chapter, I use the term "crisis" in inverted commas to indicate the fictitious nature of this phenomenon, which has commonly been used for political purposes.
3 *Acquis communautaire* is the body of common rights and obligations binding all EU member states. It represents an ever-evolving body of accumulated legislation, laws, and court decisions that constitute the body of the law of the EU, and as such has to be accepted by ascending states prior to their membership during the process of accession negotiation.
4 I use an asterisk next to Kosovo to indicate its status-neutrality, as per the 2012 Brussels agreement.
5 Irregular migration is the term proffered in European and international policy – see Morehouse and Blomfield 2011.
6 Hungarian-Serbian fence, erected by Hungary, completed in 2017; Hungarian-Croatian fence, erected by Hungary, completed in 2015; Croatian-Serbian partial fence, erected by Croatia at border crossing hotspots in 2016.
7 In late 2013 I conducted 30 interviews with a range of professionals from governmental agencies, academia, and international NGOs in Serbia, Croatia, Hungary, and France. I also conducted 17 interviews in FYR Macedonia and Kosovo in early 2015. Representatives of NGOs and IOs working on the topic in Hungary and France were interviewed in order to obtain a broader picture on trends and issues in migration and mobility, and bordering practices in Europe.
8 For example, in Serbia – Ministry for internal affairs, Office for European Integration, Commissariat for Refugees and Migration, European integration office, Committee for Asylum; in Croatia – Ministry for social policy, Croatian border police; in Kosovo – Centre for Asylum Seekers; in Macedonia – Ministry of Interior and others. International agencies and organisations that participated in the research are UNHCR Serbia, MAARI Centre, IOM, Helsinki Committee in Hungary and Macedonia, Danish Centre for Refugees, MigrEurop, and others.
9 Serbian Asylum Protection Centre, Belgrade Centre for Human Rights, Croatian Law Centre, Croatian Institute for Migration, Macedonian Young Lawyers Association, NGO Legis Macedonia, Civil Rights Program in Kosovo, and others.
10 This timeframe captures the migrant "crisis" of 2014 and 2015, and a year before and a year after the largest movement of illegalized border crossers in Europe since the Second World War. The final newspaper sample contained 226 news items and 7 TV broadcasts.
11 Only one representative of a Serbian law enforcement agency engaged in border management participated in the research.

Chapter 2

Borders, security technologies, and mobility

> Experience has taught us that [security] practices, at first only applied to foreigners, were gradually applied to everyone. ... [T]he citizen is thus rendered a suspect all along, a suspect against which all those techniques and installations need to be mounted that had originally been conceived of only for the most dangerous individuals. *Per definitionem*, mankind has been declared the most dangerous of all classes. (Agamben 2004, p. 169; original emphasis)

Introduction

The space of governance in a globalised world is defined by technology, not geography (Aas 2005). This statement is particularly true when it comes to the proliferation of borders and bordering practices in the Global North. Migration and mobility management encompasses a range of techno-social advancements that gather information about, and navigate, stratify, and regulate authorised and unauthorised mobility. As Dijstelbloem et al. (2011, p. 2) note, '[m]igration policy does not consist solely of laws and policy measures, but increasingly of technology'. Security is pursued beyond fences, walls, and border patrol guards, at and beyond physical borders. The contemporary "biometric state" has an 'almost obsessive preoccupation with where you are going and who you are' (Muller 2010, p. 8). Gathering information about who we are and where we want to go via hi-tech advancements is both omnipresent and logical. Historically, to have access to, and use of, technology translated into having power (McGuire 2012); nowadays, supreme technology and access to data mean political, economic, and military supremacy.

Since the beginning of the 21st century, scholars from a range of disciplines have focussed on techno-human interventions that aim to locate, examine, categorise, authorise, or immobilise border crossers (see Bigo 2002; Lyon 2003a, 2005; Adey 2004; Monahan 2006; Wilson 2006; Broeders 2007; Amoore et al. 2008; Aas et al. 2009; Neal 2009; Aas 2011; Van der Ploeg and Sprenkels 2011; Broeders and Hampshire 2013; Milivojevic 2013; Gerard 2014; Kinnvall and Svensson 2015; Andersson 2016; Dijstelbloem et al. 2017).

Regardless of whether you are a tourist or an asylum seeker, you will inevitably encounter many tentacles of a techno-social mobility apparatus at some point during your journey. In fact, you will likely be followed and listed in a range of online databases along the way: from the point of departure, through countries of transit, and deep into the territory of your country of destination. Technology is singled out as a critical instrument in dealing with increased mobility, a 21st century's "global security problem" (Bigo 2002). In what some authors call "cyber-fortress Europe" (see Guild et al. 2008; Milivojevic 2013; Pawlak 2014), technology serves to prevent, delay, or divert the arrival of illegalised migrants and to locate and remove non-citizens from states' territory. Importantly, these visible and invisible strategies of control have been increasingly outsourced to developing countries, including the states on the Western Balkans migration route.

This chapter examines the development, role, and use of security technologies in mobility management and border control. I use theoretical frameworks of security and pre-emption of risk (Zedner 2009; Amoore 2013; Wilson 2013; McCulloch and Wilson 2016), and Bigo's (2014) "solid", "liquid", and "gaseous" ("cloudy") borders to analyse advances and tensions pertinent to techno-social developments at physical, internal, and digital borders. I map the expansion of security technologies in the EU and set the foundation for important themes that I will explore in detail in the following chapters: a transfer of such technologies to potential and candidate states in the region and overall transformation of the Western Balkans from the backyard of Europe to a (improbable) key ally and custodian of the EU's southeast border.

Security technologies, risk, and pre-emption: the logic and developments

Security is an ambiguous concept that has dominated public policy and political discourse for decades. Given its omnipresence it is easy to forget that there is not one but many securities (Zedner 2009). Traditionally linked to the ability of a sovereign state to defend itself from external threat, security was for a long time framed around the survival of the state as a political unit (see Huysmans 2006; Zedner 2009). In late modernity, however, security is not limited to the state or external threats. Mariana Valverde (2001, p. 85) defines it as 'the name we use for a temporally extended state of affairs characterized by the calculability and predictability of the future'. Lucia Zedner, on the other hand, calls security 'the condition of "being protected from threats"' (2009, p. 14). A broad, overarching concept of security, thus, includes national, supra-national, community, social, local, environmental, human, and individual security. Merging internal and external, national and personal, community safety and international security, resulted in the multifaceted notion of security that seems to incorporate protection from almost everything – from military conflicts, terrorism, and transnational organised crime to pandemics and effects of climate change.

Security is pursued through a range of security technologies that incorporate the technology of the living (development in genetics and identification via body part prints), optical and electronic technology (laser, glass fibre networks), and information and communication technology (Ceyhan 2008). Ceyhan further argues that contemporary security technologies have been built on three sets of logic: a logic of identification of risks; a logic of management flows of goods, people, and transportation; and a logic of ambient intelligence that seeks to improve the quality and comfort of our lives. The first two logics (and, to a lesser extent, the third) underpin the development of mobility security technologies in the era of globalisation.

In the 21st century, the pursuit of national security trumps other priorities, such as welfare, education, healthcare, and, importantly, civil liberties and human rights. No price tag is too high to obtain security. While the state does not anymore have an exclusive monopoly on the pursuit for security, it has '*almost carte blanche powers* to protect it' (Neocleous 2006, p. 38; my emphasis). Security, thus, is like a fire engine, 'whose dash to avert imminent catastrophe brooks no challenge, even if it risks running people down on the way to the fire' (Zedner 2009, p. 12). The collateral damage that such pursuit causes, it seems, is increasingly accepted as the price that we simply have to pay to be salvaged from the ever-growing arsenal of threats. While objective security as such is unattainable, we keep up the chase through bipartisan support that unites the left and the right. Securitisation as the process of developing and negotiating policies in anticipation of future hazards (Buzan et al. 1998) is a political commonplace. Significantly, as Zedner drawing on Dauvergne accurately points out,

> [n]owhere is the tension between enhancing security and defensive or exclusionary policies more clearly illustrated than the contemporary politics of immigration. Finding the optimal relationship between security and the free flow of people and goods is the big dilemma of modern states and the pressure upon governments to resolve the tension between them is acute. (Zedner 2009, pp. 58–59)

The pursuit of security in mobility management aims to locate and eliminate the threat of unauthorised/"illegal" border crossers, preferably before they reach physical borders. Security technologies play an increasingly important role in an attempt to accurately identify risk and isolate wanted from unwanted border crossers. Identification of risk, however, is an ambiguous task that increasingly targets the future. Since *The Minority Report* – a science fiction short story by Phillip K. Dick, published in 1956 – the idea that technology can assist us in predicting, identifying, and eliminating risk in both crime control and migration management has been examined at length and with gusto in media and popular culture. After 9/11, and with the rise of terrorism to the pinnacle of the contemporary risk pyramid, comes our preoccupation with various techno-social advancements as likely tools for pre-empting terrorist attacks and other crimes (Lyon 2003b; Weber and Lee 2009). Evidence-based risk calculations have been increasingly eclipsed by a desire to address *potential* or *likely*, not *credible* criminal threats. Regardless how distant or dubious, risk, as Weber and Lee (2009, p. 60) note, 'must be constantly identified, managed, and, wherever possible, preempted' (see also Amoore 2013). Pre-emption, thus, is not about a particular event; it 'targets uncertain threats and imagined worst-case scenarios' (McCulloch and Wilson 2016, p. 3; see also Wilson 2013), and, as I will demonstrate in Chapter 5 in this volume, uncertain victimisation. This novel approach materialised in pre-crime society, which 'shifts the temporal perspective to anticipate and forestall that which has not yet occurred *and may never do so*' (Zedner 2007, p. 262; my emphasis). Security technologies in crime and migration management are tasked to do exactly that: predict and filter out would-be wrongdoers and/or undesirables but also those who cannot contribute to the labour markets or social fabric of the nation. Security assessment is in a direct correlation with the precarious subject, the one that is different from "us". As Barbara Hudson (2003, p. 59) suggests, we mainly respond to threats 'posed by people we do not associate ourselves with'. Thus, the "Other" has to be swiftly identified, incapacitated, and if possible excluded within, at, and beyond state borders.

The primary ground for security-driven interventions in mobility management is not a suspicious behaviour; rather, it is a suspicious identity. It is *racialised, gendered, purportedly unproductive, and precarious mobile bodies* to which these pre-emptive bordering practices stick. It is their unknowability, rather than specific threats, that makes them dangerous (Malloch and Stanley 2005). Importantly, it is their ungovernability (Weber and Lee 2009, p. 64) and their apparent inability to assimilate, to be a part of a "civilised" society and to contribute to the economy and the fabric of the nation, that labels them as unwanted. Bordering practices adhere to mobile bodies and generate labels – imprints of people's encounter with border enforcers and security technologies, indicating their (un)suitability for labour markets, asylum systems, and the overall social composition of the developed world. These labels are increasingly applied and read by security technologies in countries of origin and transit.

"Solid", "liquid", and "cloudy" borders: social sorting of mobility

Pause for a moment, and remember the last time you travelled overseas, either by a plane or by a car/train. Did you apply for visa/entry/pre-clearance online? Upon your arrival to the border crossing/passport and customs control, did you go through an automated gate? Did you have any contact with a representative of state agency or border police? If your answer is yes to the first and second, and no to the third question, you are a member of an elite club of *bona fide* travellers, a privileged class of tourists, businessmen/-women, academics, and other desirable groups of people with the right passport for whom hindrances at physical borders and beyond are trifling. If you look more closely into your travel experiences, you will notice a range of techno-social inventions specifically designed and deployed to enable your no-hustle cross-border ventures. These advances have been implemented in your home country, at physical borders, and in countries of transit and destination in order to accurately catalogue you as a wanted, approved non-citizen. Your smooth, apparently borderless journey is, however, carefully and tirelessly watched. In a software-based liquid modernity (Bauman 2000), the decision of who is in and who is out, who can cross borders and who is immobilised, is, while still in the hands of humans, processed and analysed by a range of hi-tech innovations.

Mobility imperatives in the age of globalisation have somewhat altered borders' security function as mobility *itself* became the key security concern (Popescu 2015). In order to respond to the new "reality", borders have been receiving a seemingly permanent makeover: walls, barbwire fences, navy ships, border patrols, and watchtowers are relentlessly hardening the borderlands of the Global North. Contemporary bordering processes, as Bigo (2015) notes, rest on solid borders, conceptualised as a line of demarcation. As I mentioned in the Introduction to this volume, they are borders in the most traditional sense: walls of exclusion often defended by the use of force. Solid borders are impenetrable barriers defended in the Mediterranean and at the US-Mexico border fence via the brute force of a vast military/border police apparatus. However, as I argue later in the book, solid borders can also be found away from physical borders in practices of violence and racial profiling of would-be travellers (see Chapter 4 of this volume). Apparent failure of such barriers in mobility control in the 21st century has prompted the quest for 'more sophisticated, flexible, and mobile devices of tracking, filtration, and exclusion' (Vukov and Sheller 2013, p. 225). Security technologies, such as biometrics that measure and record people's unique physiological characteristics, as well as surveillance of people on the move, have been used in contemporary border policing so much that '[t]he prime function of surveillance' – and, I would argue, security technologies more broadly – 'in the contemporary era is border control' (Boyne 2000, p. 287). It is no surprise then that the technology-migration nexus, especially when it comes to eliminating risky travellers, has captured the interest of a range of scholars in the social sciences for quite some time (Adey 2004; Aas 2005; Lyon 2005, 2007b; Van der Ploeg 2006; Wilson 2006; Wonders 2006; Squire 2010; Dijstelbloem et al. 2017). While academics have long argued that states' obsession with technology fuels the fantasy of total security (Bourne et al. 2015), the race to build bigger, better, and faster border controls is still on.

The idea that borders can be completely shut, however, is largely abandoned as '[l]ogics of passage and mobility are stronger than logics of containment' (Bigo 2014, p. 213). Solid borders are, thus, complemented (but not replaced with) liquid borders. Contemporary states, Bigo continues, are concerned more with the development and management of liquid than with defending solid borders. These borders are like 'rivers full of locks' (Bigo 2014, p. 213) that filter human mobility. In order to obtain security in mobility management states should not simply immobilise; the goal is to follow, gather information about, and govern both desirable and undesirable mobility. Border fortification and fluidity, thus, are concurrent processes. As I will demonstrate later in the book, the interplay between border fortification and fluidity shaped mobility governance in the Western Balkans during the migrant "crisis". Letting through the *right number* of the *right people* is the key logic behind these developments as '[a]gainst the political impulse to exclusion runs a powerful counter-economic impulse ... to openness' (Zedner 2009, p. 59). Borders, as Mezzadra and Neilson (2013, p. 3) would have it, 'far from serving simply to block or obstruct global flows, have become essential devices for their articulation'.

Lastly, borders are cloudy, comprised of a multitude of nodes of information, data, traces, and barcodes, collected and mined by state and non-state agencies via computer databases and information-sharing systems. As Broeders (2009, p. 34) reminds us, they 'play an important role in widening the possibilities to document, codify and store information on the activities of subjects and citizens'. People are, thus, observed, categorised, and (provisionally or permanently) detained or released, pertinent to their assessment in databases and systems for social sorting. Importantly, binary divisions of wanted and unwanted when it comes to transnational mobility are not so straightforward anymore (see Dijstelbloem and Broeders 2015) as people move in and out of each category as they encounter solid, liquid, and cloudy borders along the way.

Security technologies in mobility management, thus, include strategies, policies, hardware, and software that aim to strengthen borders and filter non-citizens (see Koslowski 2004; Brouwer 2008; Ceyhan 2008; Cote-Boucher 2008; Sun et al. 2011; Popescu 2015). They are not simply exclusive/inclusive; they enable 'a *proliferation* of different kinds of people with different statuses and opportunities' (Dijstelbloem and Broeders 2015, p. 23; original emphasis). Some of these mechanisms are explicit; they are what Dijstelbloem et al. (2011) call brute force technology, such as drones and night-vision cameras installed on high towers overlooking borderlines. Others are subtle, almost invisible – such as biometric identification technologies. Regardless of their visibility, the collection of biometric data (digital fingerprinting and iris scans), DNA tests, surveillance, motion sensors, biometric passports, and automated border control gates perform a quick, almost instant taxonomy of *bona fide* travellers, the undesirable (terrorists and the like, for whom borders remain permanently shut), and those in between (asylum seekers, illegalised non-citizens whose merit is yet to be assessed). Mobility that doesn't challenge state sovereignty and contributes to the economic and social growth of the nation is their ultimate goal: the aim is 'essentially [to keep] economies and markets open by allowing the access of people, and by permitting the circulation of labour/work force, human capital and ideas' while 'maintaining control and … staying in charge over these flows' (Geiger 2013, p. 30).

Both state and non-state agencies carry out these practices (Dijstelbloem and Broeders 2015). As Sheptycki (1998) notes, they comply, produce, and exchange knowledge about border crossers in informated space through surveillance from the land, sea, and sky. Thermo-visual cameras (static and mobile; fixed on vehicles or hand-held devices carried by border police); databases for frequent/risky migrants; carbon dioxide detectors; and a range of surveillance equipment on boats, planes, and drones identify, mark, and filter border crossers prior to, at, and post the physical border. Their focus is increasingly on the human body. Indeed, 'the body makes the ideal border, as it is always at hand, ready to be performed whenever circumstances require' (Popescu 2015, p. 103). Biometric data (biometric passports and identity cards, retina and iris scans) and facial recognition technology are key tools for reading and scanning invisible barcodes imprinted on border crossers. Contemporary "surveillant assemblage" (Haggerty and Ericson 2000) includes, for example, bone scans that can determine the age of asylum seekers (Dijstelbloem et al. 2011). Importantly, it is both desired and undesired mobility that is catalogued and labelled. To be a part of the US Customs and Border Protection's *Global Entry Trusted Traveller Program* you need to be a citizen of "trusted" states but also have to allow the US government to collect information about your biometric identity (Muller 2010; US Customs and Border Protection 2015). Similarly, the *Privium* programme allows travellers to Schiphol Airport in Amsterdam to enjoy border-free, no-wait, no-hustle travel – if you have your iris scanned by the authorities (Dijstelbloem et al. 2011). A human body, 'the universal ID card of the future' and an ultimate information storage device, is 'machine-readable' (Van der Ploeg 1999; Van der Ploeg and Sprenkels 2011).

This "migration technology" apparatus, 'a gigantic, cross-border, technology-influenced policy machine that aims to regulate the movement of aliens' (Dijstelbloem et al. 2011, pp. 6, 9), is now found in countries of origin and transit. Before I investigate its deployment in the Western Balkans, I will briefly outline the scope and many tentacles of the migration-technology machine in EUrope.

Cyber-fortress Europe?: cataloguing the "border security assemblage"

Mobility management is indeed a 'dense socio-technical environment' (Bellanova and Duez 2012, p. 110) in which technology is driven by politics, while politics (and policy) is shaped by technology. There is no doubt that mobility control has been one of the most frantic areas of policy development in the EU. While this is a context in which 'the power of the member states has traditionally been jealously guarded' (Balch and Geddes 2011, p. 23), and while EU policies have occasionally been subjected to challenges by member states (especially when it comes to asylum and honouring Dublin regulation), a gradual transfer of migration, mobility, and asylum to the portfolio of the EU resulted in a rather monolithic regime of governance (Koslowski 2001; for a detailed overview of the development of the EU migration and asylum policy framework see Huysmans 2006; Balch and Geddes 2011). In this regime, security technologies play a key role. Yet their development and distribution usually escape public scrutiny (Bossong and Carrapico 2016).

The Union's "border security assemblage" rests on networks of computer systems and databases that collect information about, and follow and analyse mobility. Surveillance as 'the focused, systematic and routine attention to personal details for purposes of influence, management, protection or direction' (Lyon 2007a, p. 14) has been the backbone of border management in this part of the world for quite some time now. The origin of the technology-migration nexus in Europe can be traced back to the 1970s and 1980s to the process of the securitisation of ID cards issued to identify undocumented migrants (Ceyhan 2008). Concerns about migration influx and porous borders that followed the process of unification led to a strong focus on integrated, hi-tech initiatives that could assist in mobility management. The abolishment of internal borders through the Schengen agreement resulted in fortification of the EU's external borders, now containing approximately 44,000 km of sea and 9,000 km of land borders (Frontex 2018a). The administration in Brussels held that '[t]he abolition of internal border controls cannot come at the expense of security' (European Commission 2018a); as such, harmonising and strengthening of external borders was perceived as the logical step forward (Huysmans 2006, p. 69). Indeed, the purported migratory threat from the former Eastern Bloc has been the initial catalyst (see Loader 2002; Bigo 2001) for what is now a seemingly unstoppable pursuit of border security in Western Europe.

The "European Information Society" (Levi and Wall 2004) has been built, expanded, and maintained through 'mass surveillance assemblage' (Levi and Wall 2004, p. 205) that is by no means an 'all-seeing eye that keeps everybody in view from one particular point' (Dijstelbloem et al. 2011, p. 10). Contemporary surveillance of both desired and undesired mobility comprises many digital and terrestrial nodes of monitoring and data collection rather than a real-life version of Jeremy Bentham's Panopticon. A wide range of state-of-the-art technology implemented in countries of origin, transit, and destination is operated by a variety of actors, including, as I will demonstrate in this book, non-EU governments and border agencies. Below, I summarise key points in the rise of the "Cyber-Fortress Europe".

Development, reach, and expansion of migration security technologies in EUrope

The year 2004 saw the adoption of biometric passports for EU citizens and biometric visas for non-EU visitors (Ceyhan 2008), and the establishment of Frontex (the European Agency for the Management of Operational Co-operation at the External Borders of the Member States of the EU, in 2016 renamed European Border and Coast Guard Agency – Frontex). Since its establishment, Frontex has been at the forefront of security technologies in Europe. As Vaughan-Williams (2015, p. 26) notes, although Frontex 'has sought to characterize itself as a technocratic risk manager and mere coordi-nator of EUrope's borders, its profile and the nature of many of its operations are now more akin to those of military-style forces'. Indeed, as Feldman (2012, p. 87) suggests, its very name implies the military-style approach to border management that it was supposed to adhere to. With its own risk anal-ysis model (Common Integrated Risk Analysis Model [CIRAM]), Frontex fosters a large network of information systems tasked with the exchange of data, risk analysis, vulnerability assessment, and operational response on a range of issues, including broad areas of mobility, asylum, migration, organ-ised crime, terrorism, human smuggling, and trafficking in people.[1] Frontex's software, hardware, and workforce is growing, as is its reach. In 2017 the agency had 1,700 officers positioned throughout the EU, while 1,500 officers from the EU and Schengen states constituted the so-called Rapid Reaction Pool. This unit was designed to bring 'immediate assistance to a Member State that is under urgent and exceptional pressure at its external borders, especially related to large numbers of non-EU nationals trying to enter the territory of a Member State illegally' (Frontex 2018a).

While in the early years Frontex focussed mostly on the territory of the Union, offshoring of border management was formalised in 2008. A "Border Package" announced that year aimed to further streamline the passage of green-, limit the access for black-, and increase the scrutiny of grey-listers of transnational mobility. The then European Commissioner for Justice, Freedom and Security, Franco Frattini, proclaimed that 'there is no alterna-tive' but to intensify the surveillance of external borders of the EU (cited in Dijstelbloem and Broeders 2015, p. 22). To do so, Frontex has commenced partnership negotiations with non-EU states and in particular those in the process of EU enlargement – candidate and potential candidate states (see Feldman 2012). New techno-social bordering practices, as Amoore (2009) has noted, now aim to visualise the unknown through annexing, dividing, and isolating people in countries of origin and transit, and in digital spaces. As such, and in addition to Frontex, the principal pillars of security-based mobility management in Europe now incorporate large database systems, in particular EUROSUR (European Borders Surveillance System), SIS (Schengen Information System) I and II, VIS (Visa Information System), EURO-DAC (a fingerprint database of applicants for asylum and illegal migrants), and eu-LISA (the EU Agency for the Operational Management of large-scale IT Systems in the area of Freedom, Security and Justice).

EUROSUR, a 'pan-European border surveillance system' (European Parliament 2013), was 'designed to become the centrepiece of Frontex's surveillance and intervention capabilities' (Bellanova and Duez 2016, p. 23). A "system of systems" (European Commission 2008a, p. 9; see also Dijstelbloem and Broeders 2015, p. 22), it includes a vast catalogue of radars, planes, vessels, satellites, and unmanned aerial vehicles (UAVs – drones) that, through "situational awareness" and "reaction capability", 'monitor, detect, identify, track and understand illegal cross-border activities', and 'perform actions aimed at countering illegal cross-border activities' (Article 3 of the *Regulation (EU) No 1052/2013 of the European Parliament and of the Council*). EUROSUR is, thus, a swarm of eyes and ears, a technological backbone of EUrope's security management. Its jurisdiction includes 'selective monitoring of 3rd country ports and coasts identified through risk analysis' and 'pre-frontier areas' as 'the geographical area beyond the external border of the member state, which is not covered by a national border surveillance system' (Articles 3(f) and 12 of the Regulation). The reach of EUROSUR, thus, extends far beyond the territory of the EU. This is often justified by the purported humanitarian nature of EUROSUR as the system was supposedly designed to reduce the number of undetected illegalised migrants in the EU, the number of deaths by saving lives at sea as well as to increase the internal security of the Union as a whole by contributing to the prevention of cross-border crime (European Commission 2018d). While in this volume I do not focus on the development and components of the humanitarian narrative that underpins the development of "border technology assemblage" (for extensive literature, debate, and critique see Walters 2011; Mezzadra and Neilson 2013; Vaughan-Williams 2015), I will flag some of its examples in the upcoming chapters, particularly when it comes to video and aerial surveillance of green borders on the Western Balkans migration route.

Remotely piloted aircrafts, popularly known as drones, are an integral part of EUROSUR. They are increasingly becoming a super-powerful weapon in border control, one that aims not only to locate but also to physically immobilise "targets of interest" (Bump 2013). They represent perhaps the least visible element of a surveillance dossier, one that can be categorised as a 'sense-and-detect' tool (Kenk et al. 2013). Frontex has been using drones in joint operations with EU member states and has over time expressed interest in acquiring its own drones (Suilleabhain 2013; Hayes et al. 2014; Csernatoni 2018). As the budget for overall research on drones reaches a mind-blowing EUR 3.8 billion, we are witnessing 'an emerging EU drone policy' (Hayes et al. 2014; see also Csernatoni 2018). Not by coincidence, the language used to describe surveillance from the sky resembles a sci-fi movie, saturated with Greek and Roman mythology: a military-style language with a plethora of acronyms describes the aircrafts, systems, and operations of Frontex, while their logos resemble army insignia. The aircrafts themselves carry mythological and/or military-style names, such as "Predator", "Avenger", or "Triton" (see Milivojevic 2016; Martin 2017). As the pursuit of security is not bound to the physical borders of the EU, Frontex drones patrol maritime borders of the EU and green borders of Turkey, Ukraine, and Serbia (Stein 2013; *ABC News*, 12 September 2014; *Press Online*, 19 October 2011). As I investigate in the following chapters, this technology-driven security-at-a-distance (Aas 2012) flourishes in countries of origin and transit. In patrolling people on the move at the fringes of the EU and beyond, drones and other border policing security technologies perform what Wall and Monahan (2011, p. 243) call the 'violent dehumanization' of transnational border crossers.

Given that migration and mobility management is closely associated with identity management (Feldman 2012, p. 117), identification database systems such as SIS, EURODAC, and the VIS have also been at the forefront of the EU's bordering practices. While they were initially established to assist in the identification of offenders, terrorists, spies, and refugees (see Feldman 2012), their task now is much broader as they aim to accurately identify *all* suspicious border crossers. The SIS, established in 1995, allows Schengen member states to share data pertinent to migration, policing, and criminal law. About 90 per cent of data in the SIS refers to 'foreigners or third-country nationals to be refused entry to the Schengen territory' (Van der Ploeg and Sprenkels 2011, p. 77). The SIS's largest sub-database records 'persons to be refused entry to the Schengen area as unwanted aliens' (Parkin 2011, p. 5). Rudimentary features of SIS and its limitations in terms of data sharing, data protection, and concerns about violations of human rights (Koslowski 2004; Broeders 2011; Parkin 2011) prompted the development of SIS II, which was supposed to enable a more efficient exchange of data, including digital fingerprints and photographs. SIS II has been identified as a potential hot spot for the violation of human rights as it stores information about both unwanted non-EU nationals that are not allowed to enter the Schengen zone and those assessed as risky (e.g. anti-globalisation protesters – see Ceyhan 2008, p. 114; for concerns regarding SIS II and violation of human rights see Balch and Geddes 2011; Broeders 2011; Parkin 2011).

The EU's techno-social advancements increasingly focus on the unchangeable "life metrics"[2] of the human body. Indeed, as Popescu (2011) argues, the human body works like a password, providing personal identification to gain access to spaces and services. Key biometric databases in EUrope's security technology assemblage are EURODAC and the VIS. Established in 1997 and effected in 2003, EURODAC is a system for the storage and comparison of the digital fingerprints of asylum seekers, illegalised migrants, and aliens found to be illegally present in the EU member states (EUROPA 2016). This system is a relatively cheap yet arguably effective tool in identifying, capturing, and removing persons derogatively called "asylum shoppers" (see Broeders 2011, p. 53). Visa applicants are registered in the VIS, another "system of systems" (Balch and Geddes 2011, p. 27). Founded in 2007, this database registers people who apply for visa in the EU, allowing Schengen states to exchange visa data (European Commission 2018b). The purpose of VIS is to facilitate checks and issuance of visas, fight abuses, protect travellers, help with asylum application, and enhance security. By collecting biometric data and digital photographs from any person applying for a visa and checking them at the external border of the EU, the 'VIS enables border guards to verify that a person presenting a visa is its rightful holder and to identify persons found on the Schengen territory with no or fraudulent documents' (European Commission 2018b). In essence, VIS verifies whether the person crossing the border is the same person who is a visa holder (Scheel 2017). The VIS also serves to identify men, women, and children who travelled into the EU legally and then overstayed their visa. Finally, the eu-LISA, established in 2011, manages the integration of EURODAC, VIS, and SIS II. Through these mechanisms, as Broeders (2011, p. 49) argues, the EU monitors and regulates the flows of all categories of migrants potentially viewed as problematic – "illegal" border crossers (SIS and EURODAC), asylum seekers (EURODAC), and visa applicants (VIS).

Migration security technologies, however, also capture green-listers of transnational mobility. EU's *Smart Borders* programme was launched in 2013 as 'a more modern and efficient border management by using state-of-the-art technology' (EUROPA 2013). The European Commission proposed this project to facilitate and reinforce border check procedures for foreign travellers (EUROPA 2013; see also Vaughan-Williams 2015). Two new security systems were introduced – the *Registered Traveller* programme, designed to 'allow frequent travellers from third countries to enter the EU using simplified border checks, subject to pre-screening and vetting' (EUROPA 2013), and the Entry/Exit System, which records the entry and exit of non-citizens, calculates the length of authorised stay, and alerts the authorities when breaching of short-term visa occurs. *Smart Borders*, thus, aims to achieve three key goals: to detect and remove the threat of visa over-stayers, to facilitate the migration of those assessed as desired migrants (business travellers, workers on short-term contracts, students, researchers, and the like), and to fill the coffers of the EU as it was estimated that 'in 2011 alone foreign travellers made a EUR 271 billion contribution to our economy' (Former EU Commissioner for Home Affairs Cecilia Malmström, cited in EUROPA 2013).

The most striking feature of this ever-expanding cyber "dossier society" (Laudon, cited in Ceyhan 2008) is its comprehensiveness and capability for an instant and exhaustive search that in seconds produces a vast amount of data about millions of border crossers and non-citizens. As such, techno-social border installations can promptly separate legitimate (desired) populations from those deemed illegitimate and suspicious. They interrupt, facilitate, or temporarily or permanently restrain people based on risk assessment and their desirability in the globalised labour market. Monitoring and surveillance are important elements in avoiding "the danger of overflows" and nurturing the growth of the nation (Bigo 2014) by fine-tuning the migration machine. As Lyon (2003a, p. 142) notes, surveillance and technology was and always will be used for social sorting, for the taxonomy of populations as a foundation of differential treatment. Importantly, while increasingly deployed in the Global South, its beneficiaries are in Brussels, Paris, or Berlin. In the following chapters I investigate the practices of "policing at distance" (Bigo and Guild 2005) in transiting states of the Western Balkans. I evaluate to what extent the techno-social mobility machine has been 'incorporated … into the externalized policing of the frontiers of Europe' (De Genova 2017a, p. 21) and its impact on people on the move in the region.

Conclusion

Giorgio Agamben's quote at the beginning of this chapter sounds ominous; indeed, it is a stark warning that shadows the development of security technologies and, as I will investigate in the following chapters, their extension to the Global South. The world in motion, in which the desire for mobility has never been greater, is increasingly a "bulimic" society where structural inclusion and exclusion happen almost simultaneously (Young 2007). The state is more than ever interested in those that cross borders and those that will cross borders in the future. Importantly, its targets are *all* subjects of transnational mobility as security assemblage relentlessly sharpens and fine-tunes its omnipotent gaze.

In border policing, sites for "smart" surveillance and regulation are borders in their multiplicity. Terrestrial and digital spaces at physical borders and deep inside state territory are locations where techno-social bordering interventions occur. Importantly, the security state performs the watch beyond its borders (Broeders 2009; Zedner 2009; Van der Ploeg and Sprenkels 2011). Physical, internal, and digital borderlands are key sites for 'surveillance, where identities, mobilities and narratives are examined by agents of the state' (Amoore et al. 2008, p. 97) and, as I will demonstrate in the following chapters, non-state actors and foreign governments. Strategies for the surveillance of mobile populations are diverse and dispersed to many points of information collection, from airports in countries of origin to "green" and "blue" borders in countries of transit. Importantly, the migration machine 'reaches the bodies of the people it aims to control and subjects them to a surveillance regime' (Dijstelbloem et al. 2011, p. 11). As such, it is not

> a machine that can be traced to a particular location or an all-seeing eye that keeps everybody in view from one particular point. Surveillance and control refers in this sense to the distribution of tasks and functions that focus on monitoring, registering and checking. These can be found in the clearly indicated points for border traffic (customs posts), but have also *extended right into the capillaries of society*. (Dijstelbloem et al. 2011, p. 10; my emphasis)

Security technologies are carried out by hospitals and welfare agencies, work-places, schools, and universities. They are so vast and geographically spread that a volume like this would be destined to fail if I tried to capture them all. Instead, I will focus on techno-social mechanisms of control carried out by state and non-state actors that observe, filter, or block men, women, and children in countries of origin and transit on the Western Balkans migra-tion route. There is no doubt that this carefully crafted sieve has been con-ceived and developed in the Global North; using an analogy from biological sciences, while its tentacles might be in Gevgelija, Belgrade, or Subotica, its brain is in Brussels, Paris, and Berlin. The EU is a 'security actor in its own right' (Boer and Goudappel 2007, p. 73), and its contemporary security assemblage amalgamates hard and soft tools of border control. Microchip passports, biometrics, and numerous databases that catalogue and exchange data about mobile bodies are underpinned by the logic of efficiency in risk management and migration flows governance. A self-sustained organism of ever-expanding cyber-catalogues, this supra-national, techno-social appa-ratus ought to address the key concern of the Global North: fast-tracking the global mobility of labour and goods, *and* identifying and reducing risks associated with migration and mobility (Aas 2005; Broeders 2007; Amoore et al. 2008). In doing so, they classify and re-classify people as privileged, unwanted, and risky, and everything in between.

Within migration security technologies criminals, victims, and crimes might be imaginary, but borders are not. As Neal (2009) notes, while '[c]rime, illegal immigration, human trafficking and international terrorism are all uttered in the same breath', supra-national hi-tech initiatives seek to address weaknesses in national border controls more broadly. The logic is 'no longer a case of intercepting the "threat" as it arrives at the border, but of "assessing" the "threats" "likely" to emerge in the future' (Neal 2009, p. 349). This logic creates what Wilson and Weber (2008) call regimes of 'punitive preemption' and 'preemptive immobilisation' of certain groups of border-crossers. Cross-border threats have been defined within a familiar context of organised crime, trafficking, illegal migration, and terrorism; yet the actual targets of such interventions are in fact undesirable, racialised, and gendered populations from the Global South. And while efforts to enhance security through exclusionary interventions make no sense and yield ambiguous returns (Dauvergne 2007, p. 545; McGuire 2012, p. 92), such interventions continue to flourish, unchallenged and uninterrupted.

The human body does not lie (Van der Ploeg 1999). The migration-technology machine captures information about unchangeable body parts (such as the iris, the retina, and fingerprints) through the use of biometrics; information is then harvested and exchanged in real-time in the outlined cyber-dossier society. Through the use of automated databases people are promptly assessed and re-assessed as "risky", "grey", or "safe" in 'fresh forms of exclusion that not only cut off certain targeted groups ... but do so in subtle ways that are sometimes scarcely visible' (Lyon 2003b, p. 150). Security technologies are potent tools for further stratification of global mobility as it is seamless, not sealed, borders that are their ultimate goal (Broeders and Hampshire 2013).

The use of security technologies in border policing often results in a "drone stare" 'that abstract people from contexts, thereby reducing variation, difference, and noise that may impede action or introduce moral ambiguity' (Wall and Monahan 2011, p. 239). Through these processes people are reduced to targets, dead bodies to numbers, and civilian victims to collateral damage. As I argue in upcoming chapters, the contemporary border security assemblage hailed as an effective and benign instrument for the further stratification of global mobility is in fact a violator of basic human rights, such as the right to seek asylum and the right to mobility. Importantly, I argue that people on the move have been refusing – and are likely to keep refusing – to be 'petrified and immobilised by the drone stare' (Wall and Monahan 2011, p. 250) through border struggles and the deployment of what I call counter-security technologies. I will return to this important point in Chapter 6 of this book. In the following chapter I map the development of techno-social interventions in the Western Balkans that targeted non-citizens transiting the region during the migrant "crisis" of the 2010s.

Notes

1 Including the Situation Centre, the Information and Coordination Network, and EUROSUR.
2 Greek words "bio" and "metric".

Chapter 3

Social sorting of non-citizens

Transiting "Other", multiplicity of borders, and strategies of control

I think migration and mobility is, if not at the very top then certainly very high on the list of priorities in the EU... [M]igration is important for their growth. ... [EU states] regulate labour migration according to needs. ... This is not about human rights; it's about business. ... The more I know about the EU policy, the more I think they are hypocritical in their approach. ... Pressure is the key word. Everything we do is dictated from the outside. (participant 4, NGO, Serbia)

Migration policies depend on the openness/closeness of the EU states to accept, or not accept workforce, migrants, and asylum seekers. When migration policies are more liberal, the number of asylum seekers [in transit] increases. (participant 31, academic, FYR Macedonia)

Introduction

In a post-Cold War era illegalised non-citizens and asylum seekers are no longer a symbol of the superiority of the West but a source of "asylum crisis" (Castles 2003) or a "system overload" (Loescher 2001). Globalisation generates a sense of anxiety that encompasses the modern state, a condition Berman (2003) calls a crisis over boundaries. Consequently, the Global North has been consumed by a fortification of borders and externalisation of bordering practices that, in turn, alters the social, political, and economic milieu in countries of origin and transit. In this chapter I chart the origins, developments, and impact of multiplication of borders on non-citizens transiting the Western Balkans. I analyse the expansion and proliferation of borders, and the regulation of the mobile population prior to, during, and after the migrant "crisis" of the 2010s. I focus specifically on measures implemented at physical, internal, and digital borders along the Western Balkans route, and argue that, as the migrant "crisis" progressed *the right number of the right people* allowed to transit through was established through the concoction of solid, liquid, and cloudy borders in the region. The goal, I suggest was never to completely immobilise border crossers that kept coming from the Middle East, Asia, and Africa but to regain control over mobility. The buffer zone and "labour reserve" in the Western Balkans, created through careful fine-tuning of bordering practices in the region, are examples of effective migration and mobility management, orchestrated by EUrope and performed by non-EU states. As I demonstrate in this chapter, prospective and candidate states on the Western Balkan migration route have seen the "crisis" as an opportunity to further their EU agenda and as a foundation for de-balkanisation of the region. Importantly, the times of increased migratory pressures have also resulted in a renewal of racism and xenophobia that also impacted on mobility management in the region.

Mobility of non-citizens in the Western Balkans: history and developments

The Western Balkans has had a turbulent and a violent past. For centuries, it was a frontier, separating the world's super-powers: first the Byzantine and Western Roman, and then the Ottoman and Austro-Hungarian Empires. It has also been a place of heightened migration between Europe, Asia, and Africa. In the 20th century the region was impacted by two world wars (the First World War and the Second World War), two regional wars (the Balkan Wars of 1912 and 1913), and the Yugoslav Wars of the 1990s.[1] For most of the last century (1945–1990), the Western Balkans has comprised two socialist states – the Socialist Federative Republic of Yugoslavia under President Josip Broz Tito and Albania, led by President Enver Hoxha. Yugoslavia was a federation of six socialist republics: Serbia (with Kosovo and Vojvodina as Autonomous Provinces), Croatia, Macedonia, Montenegro, Bosnia and Herzegovina, and Slovenia. All nation-states except for Slovenia are now a part of the Western Balkans region. While Yugoslavia was the founding member of the Non-Aligned movement (with India, Indonesia, Ghana, and Egypt) and only loosely associated with the Soviet Union, Albania remained a close ally of the Kremlin until the collapse of the Albanian Communist Party in the early 1990s (for an overview of key developments see Elsie and Destani 2015; Calic 2019). The downfall of communism in Yugoslavia, however, brought not only the demise of the socio-economic system but also a bloody civil war and various armed conflicts that lasted for almost a decade (1991–1999).

Asylum seekers and illegalised border crossers were not a common sight during the socialist times. Socialist Yugoslavia exercised utmost discretion in dealing with this delicate political issue (see Stojić-Mitrović 2014), as confirmed by participants in my research:

> Yugoslavia had a "gentleman's agreement"[2] with UNHCR; formally, we didn't accept [asylum applications of] people from developing countries [because of the policy of Non-Alignment, led by President Tito]. Yet, we let asylum seekers [stay on our territory]. Once in Yugoslavia, UNHCR processed and relocated them to destination countries. (participant 2, NGO, Serbia)

Socialist Federative Yugoslavia was in the Non-Aligned movement, so it wasn't [seen as] good practice to offer asylum to citizens of other countries in the movement. As such, the government basically said to UNHCR - you take it over, we give you access, and you give [asylum seekers] protection and resettlement. (participant 5, GA, Serbia)

The Western Balkans' recent past, as I mentioned earlier, has been tarnished by wars and political instability, which resulted in thousands of kilometres of international borders, dividing the region into adverse, mostly monoethnic states. Indeed, as Lazarova (2016, p. 32) poignantly puts it, '[i]n the last 25 years the Balkans have been among the most active producers of borders'. The term balkanisation (Szary and Giraut 2015, p. 4) is currently widely used in academia and in popular discourse to describe a social process of fragmentation into smaller, mutually hostile groups, states, or entities. During the 1990s thousands of people fled Yugoslavia to seek refuge in Western Europe, the Americas, Australia, or the Balkan region: at this time Serbia hosted the largest displaced population in Europe (Lilyanova 2016, p. 4), mostly Serbs from Croatia, Bosnia and Herzegovina, and Kosovo. In 1999, FYR Macedonia received almost 350,000 refugees from Kosovo in a period of nine weeks (Donev et al. 2002).

Towards the end of the 20th century the region experienced an incomplete transition to neoliberal market economies and a sprout of authoritarian or semi-authoritarian political regimes. While Cohen (2008) suggests that systems of governance in the region could be described as "defective", Bieber's (2012) concept of "unconsolidated democracies" more accurately captures the current tenor in the region. Newly formed states of the Western Balkans were, however, united in their aspiration to join the EU. As Bruns et al. (2016, p. 5) note, the region 'denotes the southeast European countries that represent the next strategic enlargement target of the EU'. At the time of writing, nations of the Western Balkans are in different stages of the accession process: Croatia has been a full member of the EU since July 2013 but is not yet in the Schengen (although formally in the EU, Croatia is still considered to be a part of the Western Balkans region – I will return to this point later in the book); Serbia has been in the process of membership negotiations (a final stage before full membership) since January 2014 but with only two chapters of *the acquis* closed; Bosnia and Herzegovina submitted its application for membership on 15 February 2016 and is a potential candidate state (the first step in the *Roadmap* to the accession); FYR Macedonia has been a candidate state (the second step in the *Roadmap*) since 2005 but has not yet entered the negotiation stage, mostly because of its dispute with Greece over its name;[3] Montenegro entered the negotiation stage and at the time of writing has 31 chapters of the *acquis* open and three closed; Kosovo is a potential candidate for EU membership; and Albania has been a candidate state since 2013.

Against such diverse backdrop of the accession achievements, the states of the Western Balkans (particularly FYR Macedonia, Serbia, Kosovo, and

Croatia, as the key transit countries on the Western Balkans migration route) found themselves at the epicentre of the mass influx of non-citizens leaving the war-torn countries of Africa and the Middle East. As one representative of a Serbian government agency pointed out, when the "crisis" commenced in late 2012 'we expected to [receive] about 100 people a year. ... We thought that this is going to be a temporary influx' (participant 5, GA, Serbia). However, from 2013 onwards thousands of people transited through FYR Macedonia and Serbia (and, to lesser extent, Kosovo and Croatia) towards the West. According to Frontex, the number of illegal border crossings on the Western Balkans route rose from 19,950 in 2013 to 43,360 in 2014, peaking in 2015 with 764,038 crossings only to drop to 122,779 in 2016 (Frontex 2018b). In Serbia alone, in the first five months of 2015 the number of asylum claims eclipsed the total number of claims in 2014 (Beogradski Centar za Ljudska Prava 2016). The vast majority of asylum seekers registered in Europe passed through the Western Balkans corridor: according to the UN, some 80 per cent of asylum seekers registered in Germany in 2015 arrived in the country via the Western Balkans (Cocco 2017). As a result, the EU's overarching framework of external migration and asylum policy – *the Global Approach to Migration and Mobility* – singled out the Western Balkans as a second priority (after the southern Mediterranean region – European Commission 2018c). In the midst of this turmoil, and after decades of unrests and quandaries, the region has been hailed as the new 'wardens of the European border regime' (De Genova 2017a, p. 12).

EUrope has arguably been an architect of the transformation of the region from the troubled backyard of Europe in the early 2000s to the border custodians of the EU in the 2010s. The Europeanisation of the Western Balkans, an antonym to the process of balkanisation described in Chapter 1, has been a bifurcated process of democratic (a promise of aid or membership as a reward for democratic changes) and legal conditionality (requirements regarding the adoption of *the acquis* – see Novak Lalić 2013). Both were put forward for prospective members since the EU enlargement policy officially extended to the Western Balkans in 2000. The region-tailored *Stabilisation and Association Process* (SAP), as the official EU's policy towards the region, has three main components: Stabilisation and Association Agreements as bilateral agreements that establish free trade and common political and economic objectives; economic and financial pre-accession assistance through Instruments for Pre-accession Assistance (IPA) funds; and autonomous trade measures (for more information see Giandomenico 2015, p. 45). The initial key strategy for the integration of the Western Balkans was the *Thessaloniki Agenda for the Western Balkans* (2003), which set the mechanism for implementation of the SAP. At the time of writing, both legal and democratic conditionality continue apace via the Instrument for Pre-accession Assistance (IPA and IPA2) programmes (see Trauner 2011). I will elaborate on these programmes and their importance in mobility management in the region later in the chapter.

Border management has been at the top of the agenda for the future member states since the very beginning of the process of EU enlargement. The Schengen rules have been incorporated into *the acquis* and are an important condition for candidate countries on their journey to full membership (Trauner 2011; Collantes-Celador and Juncos 2012). The Integrated Border Management (IBM) project developed for and first deployed in the Western Balkans was designed to connect the border agencies of (still somewhat confrontational) states and 'establish effective, efficient and coordinated border management, in order to reach the objective of open, but *well controlled and secure borders*' (European Partnership 2018; emphasis added). The main elements of the IBM strategy are:

• A comprehensive approach that goes beyond the security of borders to incorporate trade, transport, health, and safety;
• Inter-agency co-operation – customs, border police, and veterinary services;
• Regional and international co-operation in order to achieve border security; and
• The move from military border control to specialised police forces (Hobbing, cited in Collantes-Celador and Juncos 2012, p. 205).

To assist with the implementation of the IBM and cross-border co-operation in migration management, the EU has set up the *Ohrid Border Process* (2003) as a regional platform for establishing 'core goals and principles that would be followed in implementing agreed guidelines' (OSCE 2006, p. 11). On a bilateral level, states of the Western Balkans have been presented with an individual *Roadmap* for visa liberalisation and EU integration based on four key pillars: document security, illegal migration, public order and security, and external relations and fundamental rights linked to the movement of people (Stojić-Mitrović 2014; ESI 2018). The aforementioned instruments and processes instituted the Western Balkans as a buffer zone for the social sorting of transiting non-citizens during the migrant "crisis" of the 2010s.

Crafting a purgatory: the migration machine at the frontier

Timeline

Scholars in the area of borders, migration, and mobility principally agree that the EU has been creating buffer zones in the developing world for quite some time now, with 'neighbouring states as protective barriers' tasked with permanently or temporarily halting 'irregular migrants in transit on their way to Europe' (Zaragoza-Christiani 2017, p. 59). Under the rubric of

Table 3.1 The timeline of the development of solid borders in the Western Balkans

Time:	Action by:	Event/Place:
July 2015	Hungary	Commenced building a fence; Hungary-Serbia border
Aug 2015	Bulgaria	Border fence; Bulgaria-Turkey border
Sept 2015	Austria	Border controls; Austria-Hungary border
Sept 2015	Hungary	A 175 km fence; Hungary-Serbia border
Sept 2015	Croatia	Border closure; Croatia-Serbia border
Oct 2015	Hungary	A 348 km fence; Hungary-Croatia border
Nov 2015	Austria	Border fence; Austria-Slovenia border
Nov 2015	Slovenia	Border fence; Slovenia-Croatia border
Nov 2015	Slovenia, Croatia, Serbia and FYR Macedonia	Only Syrians, Afghans and Iraqis allowed to pass
Feb 2016	FYR Macedonia	37 km fence; Greece-Macedonia border
Mar 2016	FYR Macedonia	Border fence; Macedonia-Serbia border
Mar 2016	The EU	The EU-Turkey deal
Mar 2016	The Western Balkan route	Border shutdown

co-operation with non-EU, and in particular with potential and candidate, states, the Union 'essentially externalize[d] traditional tools of domestic EU migration control' (Boswell 2003, p. 619). Since the launch of the European Neighbourhood Policy in 2003, EUrope has been fostering what Romano Prodi called "a ring of friends", a network of countries in Eastern Europe and North Africa that benefit from partnerships with the EU without the prospect of membership (Casier 2008). The countries of the Western Balkans found themselves under additional pressure as they were next in line on the enlargement agenda. The promise of full EU membership was a dangling carrot for reforms and policy development in the region. As such, the governments of Serbia, FYR Macedonia, Kosovo, and other nations in the Western Balkans have been tasked with migration management in this part of the world (for the development of solid borders prior and during the "crisis" see Table 3.1):

> The idea is to create buffer zone that will slow down migration [in order] to minimise the pressure. [The EU] wants to enable [transit states] to do that … *so that this region becomes a purgatory* [for border crossers] on their way to the destination. (participant 2, NGO, Serbia; emphasis added)

For the West, and particularly for states in the Schengen Area, this purgatory, conveniently located outside their territory, has been perceived as necessary for the survival of the nation (and the Union). Borders have been moving outwards as new "partners" in border policing were increasingly given resources and the know-how to respond to, and regulate, migratory pressures. As the following quotes confirm, non-EU states (Serbia) and full EU members (Croatia) shared this liability. For Serbia, the Schengen border with Hungary was the key priority; for Croatia, attention was on the border with Slovenia and Hungary (Schengen borders), and Serbia (EU border):

> [Migration] bothers [the EU]: If we are better at it, their borders will be safer, better protected, and they won't have as many illegal migrants. … The EU absolutely wants to control [migrants] outside their borders, and that is us; the borders of the EU are [in] Serbia now. … We are partners, we have access to grants, and they help us a lot in drafting laws, strategies. We know what we have to do. … It is no secret the EU wants to solve the problem [of migration] outside its borders. We need to be a part of the solution, we need to develop our [mobility management and asylum] systems. (participant 8, GA, Serbia)

> The externalisation of border control is the key. … We are the buffer zone. A lot of money went into [Croatian] border control and asylum … Our biggest investments at the moment are two [asylum] centres, one of which will be in Tovarnik, near the border with Serbia. This is where [police] apprehend most of the illegal border crossers. The idea is to send a message … to smugglers and illegal migrants: we will stop you at the very gates of the EU. (participant 11, academic, Croatia)

As Croatia is the only state in the region that has succeeded in joining the EU, the pressures from the EU and the Schengen states for it to fortify its external borders were mounting prior to the 2015 "crisis". While the process of accession 'put [the issue of migration and asylum] on the map, big time… as [the Union] pressured the Croatian government to synchronise the system with the EU laws' (participant 11, academic, Croatia), demands to step up in border control seemed to intensify after the country joined the EU in 2013. Many participants in my research suggested that Croatia is at the bottom of the EU hierarchy, and mobility control is no exception. As such, the Croatian government is simply told what needs to be done. Importantly, as one of the participants pointed out, *the acquis* set 'the minimum standards [pertinent to migration management and asylum]. … For us, for Southeast Europe, these standards were quite high' (participant 12, academic, Croatia). The struggle to reach the minimum standards, and consequences if they failed to do so in the proposed timeline, were all too real for Croatian government agencies, especially border police. For the rest of the region, yet to achieve the proclaimed goal of full EU membership, these minimum standards were potentially a big stumbling point on a long road to Brussels:

> The EU open chapters 23 and 24 [of *the acquis* related to border control and asylum] at the beginning of the membership negotiations and close them at the end of the process. They know this process takes time. It is

not easy to improve border control and migration management to the standards required by the Union, especially when it comes to equipment, staffing, and training. (participant 9, IO)

As the number of non-citizens transiting through the region burgeoned in 2013 and 2014, it was clear that this very issue was going to cause a lot of headaches among political elites in the region. As I outline in the following sections, a complex assemblage of borders and bordering practices was deployed in the region prior to, during, and after the "crisis", aiming to immobilise black-listers of transnational mobility and assess those who are on the grey-list – the majority of transiting non-citizens. This process has had several important stages, and as I demonstrate, each stage was influenced, if not orchestrated, by EUrope.

Phase I (2013–October/November 2015): limited engagement

"No pressure": suspension of migration and asylum regime in the Western Balkans

The civil war of the 1990s and thousands of displaced people from the region mean that the term "refugee" in this part of the world symbolises a citizen of Yugoslavia fleeing regional conflicts (see Stojić-Mitrović 2014). As the migrant "crisis" unravelled, professionals working on the topic in the region developed unique terminology to distinguish between the two groups of refugees:

> [After the Yugoslav War] Croatian refugees were housed in [asylum centres] in Croatia. "New" refugees went there after our refugees were resettled, either because their situation was resolved … or because they moved into the houses of the Serbs [that left Croatia during or after the war]. We call them "new" refugees to distinguish this group from refugees from here, Croatian refugees, because when you say "refugee" people here think they are locals. (participant 11, academic, Croatia)

Faced with the migratory pressures of "new" refugees, states on the Western Balkans route, in particular Serbia and FYR Macedonia, initially failed to create buffer zone for transiting non-citizens. From the eve of the "crisis" in 2013 until October/November 2015, their approach to migration management was haphazard at best: it was largely a policy of *limited engagement*. As one participant from Serbia puts it, 'as soon as we got visa liberalisation [in 2009], we stopped working on asylum and [the integrated] border management. … There was *no pressure* [to build it]' (participant 18, GA, Serbia; my emphasis). Borders were, thus, mostly *permeable*, even though the physical borders in the region operated as solid barriers. Transiting states in the early stages of the "crisis" did make attempts to prevent migrants from entering their territory through border violence and military-style pushbacks. As one NGO activist from the region sarcastically put it, 'I expect to see a comic soon that will portray two border police officers … simply pushing migrants to each other, like a game of table tennis' (participant 4, NGO, Serbia). Physical borders between Serbia and FYR Macedonia, and FYR Macedonia and Greece were places where such pushbacks seemed to be a commonplace:

> We witnessed [Macedonian] police forcefully pushing migrants off a train and sending them back to Greece. (participant 35, NGO, Macedonia)

> A woman told us, panicking, that her husband managed to get to Serbia. He hid in a mosque [near FYR Macedonia-Serbia border]. … We talked to him and told him to go to police. … We phoned the officer in charge and he said Ok, no worries, we will bring him to the [asylum] centre. After a while we realised [police officer] took him back to the border. … I think a lot of people had this experience. They simply want to push them back, over the border. We often hear such stories. … We know about [migrants] who were put on a bus, taken to the border and showed off. (participant 3, INGO)

Once in FYR Macedonia or Serbia, men, women, and children encountered suspended asylum procedures for non-citizens found on states' territory. In June 2015, the National Assembly of FYR Macedonia passed amendments of *The Law on Asylum and Temporary Protection*, granting illegalised non-citizens a 72-hour timeframe to seek asylum in the country or leave the territory of FYR Macedonia. This amendment granted border crossers freedom of movement and access to public transport (Chudoska Blazhevska and Flores Juberías 2016) – or, as Beznec et al. (2016, p. 18) note, provided them with a 'de-facto transit visa'. The arrivals continued as approximately 2,000 people a day entered FYR Macedonia from Greece during August 2015 (*The Guardian*, 20 August 2015; participant 34, NGO, Macedonia). As non-citizens in transit were not under police escort or in detention, they simply kept going, leaving the territory of FYR Macedonia within the 72 hours timeframe provided for the asylum application. Given these mobility pressures, in autumn 2015 nation-states on the Western Balkans route arranged government-sponsored "formalised corridors" for people on the move (Beznec et al. 2016). The pace of transit through FYR Macedonia was such that, by October 2015, the state agencies recorded only 50 asylum applications (Lilyanova 2016, p. 6) and granted only one asylum that year (Beznec et al. 2016, p. 14).

   Once in Serbia migrants commonly expressed an intention to seek asylum, at which point police would "establish and record" their identity and issue papers that enabled freedom of movement, with a requirement to report to an asylum centre of their choice within 72 hours. In reality, however, they had 'no real obligation … to report to the centres; only if they want they [visit and/or stay] in centres' (participant 5, GA, Serbia). The expression of intention to seek asylum was not considered to be an asylum application; thus, the same person was able to express the intention to seek asylum multiple times (Kilibarda and Kovačević 2016). It is in asylum centres, however, that police were tasked with formal registration of border crossers, identity checks, and processing asylum applications. Nonetheless, as the report from Serbian NGO Beogradski Centar za Ljudska Prava (2016, p. 14) suggests, at this stage of the "crisis" agencies in charge of registering non-citizens have been actively encouraging them to leave as soon as possible (see also Kilibarda and Kovačević 2016). As such, the average stay of non-citizens in Serbia in 2015 was approximately three weeks (Lukić 2016; Milivojevic 2018a). In the same year, 557,995 non-citizens expressed their intention to seek asylum in Serbia; only 583 submitted a formal application for asylum, while a mere 30 obtained some sort of protection (16 were granted refugee status, and 14 were granted subsidiary protection – Kilibarda and Kovačević 2016). These figures suggest that transiting non-citizens used the asylum system of nation-states in the region 'as a vehicle to help them reach their final destination in Western Europe' (Šalamon 2016, p. 152). They also suggest that the asylum system in the region was set up in such a way that people on the move were unable to settle in transit states even if they desired to do so, however unlikely. According to Frontex, a lack of commitment to the issue by governments and state agencies, exemplified through formalised transit corridors, was the key reason for the increased popularity of the Western Balkans migration route during this phase of the "crisis" (Frontex 2016, p. 5).

Undoubtedly, police in Serbia, Kosovo, and FYR Macedonia were indolent when it came to processing non-citizens who expressed the intention to claim asylum as there was 'no political will to engage with … an issue that has not been considered a priority' (participant 9, IO). In other words, because of a lack of pressure from the EU and member states at this stage of the "crisis", deadlines to complete asylum procedure were frequently disregarded and asylum seekers routinely left transit states before their claim was even considered (participant 1, NGO, Serbia; participant 5, GA, Serbia; participant 30, GA, Kosovo; participant 38, INGO). As one participant from an international NGO working in the region pointed out, 'people wait, and wait for a decision that never comes, and they simply leave' (participant 9, IO). The pretence was apparent: illegalised non-citizens claimed asylum only when "caught" by police yet with a clear intention to leave transit states as soon as possible; police processed them but with minimum effort, simply waiting for the unwanted "visitors" to move on:

> A police officer told me that it is in their best interest – police's best interest – not to do anything, and let people pass [through]. They want that. (participant 24, NGO, Serbia)

I do not understand what is happening lately. … The only logical explanation is that [non-citizens] are not here long enough to … apply for asylum [in Serbia]. Police obviously refuse to act on it. (participant 18, GA, Serbia)

While the inactivity of law enforcement has been identified as a factor in non-citizens' quick transit through the region, participants in my research argued that even if the process was quicker that 'wouldn't solve the problem. The asylum seekers will simply … leave faster' (participant 26, INGO). As one state official from Serbia put it, '[migrants] just want to rest, heal, have a baby, get new clothes, eat, … get money via Western Union, and continue their journey' (participant 5, GA, Serbia). Such 'mockery of a system' (participant 1, NGO, Serbia) continued to operate in key transit states for most of 2015: people came and went, moving quickly towards Hungary or (to a lesser extent) Croatia:

[T]he police don't do anything about [illegalised non-citizens], I have no idea why. People … come and go, come and go. We never had a situation like this. I can't explain it. We had only a handful of people who got asylum and subsidiary protection. … It appears that we do have a system, but in reality - we really don't. We don't have a control [over people transiting the region], and we don't want to have a control. It is a complete chaos right now. … We play games. There is no system. (participant 1, NGO, Serbia)

However, as I witnessed firsthand while doing fieldwork in the region, the above issues were certainly not the only reason for the swift transit of non-citizens through the region in the early stages of the "crisis".

"They will attack you": expulsion of the (racial, religious, criminal) "Other"

The xenophobia and Islamophobia of the local population, remnants of recent wars and limited exposure to racial and cultural differences, also underpinned the policy of limited engagement (Lukić 2016). While the Western Balkans was certainly not alone in racially and ethnically based anti-immigration sentiment towards "new" refugees (for issues pertinent to xenophobia and racism in the EU states see Geddes and Scholten 2016; De Genova 2017b), fear of the racially and religiously different "Other" in the region had been heightened by the legacy of the Yugoslav Wars, in which religion played a key role.[4] Religiously distinctive "new refugees" were also racially and culturally dissimilar to the local population, and thus considered to be dangerous:

People in [western] Serbia have prejudices against Muslims, they were in a war [with Bosnian Muslims], so [some locals] … campaigned against [new] migrants, spreading fear. They said migrants were doing bad things, crime. As the number of migrants grew, they engaged in fear mongering, 'they will go into your house and attack you' sort of thing. (participant 2, NGO, Serbia)

The ultimate fear is the fear of unknown. Until 2009, most of the young people [from Serbia] never went abroad, didn't meet people who were different. ... We have minorities, but they are [white] Europeans. Now you have people from Somalia, Afghanistan, [with] different culture, different lifestyle so it is natural people are afraid. (participant 4, NGO, Serbia)

The growing number of non-citizens in transit generated anxiety among local populations as '[t]here are so many of them, they sleep in parks ... they are exhausted, tired, they have dark skin, don't know the language. They look awful, have beards' (participant 1, NGO, Serbia). The visual identity of the racially and religiously identifiable "Other" resulted in a series of protests against migrants in Serbia, Croatia, and Slovenia. In Croatia, non-citizens were frequently refused service in restaurants because of the colour of their skin (participant 14, NGO, Croatia). As I have written elsewhere, '[k]eeping the racially different, and presumed dangerous non-citizens on the territory of the nation was considered to be out of the question' (Milivojevic 2018a, p. 82). Permanent resettlement of non-citizens or even long-term temporary housing, however unlikely, had to be discouraged. As one NGO activist from Serbia pointed out,

I think police has orders to let them go. This comes from the top. ... [T]hey think that migrants are going to occupy Serbia. They think they are patriots, and so the best thing to do is to let them go elsewhere (participant 2, NGO, Serbia)

The racism and xenophobia of the local population resulted in a series of botched attempts to build centres for illegalised non-citizens in FYR Macedonia, Serbia, and Croatia (see Beznec et al. 2016; Lukić 2016; Milivojevic 2018a). As people continued to cross borders, reduced options for their accommodation generated a crisis of housing. "Jungles" – improvised dwellings near asylum centres or border crossings – started to pop up along the Western Balkan route, similar to 'jungles Calais in France, ... Morocco or... or shacks in Patras in Greece' (participant 16, INGO). In November 2013, during my visit to an asylum centre in Bogovađa, I witnessed approximately 200 men, women, and children living in "jungles" near the centre. While I was waiting for a formal reception with the director of the centre, Mr Stojan Sjekloća, and his team, a group of men approached me and asked if I could come with them. We walked through a dense bush, only about 300–400 m from the centre. When we arrived at their improvised shack, the men showed me a snake they had killed that morning. One of the men said, pointing to his improvised bed, 'I'm glad [a snake] didn't come in!' (Figure 3.1).

Figure 3.1 A snake killed by men in Bogovađa centre for asylum seekers, Serbia.
Source: Sanja Milivojevic.

Over-crowding, appalling living conditions, and fast approaching winter
fuelled a series of xenophobic protests by the local population in Bogovađa,
demanding the prompt removal of migrants from the community (see also
Pavlović 2016). At a round table organized in the nearby town of Lajkovac
in November 2013, a president of the local municipality explained why the
surplus of non-citizens had to be housed elsewhere:

> [W]e have army barracks here, large ammunition sheds, and stuff like
> that. They visit these facilities, but we don't know their names, we have
> no idea who they are. We don't know their past. When someone tries to
> take a picture of them, they put jackets over their heads. Why do they do
> that? Who is interested in them? There are embassies that are interested in
> these people. Why? If I ever leave my country no one would be concerned
> about me. We think, local people think this is because they must be crim-
> inals. … [P]eople found knives where migrants sleep, freshly sharpened.
> There were some syringes, drugs, and prostitution. We can't put up with
> that. That is why we organised these protests. (President of the local mu-
> nicipality, transcript from a round table in Lajkovac, November 2013)

The government of Serbia responded by opening *ad hoc* asylum centres in
Sjenica, Tutin, and Obrenovac (southern and central Serbia) but made no

attempts to fix the fraught mobility management and asylum system. Instead, similar to other states on the Western Balkan migration route, they largely disengaged with, if not enabled, mobility projects of transiting non-citizens in the early years of the "crisis".

Phase 2 (October 2015–March 2016) and 3 (March 2016–): non-entrée and border shutdown via "partnerships" in mobility management

The pressure to "fix" the migration machine in the Western Balkans was getting stronger in mid-2015. After the EU officials insisted on a change in mobility management, and after a large wave of people attempted to cross the Macedonia-Greece border, a harsh intervention of the Macedonian special police forces followed (Šalamon 2016). The Macedonian government provisionally shut its southern border with Greece at the end of August 2015 (Beznec et al. 2016), erecting temporary barbwire fences in order to stop migrants from entering their territory (see Amnesty International 2015b). Thousands of non-citizens were pushed back to no-man's land, near the border crossing Bogorodica:

> [W]hat we saw [at the border] was unpleasant to say the least. People were crying, some of them were beaten up, and every 15 or so minutes someone fainted. … We heard 6–7 shock bombs go off, and tear gas [was used] when one group tried to break through the barricades. (participant 36, NGO, Macedonia)

Hungary repeatedly urged the Serbian government to prevent migrants from crossing the Hungary-Serbia border; indeed, as one participant in my research pointed out, 'Hungarians [were] really pissed off, hundreds of people are coming in daily' (participant 1, NGO, Serbia). In June 2015, the Hungarian government announced that it would build a four-metre high border fence with Serbia and Croatia. Commenting on the terror attacks in Paris in early 2015, Prime Minister Viktor Orbán (cited in Ferzek 2015) suggested that

> [e]conomic migration is bad for Europe. We don't benefit from it, it is dangerous practice. As a Prime Minister, I will not allow Hungary to become a country of immigration. We do not wish to have minorities that are culturally different from us. We want to keep Hungary as it is.

Following the completion of the border fence on the Serbia-Hungary border in September 2015, and after violent incidents near Horgoš – Röszke border crossings on 16 September, the flow of non-citizens shifted towards the West to Croatia. Hungary responded to this change in migration flows by erecting a partial fence on the Croatia-Hungary border in October 2015 (Figure 3.2).

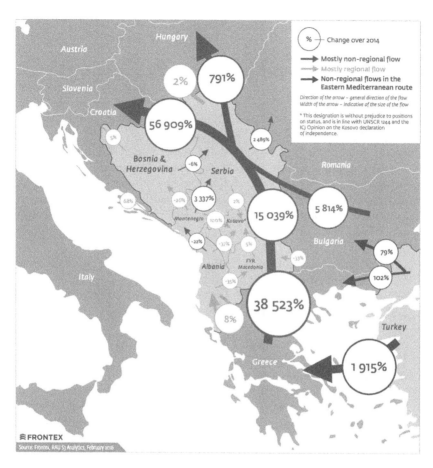

Figure 3.2 The Western Balkans migration route after the closure of the Hungary-Serbia border.
Source: Frontex (2016).

Following these developments Serbian police intensified their pushback practices (Belgrade Centre for Human Rights et al. 2017). Nevertheless, the government declared that it would not prevent migrants from transiting through Serbia. Commenting on Hungary's harsh measures towards migrants, then Prime Minister Aleksandar Vučić argued that

> [Serbia] is surrounded by fences. Yet, we are the first country [in the region] to register migrants. … We established a centre for refugees in Preševo and are doing our best to feed them. … Even though we are not yet in the EU, it is our goal to be a member soon, and *we are ready to take our share of responsibility*. Serbia is not building fences. It would be easy to do that. [The EU]

was silent when others built such fences. … I am disappointed that Greece and Macedonia used tear gas against migrants. I am confident that will not happen in Serbia. (*Blic*, 31 August 2015; my emphasis)

Vučić's narrative aligned with Angela Merkel's "We can do it" ("Wir schaffen das") policy, announced on the same day – 31 August 2015. The policy welcomed a large number of refugees and asylum seekers to Germany. However, the policy was short lived (Merkel dropped the use of the phrase in mid-September 2016) and was arguably a significant blow for Merkel and her Christian Democratic Union (CDU)-led government (Livingstone 2016). The media landscape in Serbia and the region quickly became saturated with reports on the "asylum problem", underpinned by the supposed deviance and criminality of border crossers. Tabloid and broadsheet media's headlines in no uncertain terms outlined risks non-citizens bring to the local population, the nation, and its culture:

- *Rivers of migrants*: Trains in Gevgelija filled with people *marching towards* Serbia (*Blic*, 12 August 2015; my emphasis)
- *We are facing a humanitarian catastrophe*: 50,000 refugees *rolling towards* Serbia. Shortages in water and food (*Telegraf*, 24 August 2015; original emphasis)
- *Serbia under pressure by migrants*: 7,000 migrants arrive from Macedonia every night. Another, *bigger wave* [of migrants] to follow (*Telegraf*, 24 August; original emphasis)
- *(Video and photo) Invasion of the Balkans*: Thousands of migrants wait for trains for Serbia in Gevgelija (*Kurir*, 14 August 2015; original emphasis)
- A year when migrants *conquered* Europe (*Blic*, 26 August 2015; my emphasis)
- Europe helpless against *the flood* of migrants (Vujić 2015; my emphasis).

Strident terms used to describe men, women, and children on the move included references to "illegal migrants", "legal immigrants", "immigrants", "illegals", "foreigners", and "bogus asylum seekers". Criminalised and stereotyped, they were commonly represented as troublemakers, untrustworthy, and dissimilar to the local population:

If one was getting information from the media alone, you would have a distorted picture on the topic. I now realise the extent to which the media can manipulate its readers. (participant 2, NGO, Serbia)

The terrorist narrative was ubiquitous. Tabloid media in the region widely quoted EU and NATO officials, claiming that 'terrorists could, under disguise as migrants, come to Europe and this requires a swift response' (NATO Secretary General Jens Stoltenberg, cited in *Blic*, 18 May 2015). Quoting the then President of the EU's agency for judicial co-operation, Eurojust,

Michèle Coninsx, Croatia's *Jutarnji List* reported that 'there is a *real chance* that terrorists are among thousands of migrants transiting through Macedonia and Serbia' (*Jutarnji List*, 8 July 2015; emphasis added). Serbian media followed suit, with terror-ridden headlines:

- *Serbia is a base for terrorists*: Some migrants have combat experience (*Blic*, 29 July 2015; original emphasis)
- *Terrorists hide among migrants*: Hundreds have already passed through Serbia, there is a fear that some of them are still in our country! (*Telegraf*, 22 August 2015; original emphasis)

Several government officials in Serbia claimed that 'ISIS has the aspirations to infiltrate in the Balkans' (Serbian Ministry for Internal Affairs' Undersecretary Aleksandar Nikolić, as cited in *Blic*, 29 July 2015), while the opposition urged the government to build a fence on the Serbia–Macedonia border as 'the EU is doing everything they can to keep migrants in Serbia… many of whom are potential terrorists' (*Danas*, 24 August 2015). Such claims were illustrated by images of an alleged Islamic State leader from Syria, Laith Al Saleh, who, it was argued, 'recently passed through Serbia on his way to the Netherlands' (*Telegraf*, 22 August 2015; for more details see Milivojevic 2018a). The BBC later rebutted this story, confirming that Laith Al Saleh was a plasterer from Aleppo who had been a commander in the Free Syrian Army before leaving Syria (Wendling 2015).

While the tenor in the media and among some government officials shifted, nation-states in the region kept resisting the creation of buffer zones for a while longer. In September 2015 the Serbian government passed a decree that enables non-citizens from 'countries where their life is in danger' to obtain a special pass. With this pass men, women, and children on the move could stay in Serbia for 72 hours, during which time they could access medical help, accommodation, or financial services but were not officially in the asylum procedure (Beogradski Centar za Ljudska Prava 2016). In October 2015, however, the pressure from the majority of the EU member states yielded a change in border regime in the Western Balkans. The European Commission held the regional meeting, after which, in November 2015, the policy shifted from *limited engagement* to *non-entrée*, except for the citizens of Afghanistan, Iraq, and Syria considered to be "genuine" refugees. Almost simultaneously, FYR Macedonia, Serbia, Croatia, and Slovenia announced that no "economic" migrants would be allowed to pass through their territory. States that had recently been in conflict, such as Croatia and Serbia, or Serbia and Kosovo, were told in no uncertain terms that they had to join forces in order to regain control over migration flows:

> The EU asked Kosovo to [work on] border management with Serbia but they did not ask the same from Serbia when it got visa liberalisation [prior to the migrant "crisis"]. They use visa liberalisation as a carrot for

all of these conditions. … Kosovo has done a great job in cooperation with its neighbours, including with Serbia. (participant 28, academic, Kosovo)

[P]olice from the neighbouring countries conduct mutual patrols, joint actions based on mutual agreements, even hot pursuits [of criminal groups]. The EU demands that. (participant 32, IO)

Following the March 2016 agreement between the EU and Turkey, the EU, FYR Macedonia, Serbia, Croatia, and Slovenia agreed to allow 580 asylum seekers to cross their borders per day (see Zaragoza-Christiani 2017, pp. 65–67). This deal was soon revoked, and a complete border shutdown for all transiting non-citizens was announced in March 2016 (Zaragoza-Christiani 2017, pp. 67–68). Then-Minister for Foreign Affairs of FYR Macedonia, Nikola Poposki, stated that '[i]t is clear that the absorption capacities of migrants in mainly receiving EU member states such as Germany, Austria, Sweden and others has reached a certain threshold where it cannot continue in the next year with the same pace' (cited in Chudoska Blazhevska and Flores Juberías 2016, p. 227).

While EUrope undoubtedly benefited from these processes, their "partners" in border management also hoped to profit. As De Genova (2017a, p. 20) argued, potential and candidate states saw the "crisis" as an opportunity for the re-admission of the "bad boys" of the Balkans 'into the self-anointed circle of genuine and proper Europe-ness'. For too long the Western Balkans represented a reversion to the tribal, the barbarian "Other" (Lazarova 2016), while violence and backwardness were perceived as 'an indelible part of the Balkans' (Flessenkemper and Bütow 2011, p. 168). Assisting the EU in solving the "crisis" was a chance to revamp the image of the region. In a meeting with President of the European Council Donald Tusk, the delegation of FYR Macedonia emphasised 'how their nation of two million has proved to be a reliable partner for Europe by stopping thousands of migrants from moving north' (Surk and de la Baume, cited in Beznec et al. 2016, p. 36). Regional leaders rushed to offer proof that they were indeed "good Europeans" (de Borja Lasheras et al. 2016). The de-balkanisation of the Western Balkans was under way:

The external dimension is very important for the EU, and it is clear that they want to cooperate with other states to improve systems of protection. The key task of [the European Asylum Support Office] is cooperation with non-EU states so that they would develop good asylum systems. That is no secret. This is their motivation. But it is also good [for us], if we build such system as we will be a good partner for the EU and [they] won't have problem with … asylum seekers, people who need help. (participant 8, GA, Serbia)

[W]e say to our European partners, no worries, the longer we keep them here, the less [time] they will spend at your centres. A day in asylum centre is much cheaper here. (participant 5, GA, Serbia)

The border shutdown, however, was not complete as '[t]hose still travelling on the route are either crossing borders where small numbers are allowed each day or with illegal people smugglers' (House of Lords Select Committee on International Relations 2018, p. 48). Some 1,400 illegalised non-citizens were stuck in FYR Macedonia after the border shutdown in March 2016; by September 2016 the number decreased to 200 as the majority continued on their way via Serbia (Chudoska Blazhevska and Flores Juberías 2016, p. 233; see also Beznec et al. 2016). The border shutdown was, thus, a pretence. A complete immobilisation was never the intention: the goal was to decrease the pressure on destination countries and regain control over trans-border mobility. In order to do so, the EU effectively constructed "dams" along the Western Balkan migration route that enabled the stratification and passage of a manageable number of border crossers (Zaragoza-Christiani 2017; see also Šalamon 2016). To quote Bigo again, '[l]ogics of passage and mobility are stronger than logics of containment' (Bigo 2015, p. 213). As the migrant "crisis" unfolded, the right balance of people permitted to transit through the region was reached through the concoction of solid, liquid, and cloudy borders, to which I now turn.

Cloudy borders and migration management in the Western Balkans

In Chapter 2 I analysed the development of a techno-social machine that examines, categorises, authorises, delays, or restrains mobile populations. Managing and pre-empting risk by identifying and classifying transnational mobility increasingly occurs outside of countries of destination, among "ring of friends" in countries of origin and transit. It is here that borders become the interplay of walls and locks and flows but also information, data, and barcodes, collected and mined by a range of state and non-state agencies.

The EU 'has widely been seen as a forerunner in the erosion of hard conceptual and physical boundaries with regard to a wide-range of policies' (Bossong and Carrapico 2016, p. 12). Technology has always been at the forefront of these interventions. Indeed, as Katja Franko (Aas 2011, p. 333) reminds us, one of key objectives of the EU is to 'build up surveillance resources of third world countries, particularly in Eastern Europe and Northern Africa, and enable them to take over some of the EU's surveillance labor'. Thus, the success of the techno-social migration machine increasingly rests on co-operation with neighbours (Wilson 2013, p. 147). Bigo and Guild's (2005) concept of "policing at distance" in the Western Balkans includes a range of initiatives financed and led by the EU, and implemented as a part of the EU accession process. In order to strike the right balance of border fortification and fluidity, states gradually adopted a range of requirements pertinent to the implementation of security technologies in order to obtain visa liberalisation and ultimately – EU membership.

Issuing biometric passports for citizens of the region has been one of the first requirements in the process of accession on the road to visa liberalisation. The ability to identify border crossers via unchangeable personal markers safely stored in passports' microchips has been the initial *conditio sine qua non* in the *Roadmaps*. As the following participant from Kosovo noted, the importance of biometric passports grew with the rise of illegalised non-citizens during the migrant "crisis":

> The biggest problem [for Kosovo] was that Syrians, Afghans could easily get a Kosovo passport and go to Europe... That is why [the EU] insists so much on the security of documents, and we had to [issue biometric passports]. (participant 28, academic, Kosovo)

Yet this was only the beginning of the process of the *Europeanisation* of the region via the bifurcated process of democratic and legal conditionality. The long list of requirements, conditions, and instructions stipulated in *the acquis*, regional documents, individual *Roadmaps*, and bilateral and multilateral agreements compelled would-be EU members to agree to, and install, a range of technological advancements pertinent to border security and mobility control. As one government official from FYR Macedonia explained,

> [a]fter issuing biometric passports, [FYR Macedonia had to] develop a fast link between border crossings and the central database of the Ministry of Interior, install video surveillance at all border crossings, provide appropriate technical equipment for border management, connect to relevant databases at national and European level, enable detection of forged documents, prepare risk analysis [reports for Frontex], equip police stations for state border surveillance ... and establish the Integrated Database for foreigners, which includes data on asylum, visas and migration. (participant 33, GA, FYR Macedonia)

I mapped similar developments in all the states on the Western Balkan route. To fulfil non-negotiable obligations from the *Roadmap* and to obtain a visa-free regime with the EU, for example, the Republic of Serbia signed the Visa Facilitation Agreement with the EU (in 2008); concluded a working agreement with Frontex (in 2009); issued machine-readable biometric travel documents in compliance with EU standards (in 2008); and enforced budgetary and administrative measures to ensure effective infrastructure, equipment, and information and communication technology (ICT) at its borders (in 2008 and 2009; European Commission 2008a; participant 8, GA,

Serbia). In terms of migration management, Serbia had to develop and apply mechanisms for migration monitoring, including a methodology for inland detection of illegalised non-citizens (European Commission 2008a; see also Đorđević 2009) and a functional asylum system[5] (participant 5, GA, Serbia).

While it is 'nearly impossible to obtain precise and complete information' (Geiger 2016, p. 138) on the funding that states have been receiving as part of IPA and other EU funds, such as CARDS, PHARE, and ISPA, Geiger estimates that under the regional CARDS programme alone (from 2000 to 2006) the Western Balkans cashed in more than EUR 105 million in external funds. Croatia, as the only EU member from the region, has at the time of my research exhausted pre-accession funds for the development of security technologies. In a memo obtained under the *Law on Free Access to Information* (Public Papers no. 25/13), Croatian police corroborated funding of EUR 12,070,000 through the pre-accession CARDS and PARHE project (in 2004–2005). Through IPA funds in 2009 alone they obtained additional EUR 1,483,000. Croatian police continued to use IPA I and II funds for border policing until the country joined the EU in 2013. These funds were provided specifically for the modernisation of border management and the implementation of Schengen policies, through which Croatian police purchased thermal imagining cameras, e-gates for passport control, and a range of border surveillance paraphernalia (The Croatian Ministry for Internal Affairs – The Office of the Head of Police, Memo no. 511-01-42–152–69/13, 30 December 2013).

Candidate and potential candidate states in the region continue to use IPA and IPA II. The EU's financial assistance for Serbia under IPA II funds for improving the rule of law and fundamental rights (which includes IBM, combating organised crime, and improved asylum processing and management) totalled EUR 265 million for the 2014–2020 period (European Commission 2017a), while FYR Macedonia secured EUR 83 million (European Commission 2017b). In a formal statement obtained under the *Law on Free Access to Information of Public Importance* (Official Gazette of Republic of Serbia, no. 120/04, 54/07, 104/09 and 36/10), Serbian police confirmed the purchase of a range of technological equipment with IPA funds and foreign donations (The Serbian Ministry for Internal Affairs – Border Police Memo no. 06–151/13, 14 April 2014). Similarly, a government official from FYR Macedonia outlined a wide range of technological advancements bought with foreign, mostly EU donations:

> Border police … use modern static and mobile tools and video surveillance systems, thermal imaging cameras, binoculars for day and night observation, GPS navigation devices, etc. At border crossings, we use specialized tools to check the accuracy of travel documents, check [the inside] of vehicles and cargo. … Most of the funds are donations from foreign governments and organisations, especially EU. (participant 33, GA, Macedonia)

Given that most of the region are EU candidate states, some of the border security assemblage I outlined in Chapter 2 is not yet implemented in the Western Balkans (such as EURODAC and SIS). VIS, however, has been operational in the region since September 2014 (eu-LISA 2014; The Delegation of the EU to the Republic of Serbia 2014). As such, it is Frontex that has been at the forefront of the development of cloudy borders in the region. The agency's goal is, as Mountz and Kempin (2016) note, collaborative (and efficient) policing in the Western Balkans. As participants in my research confirm, Frontex has been instrumental in designing, financing, approving, and supervising every stage of the development and implementation of the techno-social border policing assemblage:

> [W]e have continuous training programs for our staff … and members of the border police actively participate in joint operations organised by Frontex…. The National Coordination Centre for Border Management regularly exchanges information with Frontex and participates in the preparation of risk analysis in the field of border operations. (participant 33, GA, Macedonia)

> Frontex works with [Serbian] border police on data exchange, trainings, they provide equipment [for example]… thermal imaging cameras. [Police] finally managed to get optic fibre and … biometrics. VIS is also functional now. (participant 4, NGO, Serbia)

The pressure to develop an effective technology-migration machine intensified during the migrant "crisis". As non-citizens transited through the region, and mobility regime started to change, the buffer zones of social segregation were strengthened through techno-social bordering practices, mostly along the Serbia-Hungary border. This border became 'a new strategic area of deployment as intensified border checks in other areas, such as between Greece and Turkey, have led a shift in migration routes' (Martin 2013). As one participant in my research pointed out, border crossers' 'goal is simply to pass Schengen [border]. After they do so, no one stops them until they reach their country of destination. This is why the biggest pressure is on Serbia, on the northern border with Hungary' (participant 9, IO). While Serbian border police initially explicitly refused to provide any information on this topic, participants I talked to shed some light on the development of cloudy borders in northern Serbia:

> Border police said they do not have a single mobile camera for surveillance [at Serbia-Macedonia border]. They only have stationary ones. … Everything they've got from the EU went to the Serbia-Hungary border. … [This] border is a priority because the EU countries, Austria for example, pushed for it. … Austria sent a lot of money, people to patrol it. (participant 4, NGO, Serbia)

Serbia has infrared and thermal imaging cameras, mobile (vehicle-based), and a few stationary ones. ... [The border with Hungary] is completely covered with tower-based fixed cameras. ... [Serbian police] have CO_2 and pulse detection devices, to check for people in vehicles. The EU financed it all. (participant 2, NGO, Serbia)

There are no secrets: [Hungarian police] use thermal imaging cameras, mobile and... I'm not sure if you've seen the huge towers and cameras [along the border]? They cover a large area of the border. ... There is also a support from the EU border agency, Frontex, not to the extent that it happens in Greece or Italy, but it is significant. There are joint operations [with non-EU countries], several EU states send their officers and equipment to the Serbia-Hungary border. ... I think they have a very close relationship [with Serbia]. (participant 10, NGO, Hungary)

After I requested information from the Serbian police in accordance with the *Law on Free Access to Information of Public Importance* (Official Gazette of Republic of Serbia, no. 120/04, 54/07, 104/09, and 36/10), they issued a memo confirming that the Serbia-Hungary border has been monitored by the tactical balloon system "Thor-1", thermal imaging vehicles, and mobile and hand-held thermal imaging cameras for day and night surveillance. The EU financed the purchase of these systems with pre-accession funds, and their use is exclusively for border policing (The Serbian Ministry for Internal Affairs – Border Police Memo no. 06–151/13, 14 April 2014). In addition, Serbian media suggested that a drone system called "Vrabac" ("Sparrow") – comprised of three drones and a control tower – has also been used in border policing (*B92*, 1 May 2010). The first locally developed and made drone, called "Pegasus 011", was (somewhat enthusiastically) announced as a new defender of the border regime:

[Pegasus 011] looks like it came from a science-fiction movie, has an almost 20/20 vision... It is fast, precise, elegant and mostly invisible. ... While [Pegasus 011] is planned to be a flagship of Serbian military, it will be of great use in ... border policing. (*Blic*, 27 June 2011)

As one participant in my research pointed out, the Serbia-Hungary border is monitored to the extent that when people attempt to cross into the Schengen Area '[police] have already seen them via thermal imaging cameras. They think, "we will manage to get away". ... [but] it will be more and more difficult to cross borders' (participant 6, NGO, Serbia). Indeed, as the following example illustrates, surveillance of the border is so intense that police often accidentally stumble upon "illegals":

[Serbian] police were [testing new] thermal imaging vehicle. Police officers were sent to [the fields, near the border] to "role play" illegal

migrants, to be targets so to speak. A guy in charge thought he actu-
ally saw one or two illegals [on the screen]. There was some confusion,
[a person in charge did not know] what to do about it. Illegal migrants
realised they were exposed, and one ducked down quickly to avoid detection. It was comical. A person in charge said: 'he is one of ours', but
others shouted 'no, no, this is for real!' They went out there, with torches,
to look for illegals, and they caught them. (participant 18, GA, Serbia)

As a consequence of such intense surveillance, illegalised non-citizens in transit had to resort to innovative strategies to "beat" the migration-technology
assemblage. Examples such as the next one demonstrate both the length and
the extent to which people on the move have to go in order to do so:

Migrants that crossed [the Serbia-Hungary] border [and were caught and
returned to asylum centres in Serbia] tell us they rarely see police patrols.
This was very interesting. Migrants ask us '[w]here can we buy mosquito
repellent?' When we ask why they need it they say, 'you know, when
we cross border, it is woodlands and is flat. There are a lot of mosquitos.
So, they can see us. They have these little flying objects and they see
everything and detect us'... [Police] see them crossing border, all sweaty,
because of mosquitos. But now, they put insect repellent and manage to
cross. (participant 2, NGO, Serbia)

While the Serbia-Hungary border had been the focus of EUrope prior to
and during the "crisis", FYR Macedonia has also been a recipient of funds
and technical equipment from Hungary, Croatia, Serbia, Slovenia, Czech
Republic, Austria, Slovakia, and Frontex (Chudoska Blazhevska and Flores
Juberías 2016). Most of the funds obtained went to securing borders with
Greece and Serbia. As the migration flows were redirected, following the
erection of border fences by Hungary, the attention shifted to Croatia, as the
below quote confirms:

We put a lot of effort and money in border control and policing, thermal
imaging surveillance and everything else. ... The EU pressure resulted
in an increase in border police officers, an increase of police officers per
square meter of the border. Police bought two mobile thermal imaging
cameras, and [deployed them] at the eastern border [with Serbia]. This
was a big investment. (participant 11, academic, Croatia)

A well-oiled technology-migration machine has been essential for effective pushbacks at the Croatia-Serbia border as well as for filtering migrants
through the only EU state in the region. As one participant from Croatia put
it, '[C]roatian and Serbian police work well together. ... If you think about
surveillance, thermal imaging cameras and so on, this is all for one purpose

only: to push people back' (participant 12, academic, Croatia). Extensive surveillance enabled efficient social sorting of non-citizens, as demonstrated in
the following quote:

> [W]e know where they go, and we can predict where they will go too.
> We look into statistics and operational information. We also engage in
> secret surveillance, which is defined by the law. ... Technical equipment
> is expensive. But, we have stationary and mobile/handheld surveillance
> cameras. ... Rail tracks that cross borders are especially under surveil-
> lance. We don't even have to go out there [anymore]. (participant 27,
> GA, Croatia)

At the time of writing, the aforementioned border interventions are in full
swing. Money keeps flowing in as the fragile deal with Turkey is under question, and thousands of men, women, and children wait patiently in refugee
camps in the Middle East, Turkey, and Greece. The "humanitarian" spin by
the EU and Frontex is increasingly questioned by professionals in the field.
As one participant in my research suggested, 'we are facing gross violation
of human rights and human dignity, in the name of security' (participant
32, IO). Indeed, as a representative of an international NGO working in the
region pointed out,

> [t]he question [we need to] ask is about the real purpose of these tech-
> nologies. If the purpose is to save lives, we have the tools to get there,
> we have enough to do that. I don't know if the technology is serving the
> policy, or the policy serves technology. (participant 16, INGO)

Yet technology alone often fails to immobilise non-citizens in transit as
'[t]here is no technology that can bypass human willingness, when people have a profound desire and willingness do something' (participant 25,
INGO). The techno-social machine for social sorting, thus, has been de-
poloyed to strike the right balance of people who will be permitted to cross
borders. In that context, the role of the "ring of friends" in the Western
Balkans and elsewhere is essential. As one Croatian government official
bluntly put it, '[t]echnology cannot replace the "hunter": You have to use
a man. A man is the one that hunts [migrants] down' (participant 27, GA,
Croatia) (Figure 3.3).

The multiplicity of borders and bordering practices in the region outlined
in this chapter shaped a mechanism that, while under pressure during the
"crisis", was arguably successful in letting *the right number of the right people*
cross to the Global North. Its many tentacles simultaneously blocked, pushed
back, delayed, shifted, and classified people on the move, effectively creating
a manageable flow of migrants that sought access to the labour markets and
asylum systems in the West.

Figure 3.3 'Become a border hunter' recruitment poster, Hungarian border
police.

Conclusion

De Clercq (2007, p. 7; original emphasis) posed the following question a decade ago:

> if you draw a line in the sand, the wind will sweep it away in a matter of hours. If you build a fence through a globalizing labour market, will it withstand the pull and push forces on *both* sides?

Solid borders keep popping up in the Global North and the Global South, and the apparent demand for them grows as politicians call for "barriers", not a "sieve" (Bosworth 2008, p. 200); yet human mobility endures. Within the process of border externalisation, liquid and cloudy borders shift bordering practices to 'a more fluid landscape built on overlapping, and often contradictory, history of mobility and exchange' (Raeymaekers 2014, p. 168). The process of EU expansion has profoundly altered mobility governance in the Western Balkans, as was evident prior to, during, and post the migrant "crisis". As a consequence, migration and mobility control in Europe has been subcontracted to non-EU ascending states through regional strategies, individual *Roadmaps*, and the acceptance of the *acquis*. As I demonstrate in this chapter, the sites of enforcement were physical, internal, and digital borders in the region.

Bordering practices that slow down or immobilise people increasingly occur in the Global South – in the Serbia-Hungary borderlands, at border crossings in FYR Macedonia, and in the political rhetoric of the government officials of Kosovo. Indeed, potential and candidate states in the region have been pressured to harmonise their legislation, policies, and practices with the EU, and to "do border" on its behalf. Through the implementation of requirements set in the EU policy framework, future members have to demonstrate both the capacity and the willingness to become a new frontier of the EU's border regime. These "genuine partnerships" are, however, a simple transfer of the mechanisms of border control to potential and candidate states.

The Western Balkans, with its complex history of mobility, has been at the forefront of this process in Europe over the last two decades. The externalisation of bordering practices in the region has been meticulously planned and executed within the (ongoing) process of EU accession. After a turbulent period in the 1990s, the region has emerged as a place where seamless borders of the EU materialise, a key checkpoint where illegalised non-citizens are identified, stratified, labelled, filtered, or (temporarily or permanently) immobilised. In doing so, the Western Balkans seemingly transformed from one of the most troubled regions of Europe to its chief border custodian. EUrope has established yet another important frontier where the social sorting of people takes place.

Through the application of bordering strategies along physical, internal, and digital borders in non-EU spaces, the Union and its member states have successfully regulated mobility of non-citizens transiting through the region. The deployment of ever-expanding techno-social interventions in the region is there to address the key concern of the Global North: facilitating mobility of labour and goods, *and* identifying and reducing risks associated with such mobility. Striking the balance of people who will be allowed to cross – people assessed as useful in the labour markets or as genuine asylum seekers that will validate the supposedly humanitarian nature of the asylum system of the West – is the process in which solid, liquid, and cloudy borders in countries of transit come together. Importantly, nations that were in conflict 20 years ago joined forces to accomplish this important task.

The migrant "crisis" amplified and accelerated a process that has long been in the making: the process of de-balkanisation of the Balkans. Yet the techno-social migration machine positioned in the Western Balkans was undoubtedly fragile during the largest influx of non-citizens in Europe after the Second World War. Multiple failed attempts by the state agencies of FYR Macedonia, Serbia, and, to lesser extent, Kosovo and Croatia to categorise green-, grey-, and black-listers of transnational mobility among thousands of non-citizens that transited through the region have been resented, if not condemned, by the EU and its member states, in particular Hungary and Austria. The dramatic changes in border regimes described earlier resulted in restoring much-needed control on the second largest migratory route in Europe. There is no doubt that security technologies played an important part in this complex social process. Cloudy borders are often deployed at geographical borders; while more covert than the razor-wire border fences in the region, they are 'at least as effective in obstructing migrants' (Bossong and Carrapico 2016, p. 10). These processes have been the chief, albeit not the only, driving force for changes in migration regimes along the Western Balkan migration route. Xenophobia and Islamophobia also played an important role in fine-tuning the techno-social migration machine in the region.

The "crisis" subsided in 2016. In order to consolidate the newly established "stability" and 'strengthen cooperation in the fields related to border management and monitor the flows on key migratory routes outside the EU' (Frontex 2017b), in 2017 Frontex appointed a liaison officer in Serbia. The Union is, apparently, preparing for future migratory pressures and is currently negotiating with Serbia and FYR Macedonia its new mandate that will allow the agency to operate in non-EU states if a neighbouring state 'requires assistance due to high migratory pressure' (Frontex 2017b, p. 3). In June 2018, Austrian and Danish governments confirmed that they are considering plans to build camps for migrants expelled from the EU, with the Western Balkans as a potential host site for such camps (B92, 15 June). Clearly, the region remains a key strategic point for the future management of non-citizens, pertinent to the stability of a delicate agreement between the EU and Turkey. This part of the world still 'holds some of the keys to managing the refugee flows' (de Borja Lasheras et al. 2016, p. 3), and as such, its role in mobility management is far from over. As one participant in my research warned, the migration machine in the region 'will certainly be stricter, as we move forward. The EU mechanisms are changing, so we have to follow. ... If they want to implement something, we have to do it, too' (participant 8, GA, Serbia). Judging from Serbian President Aleksandar Vučić's recent suggestion that migrants can assist in addressing brain-drain and negative population growth in Serbia (*Srbija Danas*, 18 March 2018), it seems that Serbia and the region are ready to follow such a lead. In the next chapter I examine state strategies of filtering and immobilising citizens, yet another crucial undertaking essential for the Western Balkans' EU future.

Notes

1 The "ten-day war" in Slovenia in 1991 and conflicts in Croatia, 1991–1995; Bosnia and Herzegovina, 1992–1995; and Kosovo, 1998, and the NATO bombing of the Federal Republic of Yugoslavia in 1999.
2 An informal, non-written, and non-legally binding agreement between two parties.
3 In June 2018, the governments of FYR Macedonia and Greece reached an agreement that was set to change the name of the country to the Republic of North Macedonia. However, Macedonian President Gjorgje Ivanov and his political party were not in support of this deal, and violent protests erupted in the Macedonian capital, Skopje, in June 2018. Citizens of Macedonia voted on the issue in a referendum set for 30 September 2018, with no conclusive outcome. The question posed to people directly linked the name change to the EU and NATO future of the country: 'Are you for EU and NATO membership by accepting the agreement between the Republic of Macedonia and the Republic of Greece?' The Parliament of FYR Macedonia had the power to vote for a name change as the nature of the referendum was "consultative" (see Kuzmanovski 2018). Indeed, the Macedonian Parliament voted for a name change on 20 October 2018, renaming the country the Republic of North Macedonia. The Greek government also faced a confidence vote as an outcome of the deal but survived the challenge. The Greek Parliament was set to vote on the issue in early 2019 (see Santora and Dimishkovski 2018).
4 In the Yugoslav Wars of the 1990s predominantly Orthodox Serbs fought predominantly Catholic Croats and Bosnian Muslims.
5 For the detailed history of the development of asylum system in Serbia and FYR Macedonia see Beznec et al. 2016.

Chapter 4

Social sorting of citizens

"Bogus" asylum seekers and proliferation of borders in the Western Balkans

> The choice for us in this case is very clear: either we export stability to the Balkans, or the Balkans export instability to us. (Former EU Commissioner for External Relations Chris Patten, cited in Brzakoska Bazerkoska 2016, p. 241)

> It is not freedom that creates instability, but the suppression of freedom. (Former German President Helmut Kohl, cited in Flessenkemper and Bütow 2011, p. 162)

Introduction

In the previous chapter I outlined one stream of the migrant "crisis" of the 2010s: transit of non-citizens through the Western Balkans. I chronicled strategies that target people on the move through the development of solid, liquid, and cloudy borders implemented at border crossings, within transit states, and in digital spaces. An additional stream of transnational mobility occurred in the region around the same time: a significant number of citizens of Kosovo, Serbia, FYR Macedonia, and Albania applied for asylum in the EU following visa liberalisation in 2009 and 2010. Local authorities found themselves under additional pressure, already troubled by ongoing requirements to manage people in transit. European governments and EU officials repeatedly urged political leaders and governments in the region to regain control over mobility of its citizens and to preclude "bogus" asylum seekers from applying for asylum in the EU. As such, the process of re-bordering in the Western Balkans has largely been bifurcated: one set of interventions focussed on regulating mobility of non-citizens; the second, outlined in this chapter, was directed at local populations.

Mobility as a 'freedom to choose where to be' (Bauman 1999, p. 40) is undoubtedly 'an essential element of human nature' (President of the 61st session of the UN General Assembly Sheikha Haya Rhashed Al Khalifa, cited in Kalm 2010, p. 32). The reality of the contemporary world is the movement of people (Bergson, cited in Adey 2009, p. 6) or, to be more precise, a desire for mobility. As such, transnational mobility in the 21st century is 'not an exceptional but a normal phenomenon' (Kalm 2010, p. 32). Nevertheless, as widely documented in the literature and as I demonstrated in the previous chapter, mobility of people from the Global South has been progressively challenged and regulated through a series of interventions in countries of destination, origin and transit. As Janet Wolf (1993, p. 253) eloquently puts it, 'we don't all have the same access to the road'. People are governed 'along the lines and rivers of mobility flows' (Adey 2009, p. 10), and their ability to cross borders has been contested every step of the way.

While states commonly place restrictions on non-citizens' right to enter their territory, the issue is more complex when it comes to the right of people to leave their own country. As citizens, we can be warned about leaving but not prevented from departing, except in the most extraordinary circumstances (Commissioner for Human Rights 2013, p. 8). Such circumstances have to be deemed necessary to protect national security, public order, public health, or the rights or freedoms of others. They also have to be provided by law and subject to a proportionality test (Commissioner for Human Rights 2013). Yet, as this chapter demonstrates, limitations on the freedom of movement of nationals − a basic human right guaranteed in the *Magna Carta* (Adey 2009, p. 105) and subsequent international human rights instruments, such as the *Universal Declaration of Human Rights*, the *International Covenant on Civil and Political Rights*, and the *European Convention on Human Rights* − have been widely implemented in the Western Balkans during the "crisis". Importantly, such restrictions were not necessary for the national security, public order, or public health of the communities and people of the region. *A contrario*, they were regulatory mechanisms authorised by EUrope set to reinstate control over border crossers in times of increased mobility pressures.

This chapter analyses the origins, developments, and effects of bordering practices in the south-east flank of the EU that target citizens of the Western Balkans. Building on scholarship that has looked into the mobility management in Africa, the Middle East, and Asia (see, for example, Boswell 2003; Hyndman and Mountz 2008; Vaughan-Williams 2011; Ikuteyijo 2014; Bossong and Carrapico 2016; Casas-Cortes et al. 2016; Infantino 2016), this chapter maps the migration machine in Serbia, FYR Macedonia, and Kosovo,[1] and examines the consequences of bordering practices in the region that specifically target citizens aspiring to temporarily or permanently migrate, seek asylum, and/or seek access to labour markets in Western Europe. The chapter also investigates the role of the EU and its member states in such developments in the region and their overall impact on human rights of people on the move. An important part of the analysis is a narrative of "bogus" asylum seekers and an examination of requirements put forward by the EU in order to regulate citizens' access to the Union and the Schengen Area of free movement.

In terms of the structure of the chapter, the overall history of mobility of citizens of the region and two case studies (Serbia/FYR Macedonia and

Kosovo) are outlined first for clarity reasons, followed by an analysis and theoretical engagement with those developments. While the debate about the (il)legality of bordering practices in the Western Balkans is deliberately omitted, their compatibility with human rights standards, including the right to leave the country and the right to seek asylum, is interrogated throughout the chapter. This chapter predominantly focusses on the racially and ethnically different "Other" by looking at how intersections of nationalism and racism in the region limit the migratory projects of (in this instance local) grey-listers of transnational mobility. I argue that bordering practices against the citizen "Other" are indeed racist as they violate the principle of non-discrimination (Article 2.1 of the *International Covenant on Civil and Political Rights* and Article 5(d) of the *International Convention on the Elimination of All Forms of Racial Discrimination*) and contradict the requirements set in individual *Roadmaps* for visa liberalisation. Moreover, I suggest that such practices serve to control the pace of movement of people from the region to the EU. They largely rest, I contend, on the border guards of countries of origin that authenticate the legitimacy of citizen-travellers on behalf of destination countries. It is border police that, like detention centres in Mezzadra and Neilson's (2013, p. 132) *Borders as Method*, perform the function of regulators of the time and speed of people's access to the labour markets and asylum systems in the West. When those mechanisms fail, deportation and other instruments of emerging punitive regimes of the Global North are activated in order to abate over-saturation of undesirables (see Bosworth et al. 2018). I commence this chapter with a review of key issues pertinent to mobility of men, women, and children from the region.

Mobility of citizens from the Western Balkans: history and developments

It was early September 2013. I flew from Vienna to Budapest on a small jet with just over 70 passengers on board. At the Ferenz List Ferihegy International Airport, a flight attendant announced that passport control was going to be performed at the tarmac and not inside the airport building, which is a standard practice for air travel. This was particularly surprising, given that the trip was entirely within the Schengen Area of free travel. I asked the flight attendant to explain the rationale for such practice. At that point I spotted a group of Roma passengers, sitting at the back of the plane. Dark-skinned and loud, they were visible but certainly not disruptive. The flight attendant calmly replied, 'Ms, this passport check is not for you. Please do not worry and put your passport back to your bag'. At the tarmac I spotted a police van. They quickly put the Roma family in and whisked them out of sight, flashing lights on. Flustered, I went inside to have a cup of coffee and collect my thoughts. As I was about to leave I saw the family being escorted out of the building. I kept wondering what had happened to them long after they were gone. This story, although geographically situated in the Schengen Area of purported free movement, is a good starting point for mapping mobility controls in the Western Balkans, where such freedom is not assured, not even by the letter of the law.

The history of the Balkans is one of both forced and voluntary mobility. As Bonifazi and Mamolo (2004, p. 519) note,

> [t]here is hardly another region of the world where the current situation of migrations is still considerably influenced by the past history as in the Balkans. Migrations have been a fundamental element of the history of the Balkans, accompanied by its stormy events.

The Yugoslav Wars that engulfed the region in the 1990s created the largest flow of forced migration in post-war Europe (Krasteva 2015). As outlined in the previous chapter, conflicts caused population movements, accompanied by the expansion of the Balkan's fluid borders and internal political instability. Indeed, as Alice Hills (2006, p. 123) suggests, borders 'dominate the security agenda' in 'a region of traditional smuggling routes, organised crime and corruption'. While perhaps somewhat exaggerated, this assertion reflects on some of the challenges the region has been facing for quite some time. Civil wars in the 1990s that caused thousands of people to flee Croatia, Bosnia and Herzegovina, and Kosovo; remnants of the socialist past accompanied by a (more or less successful) transition to neoliberal economies; a rise of unconsolidated democracies; ongoing political unrest and economic crisis; border disputes and the ambiguous status of Kosovo[2]; as well as organised crime and corruption make the Western Balkans a place of forced and voluntary migration. As Zimmerman and Jakir (2015, p. 14) argue, the region is a 'European "super-periphery"', marked by high unemployment, fragmentation, deindustrialisation, and political instability. The Western Balkans has long been constructed as an (linguistic, political, social, cultural, and ideological) outcast in the EUropean public and political discourse (see Komel 2015; Norris 2015). The precarious position of the region is best illustrated by de Borja Lasheras et al. (2016, p. 2), who called it the EU's "soft underbelly".

Yet, as outlined in Chapter 3, since the end of the tumultuous period of the 1990s, the Balkan states have been unanimous in their desire to join the EU. The powerful idea of the EU found its promoters in unlikely protagonists (such as Serbia's current centre-right pro-EU government, which was formed by former political allies of Slobodan Milošević). The accession of the Western Balkans to the EU has largely been a process of ongoing *conditionality*, to an extent that political elites in the region commonly refer to the Union as an 'annoying and tyrannical teacher constantly giving [us] new tasks' (Croatian journalist Tihomir Ponoš, cited in Zimmerman and Jakir 2015, p. 12). Adopting the EU's model of externalised border management was 'a first step in the process of integrating [the Western Balkans] into the EU' (Celador and Juncos 2012, p. 202). In that respect, the flow of both non-citizens and citizens had to be managed through the gradual (and conditional) process of visa liberalisation and other strategic frameworks I outline below. Local grey- and black-listers of transnational mobility who did not meet the threshold needed for accessing the asylum systems or labour markets of the West had to be controlled at the very source – in Serbia, Kosovo, and FYR Macedonia.

On paper, however, ensuring mobility of citizens was one of the key require- ments for candidate and potential candidate states. The individual *Roadmaps* for visa liberalisation stipulated a range of conditions pertinent to the freedom of movement that had to be fulfilled in order to obtain visa-free regime with the EU (previously mentioned requirements to issue biometric passports and requests to implement policies regarding minorities and non-discrimination rights – Kacarska 2015). As a part of the reporting process and implementa- tion of *the acquis*, prospective members had to provide data on the migration of their citizens to the EU and a report on the steps taken to reduce irregular migration (European Commission 2015a). Notably, the Western Balkans' rep- utation as the backdoor of Europe quickly re-emerged in EUrope's pubic and political discourse after visa liberalisation in 2009 and 2010.[3]

Visa-free regime granted to citizens of Serbia and FYR Macedonia re- sulted in an increase of asylum applicants in the EU. The overall number of claimants rose by 76 per cent in the year after the liberalisation (Trauner and Manigrassi 2014) and, as the EU officials claimed in 2015, 'has been rising steadily since' (European Commission 2015a, p. 3). During the first year of the migrant "crisis", in 2014, asylum applicants from the Western Balkans reached 110,000 persons (EASO 2015), only to peak at almost 180,000 in the first three quarters of 2015 (Lange 2016). The total amount of asylum appli- cations from the Western Balkans in the period 2009–2015 reached 538,140 (Malaj and de Rubertis 2017), while the percentage of citizens from the re- gion in the overall pool of asylum applicants in Europe grew to 17 per cent at the end of 2014 (the second largest number of applications after Syria – EASO 2015). People aiming to seek asylum and/or access labour markets in the EU typically travelled from the Serbian capital city of Belgrade to Subotica on the Hungary-Serbia border, where they crossed into the Schengen Area and onwards, mostly to Germany (EASO 2015). The flow from the region was 'clearly seasonal', climaxing in the winter months (see Korićanac et al. 2013; Lukić 2013). Kosovo applicants were mainly ethnic Albanians, while those from Serbia, Bosnia and Herzegovina, and FYR Macedonia were mostly Roma (EASO 2015). Only about 4 per cent succeeded in obtaining asylum or subsidiary protection, one of the lowest recognition rates of any country of origin (EASO 2015, p. 36). A growing number of unskilled labourers and "bogus" asylum seekers, as they were frequently called, rekindled accounts of the Balkans as a place where 'violence and backwardness are an indelible part' (Flessenkemper and Bütow 2011, p. 168) of the fabric of the region. The discriminatory language depicting asylum claimants as "unwanted invaders"

(Parker 2015) and "illegals" (Brouwer et al. 2017b) has been neatly interwoven into EUrope's media landscape, targeting in particular Roma and migrants from Kosovo.

While there is no doubt that the movement of people intensified after visa liberalisation, some commentators assessed such growth as "insignificant" in the context of the overall numbers of third-country nationals that enter the EU annually (see Commissioner for Human Rights 2013, p. 43). The influx of citizens of the Western Balkans, however, endangered a visa-free regime, even before its peak during the "crisis". In 2011, the EU introduced the safeguard clause, which allowed temporary interruption of visa-free systems 'in exceptional and well-defined circumstances'. One such circumstance was a substantial and sudden increase in the number of asylum applications (Sommo 2011). Following Frontex's annual statistics for 2013, which suggested that the number of undocumented crossings of citizens of the Western Balkans was comparable to the number of non-European migrants in transit (European Commission 2015a, p. 4), the European Parliament adopted a resolution in December 2013, introducing such a "protective mechanism" (European Commission 2015a) against the nations of the Western Balkans. In 2014, the European Commission further responded to the "crisis" by opening post-visa liberalisation missions in Serbia and FYR Macedonia (Kacarska 2015), while the states with the largest number of asylum applications (such as Germany) declared Serbia, FYR Macedonia, and Bosnia and Herzegovina as safe countries of origin, shortened the asylum procedure for their citizens, and cut allowances and benefits for asylum seekers from the region (Heuser 2014; EASO 2015). The European Commission urged the candidate and prospective candidate states to implement measures in order to regulate the influx of their citizens and establish a monitoring mechanism to 'evaluate the sustainability of reforms aiming to uphold the scheme's integrity' (European Commission 2015a, p. 2; see also Kacarska 2015). In order to avoid the suspension of the visa-free regime, countries of the Western Balkans were requested to

> increase targeted assistance to minority populations, especially Roma people; enhance operational cooperation and information exchange with neighbouring states, EU member states and relevant EU agencies; investigate and prosecute facilitators of irregular migration; enhance border controls in compliance with citizens' fundamental rights; and organise information campaigns about the visa-free travel scheme. (European Commission 2015a, p. 5)

It is against this backdrop that an additional arm of the migration machine for social sorting has been developed in the region. Policies and practices of "doing border" have, once again, been offshored to non-EU states and their border management agencies. Somewhat different from the flows of non-citizens, mobility of the local population has been regulated mostly through "walls" and "locks" at the physical and, to some extent, internal borders of the region.

Reinforcing purgatory: citizen "Other" in a holding pattern

While the EU has identified "bogus" asylum seekers as an important political issue since the early 2000s (see Lukić 2016), a stern warning by the Union that unwanted border crossers have to be kept at home by all means came after the visa liberalisation of 2009 and 2010. Since 2011, countries with the largest numbers of asylum seekers, led by Germany, issued a range of demands to the governments of Serbia, Kosovo, and FYR Macedonia to restrict their citizens' (mostly Roma and Kosovo Albanians) access to labour markets and asylum systems in the West. While addressing causes of transborder mobility (such as racism and nationalism, ghettoisation, and the poverty and high unemployment of Roma– see Grupa 484 and Nexus 2012; Sardelić 2014; Leko 2017) would arguably be a more logical and effective response to the issue, EUrope's push to regulate mobility triggered a range of drastic measures that prevented people from leaving the region. Two main strategies to restrict the movement of the local "Other" have emerged: legal reforms that criminalised the abuse of visa-free regime and the racial profiling of non-citizens at border crossings (Kacarska 2015). Such measures violated people's human rights, in particular the right to leave the country and the right to seek asylum. In the following section I focus on Serbia and FYR Macedonia's responses to the "bogus" asylum seekers "crisis" as their responses have been almost identical. I present the case study of Kosovo later in the chapter as an anomaly that summarises the tumultuous nature of bordering practices aimed at citizens of the region.

'Bogus asylum seekers risk everything': rescuing visa liberalisation and the EU future in Serbia and FYR Macedonia

Applicants from Serbia (with Kosovo[4]) constitute a share of 60–80 per cent of the total asylum claims from the region since visa liberalisation in 2009 (EASO 2015, p. 5; see also European Commission 2015a). Data by Frontex (2013) indicate that 15,900 asylum seekers from Serbia were registered in 2012 (mainly in Germany), an increase of 38 per cent compared to 2011. At the same time, only about 1 per cent of asylum applications were approved, making the asylum recognition rate in the EU/Schengen Area at 2.7 per cent (European Commission 2015a). An isolated research project on the topic conducted by a group of Serbian NGOs in 2012 and 2013 indicated that the 'key reasons why citizens of Serbia seek asylum in the Western Europe are deeply rooted in extremely difficult economic and social circumstances of, in particular, Roma minority' (Korićanac et al. 2013, p. 5). Roma are, undeniably, 'the most marginalized and discriminated ethnic minority in Europe' (Malecki 2014, p. 111). As Askola (2011, p. 49) argues,

> Roma have historically been and continue to be constructed as Europe's outsiders, experiencing discrimination and marginalisation, and Romani women in particular are situated as subjects of multiple and intersectional discrimination.

During Elizabethan times in England, Roma were subjected to exile and executions as well as limited mobility (Pickering and Weber 2006, p. 6). In modern-day Europe they are persistently at the very margins of society, with high rates of unemployment and poverty, and low rates of education and well-being (Commissioner for Human Rights 2013; Vukelić 2013; Cherkezova 2014; Ferreira and Kostakopolou 2016). It comes as no surprise then that Roma in Serbia are in a very precarious situation. According to Korićanac et al. (2013, p. 13), they are over seven times more likely to live in poverty, with over 56 per cent of Roma children living under the poverty line.

In public discourse, Roma have frequently been labelled as '[people] not willing to work who want easy money' (participant 4, NGO Serbia). Yet employment opportunities for Roma in Serbia are scarce at best. While key national strategies[5] identify Roma as vulnerable because of poor living conditions, poverty, social exclusion, discrimination, lack of education, and a high rate of unemployment (Ministarstvo za ljudska i manjinska prava 2010; Korićanac et al. 2013; Vujadinović et al. 2013), and while they are the biggest group of Serbian citizens returned from the EU in accordance with bilateral readmission agreements, measures for the social inclusion of Roma have been piecemeal (participant 4, NGO, Serbia). The Serbian Prime Minister at the time of the "crisis", Aleksandar Vučić, called Roma 'traditionally poor people', suggesting that poverty is a part of their heritage and history, not linked to racism or discrimination (Bojić 2017).

The migration of Roma is undoubtedly seasonal. They leave Serbia to survive harsh winters, and, as one respondent pointed out, 'a vast majority... go [to the EU] to access allowances. ... It is better for them, financially, to leave, seek asylum, get the money and come back after the winter' (participant 8, GA, Serbia). Serbian media frequently reported about a monetary "reward" Roma were "given" in the EU:

> Even if their claim is rejected, they come home as "richlings". ... The risk pays off. Roma returnees from France or Germany testify about a generous monetary support of up to EUR 2,000 a month. With that money, even if they are immediately deported, they can live [in Serbia] for a year. ... The time [they spend in the asylum procedure] is sort of a rest, a break from daily struggles. (Lukić 2013, p. 33)

Thus, in the Serbian public discourse Roma border crossers have been constructed as risk-takers while the 'asylum system in [the EU] is the only way
[for Roma] to secure a decent life, notwithstanding the length of stay and
negative consequences' (Korićanac et al. 2013, p. 10; participant 4, NGO,
Serbia). The unbearable reality of the daily lives of many Serbian Roma,
thus, leads to risky journeys into the unknown. Nevertheless, according to
participants in my research, there is an obscure deviance and opportunism
that underpins such endeavours:

> When they seek asylum in Germany, Sweden, or Belgium, Roma wait
> there while the procedure finishes. During this time, they get financial
> assistance. Some countries have allowances for people who pull out from
> the asylum process. When you have so many poor people as you do in
> Serbia, it is *not surprising that many see this as an opportunity to profit.* ...
> They don't need visas anymore, so they jump on a bus, go to Germany,
> apply for asylum, and *come back after two months with money they couldn't get
> here in six months.* (participant 9, IO; my emphasis)

In 2011 and 2012, EU officials frequently used Serbian broadsheet and tabloid
media to warn the government and citizens of Serbia about the possible can-
cellation of visa-free regime if asylum pressures continued. At the same time,
media furthered the stereotype of the "deviant Other" by potraying citizens
seeking asylum as professional beggars and social parasites, who ultimately
fail in their quests:

- Bogus asylum seeking as a profession, *B92*, 18 October 2012;
- Bogus asylum seekers: Poverty sends fugitives back home, *Večernje Novosti*, 18 October 2012.

While Serbian authorities initially failed to explicitly mention Roma in
the media, European officials and foreign commentators did not shy away
from such statements. For example, Alexandra Stiglmeyer, senior analyst
for the European Stability Initiative, suggested in 2012 that 'the majority of bogus asylum seekers are Roma. So, if Serbia or FYR Macedonia
starts taking Roma off buses, that would be ethnic discrimination' (cited in
B92, 18 October 2012). Roma were soon singled out as a major threat to
Serbia's visa-free regime as the then Minister of Interior warned that they
might even 'endanger Serbian national and state interests if they seek asylum
abroad' (Chachipe 2012, p. 90). Participants in my research also saw Roma
"bogus" asylum seekers as one of the biggest obstacles on Serbia's road to the
EU (participant 4, NGO, Serbia; participant 8, NGO, Serbia). As one NGO
representative suggested, this is simply because '[the EU] is impacted by this
issue, much more than [transiting non-citizens]'. As such, she continued, the
Serbian government can find itself in a situation where '[w]e are supposedly

on our way to the EU ... negotiating accession to the EU, but we might have visas again' (participant 4, NGO, Serbia).

As the "crisis" intensified in 2013, Serbian media further focussed on the link between "bogus" asylum seekers' ethnicity and the potential demise of visa-free regime, and what needs to be done to avoid such a fate:

- Asylum seekers: Roma will bring visas back, *Večernje Novosti*, 28 January 2013;
- An increase in bogus asylum seekers can lead to the cancelation of visa-free regime, *Politika*, 12 September 2013;
- Bogus asylum seekers "wobble" visa-free regime, *Blic*, 20 December 2013;
- [Chief of Serbian Police] Veljović: Reducing the number of bogus asylum seekers is a priority, *RTV*, 29 October 2013.

Contrary to research (Korićanac et al. 2013, p. 12), media reports often implied that Roma were 'mistaken when it comes to asylum, ... [and] are misinformed and led to believe something that is not true' (Serbian Roma rights activist and former deputy Director of the Office for Human and Minority Rights Dragoljub Acković, cited in Lukić 2013, p. 33). In a series of articles commissioned by the Norwegian Embassy in Serbia, prospective asylum seekers were warned that

> [w]hen people apply for asylum in the EU they are housed in asylum centres. Then they wait, and wait. Finally, their application is granted, or they are deported. Sometimes asylum seekers end up in prison. The situation is not as great as one might think. (Lukić 2013, p. 32)

Further, media frequently implied that asylum seekers from the region were economic migrants, not asylum seekers. Their asylum applications, it was argued, can have consequences both for the applicants and for the nations from which the "invaders" originate (see Lukić 2013):

> *Spending many hours in lines in front of embassies* of Italy, Germany, France, Belgium and other European countries *can soon become a gloomy reality for Serbian citizens*. In order to protect its borders from *an invasion of so-called bogus asylum seekers*, the EU indicated to the governments of the Western Balkan that the time has come to take warnings about suspension of visa-free regimes very seriously. (Pantić 2013, p. 22; my emphasis)

To address these concerns, in 2011 the Serbian government launched a campaign to 'educate its citizens' (participant 8, GA, Serbia) about the perils of irregular migration to the EU (Vukosavljević 2011). Cities and towns in southern Serbia with a large Roma and Albanian populations, border crossings on the Serbia-Hungary and Serbia-Croatia borders, and Belgrade's Nikola Tesla International Airport were at the forefront of the campaign (see Chachipe 2012, p. 88). At the time of writing this book, posters authorised by the Serbian government still greet travellers at passport control booths. They send a stark warning to locals aiming to seek asylum or access labour markets in the EU about the consequences of such actions. This is clearly suggested in the title: 'Bogus asylum seekers risk everything'. The text of the poster is as follows: 'The financial aid that they receive will be cancelled. They will be deported to Serbia. They will be banned from entering the EU for a period of time'. Small print reads, 'Visa liberalisation does not mean the right to work, unlimited stay, and political asylum in the EU member states' (my translation) (Figure 4.1).

Figure 4.1 'Bogus asylum seekers risk everything' poster (top) at Belgrade Nikola Tesla Airport's departure passport control booth.
Photo credit: Sonya Adams, March 2018.

As the effectiveness of education campaigns in reducing mobility is often marginal (see Pécoud 2010), these were complimented with legal reforms that set the foundation for the further reinforcement of solid borders in the region. In 2011, Serbia adopted Article 5 of the *Schengen Borders Code* and passed a special decree[6] that gave border police extra powers, including the right to interrogate travellers about their migration history and future plans. As such, Serbian police had the right to inquire about the purpose of the travellers' trip and request that they present a return ticket, invitation letter, medical insurance, finances, and proof of accommodation in their country of destination (Vukosavljević 2011). In December 2012, the Serbian parliament passed a law criminalising the abuse of the right to seek asylum abroad (*The Criminal Codex of the Republic of Serbia*, Official Gazette 85/2005, 88/2005-isp., 107/2005-isp., 72/2009, 111/2009 and 121/2012). As one government official from Serbia suggested, this led to 'us controlling [our citizens] but this is something Hungarians should do'. Nevertheless, as she continued,

> [Serbian police] cannot prevent people from crossing borders, they have the right to do so. Our hands are bound in that sense. … Article 5 of the Schengen Border Code stipulates what citizens that cross borders have to have, what border police can ask them – for example, a return ticket, invitation letter, health insurance, money, accommodation and so on. We now check if our citizens have all that, when they travel to the EU. But if they do, we can't prevent them from leaving. That is impossible. (participant 8, GA, Serbia)

It appears, however, that law enforcement's hands have not been so bound after all. The head of the Serbian border police, Nenad Banović, confirmed in a media interview that over 250 Serbian citizens were returned to Serbia in January and February of 2011, before the introduction of the outlined radical measures (*RTS*, 10 March 2011). From February to November 2011, 1,715 people were prevented from leaving the country (Chachipe 2012), among them a Roma family that was banned from boarding a flight to go to a wedding in Sweden (*Večernje Novosti*, 1 December 2011). Precluding Serbian citizens from leaving the country has largely been a discretionary power of border police officials. Thus, they have no obligation to provide an explanation or a statement containing a reason for such a decision, making it impossible for unsuccessful border crossers to challenge it in a court of law (see Kacarska 2015). In addition to frequent and arbitrary returns, people who were permitted to cross borders have routinely been warned that any potential asylum claim they make in the future will not be successful (participant 4, NGO, Serbia). Such practice is not surprising, given that any movement of Roma – even within the Schengen Area, as demonstrated in the story from the beginning of this chapter – is deemed to be suspicious and risky. Racial profiling at the gates of EUrope is alive, so much so that state agencies openly talk about practices of "profiling", as the following example illustrates:

> [Roma] have been increasingly stopped at border crossings and asked how much money they have. This is a violation of their human rights. Police calls [this practice] as it is. We don't blame [Serbian police] for do- ing this - the EU demands it. Yes, they tell us - 'we do profiling'. When we ask 'how do you "do profiling"', it is clear. When [police] stop a bus, you see who they take off. (participant 4, NGO, Serbia)

Practices of profiling proliferated during the migrant "crisis" of 2014–2015. The Minister of Interior in the Serbian government at the time left little doubt as to who was the target of border pushbacks, stating that '[n]o one from [Albanian and Roma] communities will be able to leave the country if they do not have a return ticket, means to support their stay, and cannot state the reason for the journey' (Ivica Dačić, cited in Kacarska 2015, p. 372; see also *B92*, 8 May 2011). Pressured by the EU, the Serbian government toughened its rhetoric, declaring that the state would 'reinstate the order' by making abuse of visa-free regime 'an ugly past'. It also promised to 'take repressive, restrictive measures to stop abuses, and… fiercely punish [abusers of the sys- tem]' (State Secretary of the Ministry of Internal Affairs, *Sky Plus* 2014). In 2014 Serbian authorities refused the right to leave the country to more than 6,500 Serbian citizens 'unable to justify the purpose of their stay in the EU' (European Commission 2015a, p. 6). The government also suggested that it would cover the costs of repatriation for 10,000 asylum seekers from Europe in order to eliminate the threat of the return of visas (Riegert 2012). Visa-free regime as 'the single most valued prize in the European integration process' (*The Economist*, 5 January 2013) and the foundation of the state's EU future had to be saved at all costs. As the Serbian Commissioner for Refugees (cited in Rujević 2017) summed it up, '[w]e say [to the German authorities]: "How can we help you? Shorten the procedure. Serbia is a safe country; return them to us in 24 hours". You don't need to be too smart to figure it out'.

These strategies yielded results that pleased the administration in Brussels. The pushbacks grew, while the number of applications for asylum from Ser- bian citizens dropped by 55 per cent in 2016 compared to 2015 and to 41 per cent between the second half of 2016 and the first half of 2017 (European Commission 2017c). Serbia's visa-free regime and its European future was safe for the time being (Figure 4.2).

FYR Macedonia followed the path set by their northern neighbours. In 2009, the Prime Minister announced that visa liberalisation was 'a small step for the EU, but a giant leap for Macedonia' (cited in Trauner and Manigrassi 2014). It is no wonder, then, that the government was ready to defend no-visa policy with the EU by all means. While the authorities took steps to improve the integration of Albanian and Roma minorities into the country, similar to

Figure 4.2 'We can help you' poster at Belgrade Nikola Tesla Airport's arrivals. The text of the poster is as follows: 'Counselling centre for return-ees' (my translation). A Catholic church-run charity, Caritas Serbia, authorised the poster (logo in the top right corner).
Photo credit: Sanja Milivojevic, March 2018.

developments in Serbia the focus of the Macedonian authorities was mostly on solid borders. The parliament passed a law criminalising the abuse of the visa-free regime, and in 2012 four people were imprisoned for this crime (Mackic, cited in Kacarska 2015). FYR Macedonia also passed an amend-ment to the *Law on Travel Documents,* stipulating that citizens who have been forcibly returned to or expelled from another country shall not be issued a passport, or their existing passport shall be confiscated for a period of one year (Mahmut and Bikovski 2014). This is yet another direct violation of the right to leave the country as guaranteed in the international law and the *Roadmap.*

Similar to regulating the migration flows of non-citizens, the governments of the region focussed on mutual cooperation in order to address the issue of "bogus" asylum seekers. FYR Macedonia opened joint law enforcement centres with Serbia and Kosovo; enhanced cooperation with Frontex; and, importantly, 'considerably strengthened border controls, leading to a 41 per cent increase in exit refusals in 2013' (European Commission 2015a, p. 5). Macedonian parliament passed a law allowing border police the discretionary power to 'temporarily suspend the right to travel on only the suspicion of being a potential "failed asylum seeker" as well as carrying on border checks based on ethnic profiling' (Trauner and Manigrassi 2014, pp. 136–137). As Mahmut and Bikovski (2014, p. 25) note, between 2011 and 2013, 74 Roma were prevented from exiting the country, and 24 had their passports revoked.[7] In 90 per cent of the cases analysed by the European Roma Rights Centre, only Roma were asked to provide evidence pertinent to their journey; 30 per cent were told they could not cross the border because of their ethnicity (Mahmut and Bikovski 2014). These numbers were probably underestimated as the Commissioner for Human Rights' (2013, p. 48) report suggests that between December 2009 and November 2012 approximately 7,000 citizens of FYR Macedonia were refused exit, and their passports were frequently confiscated. Unsuccessful border crossers' travel documents were imprinted with the words "AZ"[8] (Kacarska 2015), labelling them as perpetual black-listers of transnational mobility.

While such policy, to put it mildly, 'teeters on the racist and the illegal' (*The Economist*, 5 January 2013), its impact was clear: the number of refusals grew, and there was a significant decrease in asylum applications from the country in 2015 and 2016 (European Commission 2017c). With these bordering practices FYR Macedonia effectively created 'a padlocked cage' for Roma (Mahmut and Bikovski 2014) and arguably succeeded in keeping the visa-free regime alive.

In the few short years after visa liberalisation the number of border crossers from Serbia and FYR Macedonia faded through the interplay of solid and liquid borders in the region. The outlined measures reduced the "pressure" on labour markets and asylum systems in the EU/Schengen Area through overt discrimination of the ethnically and racially different "Other":

> Whereas in block four [of the *Roadmap*, the European Commission and EU member states] demanded us to ensure the freedom of movement without any discrimination, what they demand now is basically that if there is an Albanian, or Roma or a poor person at the border to treat him/her differently. (NGO activist, cited in Kacaska 2016, p. 372)

Such bordering practices contravene not only requirements set for Serbia and FYR Macedonia in individual *Roadmaps* but, more importantly, those set in the *European Convention of Human Rights*, the *Universal Declaration of Human*

Rights (for detailed analysis on this, see Flessenkemper and Bütow 2011; ERSTE Stiftung and ESI 2013; Mahmut and Bikovski 2014), and Constitutions of Serbia and FYR Macedonia. While both countries were successful in developing mechanisms for regulating mobility of ethnic and racial minorities from their territory, Kosovo's target was the majority of its populace.

'Kosovo is what you fought for... now go back and rebuild it': a puzzling case study of mass migration and unlikely alliances

Similar to other nations in the region, migration 'has been an important livelihood strategy for a significant share of Kosovo's population and is likely to remain so in the foreseeable future' (Gashi and Haxhikadrija 2012, p. 6). After declaring independence from Serbia in February 2008, Kosovo had been singled out as one of the European countries of origin with the highest number of migrants (Möllers et al. 2017b). With an overall unemployment rate of 33 per cent and a youth unemployment rate of a staggering 57 per cent, Kosovo citizens are among the poorest in Europe (UNDP 2016). Their desire for cross-border mobility has been juxtaposed with limited opportunities. Kosovo is the only country in the Western Balkans that does not have visa liberalisation regime with the EU, making it 'one of the most isolated places on earth' (European Stability Initiative, cited in Kacarska 2015, p. 370). At the same time, political tensions that are still present in the region, such as Serbia's refusal to recognise Kosovo as an independent state, further contribute to instability. As such, Kosovo citizens were not allowed to travel through Serbia with Kosovo passports or identification documents until 2012, when the EU pressured the Serbian government to allow such an arrangement (Bytyci and Than 2015). In another important development, as Serbia considers Kosovo an integral part of the Republic of Serbia, citizens of Kosovo were allowed to apply for a Serbian passport that would grant them access to visa-free travel to the EU. In January and February of 2015 alone, approximately 60,000 Kosovars applied for a Serbian passport (Möllers et al. 2017a).

It was against this backdrop that approximately 100,000 citizens of Kosovo left the country to seek asylum in the EU in 2015 and 2016 (Möllers et al. 2017a; see also Friedrich Ebert Stiftung 2015). Dubbed by a German consulate official in Prishtina as 'an avalanche of asylum seekers' (*RTS* 2015), up to 1,000 people a day travelled from Kosovo to Serbia and further to the EU, mostly without papers. About 10,000 Kosovars applied for asylum in Hungary in January 2015 alone, compared to 6,000 applicants total in 2013 (Murati 2015). In Germany, the number of applicants from Kosovo doubled compared to that in the month of December 2014 (*RTS* 2015). Kosovo border officials argued that they were unable to stop citizens from crossing borders as there was no legal basis for such a ban. As one participant from Kosovo pointed out,

[p]eople legally cross [t]he border with Serbia, so Kosovo police can't stop them. ... You cannot limit peoples' freedom. If a citizen of Kosovo ... says at the border: 'I want to have a cup of coffee in Belgrade', you cannot deny his freedom of movement. (participant 28, academic, Kosovo)

The motivation for such a sudden influx of border crossers remains largely unknown.[9] While there is a recognition that 'people leave due to harsh economic conditions' (participant 38, NGO, Kosovo), as the following quotes suggest, migratory flows from Kosovo were not spontaneous. While initially haphazard, the journeys of Kosovars towards the West were supported by local "entrepreneurs" in the countries of origin (Kosovo) and transit (Serbia):

People saw their neighbours pack up and leave, and it did not look dangerous. So, they hopped on a bus and went to Serbia. [Smugglers] waited for them in Serbia, everything was organized. ... Every night, ten or fifteen buses left Prishtina for Belgrade, and it was all legal. (participant 28, academic, Kosovo)

The agreement signed with Serbia allows Kosovo citizens to cross the border with Serbia with an identification document. Up to this point everything is legal. They cross Serbian-Hungarian border illegally. ... There were organized groups [in Kosovo and Serbia], ... people paid huge sums of money to be able to cross the border with Hungary. (participant 28, academic, Kosovo)

In order to reduce the number of asylum applicants from Kosovo, Germany changed its asylum procedure to "urgent", while state agencies were allowed to carry out a forcible return of Kosovo citizens (Cani 2015). The German government declared Kosovo a safe country of origin, which further accelerated the rate of rejection of asylum claims (Stute 2015). The EU states kept sending thousands of Kosovars back: in 2015–2016 the number of repatriated citizens surpassed 26,000 (Möller et al. 2017a). As one participant from Kosovo pointed out, '[t]he response of the EU representatives to this issue was simple: Kosovo is what you fought for, now you have it – go back and rebuild it' (participant 28, academic, Kosovo).

Similar to scenarios in Serbia and FYR Macedonia, "bogus" asylum seekers were identified as a threat to the visa-free regime that Kosovo was yet to obtain (participant 28, academic, Kosovo; participant 37, IO). The government of Kosovo launched several prevention campaigns to preclude people from applying for asylum in the EU. The target, however, was not racial or ethnic minorities, but the majority of Kosovo's population. Media reports in Prishtina and other cities were saturated with images of '[refugee] camps in bad conditions, so people slowly started coming back. [The government] also pressed charges against several [smuggling] groups' (participant 28, academic, Kosovo). While the authorities could not resort to profiling like their

Serbian and Macedonian counterparts, they did something that only a few years before would have been considered impossible: they shared the task of immobilising Kosovo citizens with their long-time adversary – Serbian border police. As the following quote confirms, cooperation with Serbia was crucial in preventing "bogus" asylum seekers from Kosovo from getting to the EU:

> One clear example [of cooperation between Serbian and Kosovo police] is when [a group of smugglers tried to enter] Serbia. On the Kosovo side they recognised the van [as suspicious], but everybody had [Kosovo] documents, so they couldn't stop them…. [There was] a van full of people, a driver was a Serbian national doesn't speak a word of Albanian, and passengers were Kosovars from different parts of Kosovo, they didn't know each other … When you see something like this the flag goes up. Kosovo authorities passed the information to the [Serbian] side and they were denied entry into Serbia. … I think we had about 6,000 or 7,000 prevented departures total [in this way]. (participant 37, INGO)

This partnership between Serbia and Kosovo in mobility management was thought to be beneficial for both states as they hoped to pick up extra points with the administration in Brussels. Kosovo was particularly keen to work on this issue with Serbia, hoping to obtain a much-desired visa liberalisation with the EU. Nonetheless, as one participant in my research pointed out, '[the EU] intentionally kept visa liberalisation as a carrot [to enhance Kosovo's] relationship with Serbia' (participant 28, academic, Kosovo). While this "crisis" was unfolding, the Serbian government claimed that they could not stop the movement of Kosovars towards the West, even though Belgrade insisted, as it still does, that Kosovo is a Serbian territory. The then Serbian Prime Minister had a clear message for the EU, saying that the Union

> [t]old us to give Kosovo Albanians freedom of movement. We gave them that. Now you want us to restrict [it]. Please just tell us: should we allow it or deny it? But please do not say that Serbia is to blame for this. … Whatever you tell us to do, we will do it. (cited in TV N1, 12 February 2015)

What Serbian officials ultimately did was the following: in the space of two days in February 2015 (7–9 February), Serbian police stopped 4,400 people at the border with Hungary (Medić 2015). Almost all were citizens of Kosovo or, in the eyes of the Serbian law, citizens of Serbia, trying to cross Serbian borders. It is here, in the processes of immobilising citizens-yet-non-citizens at the physical borders of Kosovo and Serbia, that one can fully appreciate the absurdity of borders and bordering practices in the Western Balkans in all their complexity.

Conclusion: solid and liquid borders targeting citizens of the Western Balkans

Governing transnational mobility in countries of origin happens at many points and junctures. Contemporary borders, as Wonders (2006) argued over a decade ago, are semi-permeable in a multitude of ways. They are flows and locks, as well as walls and fences, that categorise people and regulate the pace of mobility flows. The operational arms of the migration machine that filters people on the move have been outsourced to the Global South: in the 21st century, migration management increasingly happens in countries of transit and countries of origin. Subjects of such management are both skilled and un-skilled workers and asylum seekers, for whom "circular" migration manage-ment is advocated – one that is fluid and provides a steady supply of cheap and flexible labour to meet the demand in countries of destination (see Kalm 2010).

A ring of novel solid and liquid borders has been designed and carried out by (mostly) law enforcement agencies in the Western Balkans, effectively *do-ing border* on behalf of the Global North. During the "crisis" of asylum appli-cants from the region, states responded to the EU requests by submitting their citizens to a range of bordering practices at physical and internal borders. Narratives of "bogus" asylum seekers or "economic migrants" were carefully crafted in the media and public discourse, accompanied by "education" cam-paigns that aimed to keep prospective border crossers at home. Through the enforcement of solid borders, citizens of Serbia and FYR Macedonia were subjected to pushbacks that resulted in the violation of their human rights and discrimination against the racially and ethnically different "Other". This has caused the (temporary or permanent) disruption of mobility, mostly of non-white and ethnically diverse populations from the region. While such processes have clearly been instigated and fostered by the Global North, the outcry over such discriminatory practices fell on the states and governments of the Western Balkans. Yet again, the EU's scruples in mobility management have been upheld. Indeed, in the *Roadmaps* and the *acquis* there is an explicit requirement for freedom of movement without discrimination; it is in the laws and discretionary practices of law enforcement and other agencies in the region that discriminatory and racial practices supposedly take place. The hy-pocrisy of EUrope has never seemed more transparent than on this very issue.

While border studies increasingly stress the importance of the multiplicity of borders and the process of the detachment of borders from the territory of the nation (see Sassen 2006; Weber 2006), physical borders and their enforce-ment apparatus still play an important role in mobility management. The bor-der police of nation-states of the Western Balkans, often considered the "soft underbelly" of Europe, have now been promoted to the guards of the EU's migration regime, with the ability to effectively govern transnational mobility. They are at the forefront of the migration machine that aims to deliver a much desired 'dream of correlating migratory movements with perceived economic and social needs established by statistical analyses of labor market dynamics, demographic studies, and political priorities' (Mezzadra and Neilson 2013, p. 138). Such practices are barriers that, like water dams, hold and release the number of people that corresponds with demands for both the skilled and the unskilled labour market, political prestige, and the overall assessment of "optimal" migration flows. These zones of interruption, waiting, and holding (Mezzadra and Neilson 2013) are, similar to the zones that filter non-citizens described in the previous chapter, marked with controversy. Border enforcers in potential and candidate states are tasked with decision-making that is undoubtedly discriminatory, racist, and illegal. The construction and enforcement of the "bogus" asylum seeker profile serves to streamline this process. As demonstrated in the case study of Serbia, framing citizens as racially and ethnically different "Others" with no right to asylum locates the Roma minority (or Kosovo Albanians, in the case of FYR Macedonia) as a key threat to the nation's visa-free regime and – ultimately – the EU membership. The pushbacks (done on behalf of and for the benefit of the West) are conceptualised as a task necessary for the survival of the nation and its European future. As state agencies of the Western Balkans perform this important task, the administration in Brussels and member states of the EU have been reluctant to condemn such discriminatory practices; after all, they are the key beneficiaries of such interventions. The outlined practices eliminate the *fragmented refugee subject* (Kmak 2015) from the Western Balkans – the "Other", "bogus" asylum seekers that want to defraud the asylum system or penetrate the labour market, whose mobility is therefore both illicit and immoral.

Étienne Balibar (2002) and Leanne Weber (2006), amongst others, argued that people from different social groups experience heterogeneous borders in different ways. Indeed, race and ethnicity are an integral part of the border regimes around the world. As Brouwer et al. (2017b) demonstrate in their study of crimmigration controls in border areas of the Netherlands, racism can be traced to the bordering practices of developed EU member states. Unsurprisingly, race and ethnicity play an important part in bordering practices in the Western Balkans, a region where race, religion, and ethnicity have been *the* cause of wars and unrests for centuries. As this chapter demonstrates, Roma bore the brunt of discriminatory bordering practices in the region. To quote Saskia Sassen (2014, p. 18), 'Europe has failed Roma for centuries', and keeps doing so. Through the bordering practices and policies mapped earlier, designed in Europe, and implemented in the Western Balkans, Roma are framed as

> a mobile (racialized, criminalized) menace to the stability and integrity of (Western) European "civilization", whose flight from protracted poverty and entrenched marginalization must not even conceivably be apprehensible as the mobility of refugees fleeing institutionalized persecution and structural violence within Europe. (De Genova 2017a, p. 20)

In addition to racial discrimination, there is evidence of significant ethnically based profiling at the outer border of the EU. Through limitations on the right to leave the country in instances of increased transnational flows, ethnic Albanians from Kosovo and FYR Macedonia join Roma as "off-white" and religiously different outcasts that have been subjected to a strictly regulated opportunity to access both the labour market and the asylum systems of the EU. The borders of Europe, thus, have been underpinned by the postcolonial politics of race that 'refortifies Europe-ness as a racial formation of whiteness' (De Genova 2017a, p. 21). Yet a limited number of low skilled, racialised bodies will ultimately be sieved through to meet the demand for (marginalised and exploitative) labour in the Global North. Borders, as Panagiotidis and Tsianos (cited in Mezzadra and Neilson 2013, p. 183) argue, seek to 'produce governable' and, I would argue, economically and politically useful 'mobile subjects from ungovernable flows'. As this analysis suggests, the role of physical border is still central to this quest.

A case study of Kosovo, however, indicates all the intricacy of such projects in complex social settings like the Western Balkans. Set to ensure the European future of Kosovo, restrictions imposed on Kosovo's citizens initially yielded unlikely alliances between former enemies. Nevertheless, things can turn ugly very quickly, especially in this region. Blaming Kosovo Albanians for the potential disruption of visa-free regimes in Serbia and accusing Serbian authorities of non-engagement when it comes to stopping Kosovo citizens at their borders are just some scenarios that can easily rekindle animosities of the recent past.

The Global North demands control of border crossers passing through but also people from the region. Through interventions outlined in this chapter, the governments of Serbia, FYR Macedonia, and Kosovo effectively precluded their citizens from accessing fundamental rights and freedoms, such as the freedom of movement and the right to seek asylum. Indeed, 'one of the most egregious human rights abuses common to totalitarian regimes is the closure of their borders' (Commissioner for Human Rights 2013, p. 10). The negative and inevitable consequences of these processes, such as racial profiling and governing mobility through the race and ethnicity of border crossers, are, it seems, a price that potential and candidate states are willing to pay to get much needed political points for the big prize – their EUropean future. However, as European refugee and Roma rights activists have warned, '[t]he idea that citizens would eventually be hindered from leaving their country on the grounds of their ethnic background is unbearable to us against the background of German and European history' (cited in Angelos 2011). Those accountable for such violations are in Belgrade, Skopje, and Prishtina, as suggested in the Council of Europe's Commissioner for Human Rights (2013) report but also among those that designed and uphold the 'white Schengen' (Heuser 2014, p. 78). In the following chapter I look at practices of governing mobility of women border crossers through counter-trafficking strategies developed and implemented in the region.

Notes

1 While a country of origin for citizens seeking asylum in the West, Albania was not included in this research as it is not located on the Western Balkans migration route.
2 At the time of writing Kosovo is not recognised as an independent state by five EU member states – Spain, Slovakia, Cyprus, Romania, and Greece. Serbia also does not recognise Kosovo as an independent state.
3 Serbia, Montenegro, and FYR Macedonia got visa liberalisation in 2009; Albania and Bosnia and Herzegovina got this in 2010. At the time of writing Kosovo is the only country without visa-free regime with the EU.
4 In some statistics Kosovo features as a part of Serbia, while in others it is represented as an independent state, thus the discrepancy in the numbers.
5 *Strategy of reintegration of returnees based on the readmission agreements* and *Strategy for the improvement of the Status of Roma in the Republic of Serbia*, adopted in 2009 and 2010.
6 *Uredba o bližem uređivanju načina vršenja policijskih ovlašćenja policijskih službenika granične policije i dužnostima lica koje prelaze državnu granicu*, Službeni glasnik RS br. 39/2011.
7 Mahmut and Bikovski (2014) suggest that these numbers are not definite as there were an additional 50 cases that were not officially registered.
8 Short for "azil" – "asylum", indicating the reason they were refused the right to leave the country.
9 Möllers et al (2017) single out political instability, economic hardship, and a range of facilitators that encouraged people to leave. Interestingly, the International Organisation for Migration (IOM) suggested on its official Twitter account that a 'sharp rise in #asylum applications may be driven by #SocialMedia' (IOM Twitter post, 13 February 2015). Möllers at al. (2017) also suggest that Facebook played an important role in 'luring' people to seek asylum in Germany.

Chapter 5

Bordering women, via trafficking

Gender and mobility of non-citizens

Contemporary state's efforts to combat "trafficking" go hand in glove with their wider actions against "illegal" migration. ... The measures employed by contemporary states in an effort to immobilize would-be migrants and drive out those who succeed in entering or remaining in their territory without authorization have nothing to do with protecting human rights. (O'Connell Davidson 2015, p. 130)

I look into [the] future. For my child, [the] future [should] be better. ... I wish better for my child. This is why I always have to be strong. ... I have to look [to] the future. 'Thank you for bringing us here', my child [will] say, 'be strong, you are fighting for us'. I just think about that. Sometimes I'm crying. I'm crying, why [did] you come, if you stay[ed] it [would] be better. But I always, I close that door. I open the future doors. The future will be better for me. ("Khandan", Iran)

Introduction

While risking being overly (albeit unavoidably) repetitive, I would like to begin yet another chapter with a widening mobility gap as an opening argument. As this chapter is about mobility of women from the Global South, or lack thereof, it is important to remind ourselves that 'profit-driven, uncoordinated and uncontrolled globalisation... does not translate into the growth of equality' (Bauman 2011, p. 50). Inequality is perhaps most apparent in the hierarchy of mobility of the global population: according to the United Nations' Department of Economic and Social Affairs (2015), most migrants originate from middle-income countries. However, inequality is not simply geographical; it is gendered too. The feminisation of survival (Sassen 2000) leaves households and communities in the developing and developed world increasingly dependent on women's labour. The feminisation of the global labour market and migration are an outcome of, *inter alia*, shrinking employment opportunities and worsening living conditions in the Global South. Currently, women comprise about half of all international migrants (UN Department of Economic and Social Affairs 2015; Hennebry et al. 2016) and half of over 25 million refugees worldwide (UN Women 2018). For the majority of women, legal options to cross borders are limited (Morrison and Crosland 2000; Pickering 2011; Segrave 2017).

Within a growing population of illegalised migrants across the world, 'the most vulnerable are often the least visible: women and children' (APC/CZA 2013b). While lack of opportunities does not hinder their desire to pursue a better life, nor their longing for international mobility, women are less likely than men to reach their country of destination. Their journeys are delayed as women frequently get stuck in countries of transit due to financial constraints, violence, abuse, exploitation, and pregnancy, and because they travel with children (Freedman 2007; Pickering 2011; Turek 2013; UNFPA 2013). Thus, as Marchand (2008, p. 1387) argues, '[i]t goes without saying that the migration – violence nexus is gendered'.

In this context human trafficking has been singled out as a major risk for women border crossers, as '[w]omen and children fleeing violence are especially likely to become victims of traffickers and smugglers' (European Parliament 2016, p. 7). A recent report by the UN Special Rapporteur on Trafficking in Persons noted that trafficking is 'often interlinked with mixed migration movements, encompassing various categories of persons on the move, including refugees, asylum seekers and migrants travelling, mostly in an irregular manner' (UN General Assembly Human Rights Council 2018, p. 3). Female migrants, it is commonly argued, might enter the migratory process independently or with a smuggler, but their journey often turns 'into trafficking at a later stage' (UN General Assembly Human Rights Council 2018, p. 4). This anxiety about women's mobility is not new. As Ratna Kapur (2016, p. 25) argues, the last decade has brought 'an extraordinary proliferation of law regulating cross-border movements, in the area of trafficking as well as people smuggling'. In contemporary public discourse and policy debates women migrants are often portrayed as victims lacking agency and in need of protection and/or rescue. Finally, the role of technology as a potential facilitator of trafficking and a tool that can potentially prevent exploitation has also been emphasised (and rebutted) in the literature (see Latonero et al. 2012; Musto and boyd 2014; Milivojevic and Segrave 2017).

This chapter follows a road less travelled. It builds a picture, however incomplete, of the potential intersections of gender and borders in the Western Balkans, and their impact on women non-citizens prior to, during, and after the "crisis". The chapter documents the multiplicity of borders and bordering practices, deployed as conventional and "humanitarian" interventions in the region, and highlights their role in regulating women's transborder mobility. While there are important limitations in terms of scope, data, and analysis, this chapter unpacks yet another important part of the puzzle and further assists in deciphering the mobility machine in this part of the world.

A migration-trafficking conundrum

The border hardening described in previous chapters has undoubtedly shifted transnational migration patterns towards riskier, less-accessible borderlands. A lack of legal options results in migrants' reliance on illegalised, undocumented alternatives (Boswell 2003; Lee 2011). Yet, as Pickering (2011, p. 1) notes, 'the experience of extra-legal crossing is significantly different for women'. Their journeys are more dangerous, even lethal (see Weber and Pickering 2011; Gerard and Pickering 2012; Pickering 2013; Pickering and Cochrane 2013). Physical and sexual violence at the hands of smugglers, state agents, and fellow migrants in countries of origin and transit are common experiences for women, already in a precarious position because of the hazardous routes they have to take. As such, the number of women who reach the Global North is disproportionally small. For example, at the peak of the migrant "crisis" approximately three-quarters of asylum applicants in the EU, including Norway and Switzerland, were men (Connor 2015). Punitive bordering practices increase the demand for people smugglers (Koser 2001), whose "helping hand" in the context of extra-legal border crossings can expose women to exploitation and abuse, including human trafficking (Koser 2000, 2001; Morrison and Crosland 2000; Boswell 2003; UNHCR 2006; Aas 2007; Akee et al. 2010; Galonja and Jovanović 2011; Korićanac et al. 2013; McAdam 2013; Turek 2013; Brunovskis and Surtees 2017).

For almost 30 years human trafficking/trafficking in people has been observed and analysed by international policy-makers, governments, law enforcement, activists, and academics from a range of disciplines. Described as a 'dark side of globalization' (Apap et al. 2002; Berman 2003), concerns around trafficking followed a period of heightened mobility in Europe after the collapse of the Iron Curtain. It was at this point in history that trafficking was irreversibly linked to "illegal" migration (Lazaridis 2001) as commentators argued that the collapse of hard borders between the communist East and the capitalist West would lead to the exploitation of thousands of women, primarily in the sex industry (see Segrave et al. 2009; Milivojevic and Pickering 2013). While a 'doomsday' scenario (Cohen 1991) of migration floods and women's sexual slavery never befell, trafficking has ever since been firmly positioned as a cross-border crime issue (Lee 2011; Milivojevic and Segrave 2017; Segrave et al. 2018). In the international context, it has been regulated in the *Protocol to Prevent, Suppress and Punish Trafficking in Persons, Especially Women and Children*, supplementary to the UN Convention against Transnational Organized Crime (in further text "the Protocol"). Constructed as a transnational and/or organised crime issue, the law and order zero tolerance approach dominated both national and international responses to trafficking. In a 'the tsunami of counter-trafficking policy and legislation that followed in the wake of key international commitments in 2000s' (Segrave and Milivojevic 2015, p. 132), the definition of trafficking has been clarified and simplified, only to remain ambiguous. As Chuang (2014, p. 610) points out, we are still in a 'definitional muddle' when it comes to conceptualising trafficking. I, along with many critical feminist scholars, consider trafficking to be a form of exploitation that can happen to migrants when they have limited options to move across and within borders via regularised routes, an exploitation that is rooted in various state practices that create, further entrench, or contribute to their vulnerability (Milivojevic et al. 2017).

Trafficking has been constructed as a gendered issue from the very beginning of this renewed national and international engagement as women border crossers 'tend to embody a particular kind of "powerlessness" in the Western imagination' (Malkki, cited in Freedman 2010, p. 193). In the media and public discourse women migrants are often portrayed as helpless victims of traffickers (Andrijasevic 2007) but also their culture (Freedman 2010) and people smugglers (Sanchez 2013). As such, contemporary policy responses to the vulnerability of women migrants build on the notion of agency-deprived victims in need of protection. They are to be "rescued" from trafficking and other perils through "traditional" bordering practices – border controls in countries of origin and transit but also "humanitarian" interventions designed to prevent their likely future victimisation (Andrijasevic 2007; Nieuwenhuys and Pécoud 2007; Milivojevic and Pickering 2008; Pécoud 2010).

The Global North's counter-trafficking framework has largely focussed on the prosecution of traffickers and coordination and cooperation of border agencies in order to prevent exploitation and victimisation. Since trafficking has a clearly defined (often putative) crime victim in need of rescue (Lee 2011; Pickering 2011), immigration and law enforcement agencies have commonly been tasked with the job (see Weber 2003; Ham et al. 2013; Gerard 2014). The Protocol in Article 11 provides that nation-states 'shall strengthen, to the extent possible … border controls as may be necessary to prevent and detect trafficking in persons' (UN 2000) without specifying what such border control should entail (Edwards 2007). The *Recommended Principles and Guidelines on Human Rights and Human Trafficking* put in place safeguards against the exploitation of migrants, including the indicators of potential trafficking that should assist law enforcement in identifying victims of trafficking. One indicator of women's vulnerability are cases where women express agency (as the capacity and potential to make choices and decisions about their own life – Mahdavi 2014, p. 12) in an "inappropriate" way. When there is "too much agency", for example when women are identified as potential sex workers or when they travel alone, they are carefully watched and regulated (see Ham et al. 2013). As Kempadoo et al. (2005, p. 29) noted over two decades ago, there is 'a bias that women and girls need constant male or state protection from harm, and therefore must not be allowed to exercise their right to movement'. As I demonstrate in this chapter, this bias is very much alive today.

While some nations overtly restrict women's migration opportunities in order to prevent their impending victimisation (Gozdziak 2015), others do so more subtly through counter-trafficking mechanisms. Saving "trafficking Cinderellas" (Doezema 2000) from sexual exploitation has been a key rationale for the introduction of restrictive policies for women migrants (Apap et al. 2002; Freedman 2007; Segrave et al. 2009; Lee 2011; Milivojevic and Pickering 2013; Milivojevic et al. 2017). At the same time, the narrative of evil traffickers serves as 'a *suitable enemy* for the reinforcement of state power' (Nelken 2010, p. 490, original emphasis). Thus, restoring order at the border can be accomplished only through the criminalisation of trafficking, prosecution of traffickers, and implementation of border regimes in both the terrestrial and digital sphere that stratify and regulate the scope and pace of women's mobility (see Boswell 2003; Segrave et al. 2009; Berman 2010; Gerard and Pickering 2012).

It is against this backdrop of counter-trafficking developments that Europe faced increased migratory flows in the 2010s. As scholars began to chart women's vulnerability to violence in times of increased mobility (see, for example, Freedman 2016), the "crisis" seemed to 'expose serious protection gaps' when it comes to potential victims of trafficking (UN General Assembly Human Rights Council 2018, p. 4). The European Commission launched a comprehensive *European Agenda on Migration* on 4 March 2015, calling for a more robust approach in fighting irregular migration and dismantling smuggling and trafficking networks (European Commission 2015b, p. 6). Indeed, this key policy document suggested that trafficking and smuggling are interlinked as migrants, while often commence their journeys voluntarily, are vulnerable to sexual or labour exploitation along the way (European Commission 2015b; see also Dimitriadi 2016). Identification of victims, it was argued, is difficult at arrival areas or in transit countries

> due to little awareness of the indicators of trafficking in persons and of victims' needs among first responders, and an unwillingness from the potential victims themselves to be identified and registered in a country that is not their intended country of destination. (UN General Assembly Human Rights Council 2018, p. 4)

As the "crisis" intensified, the international community's focus was, yet again, on governments in countries of transit, including those on the Western Balkans migration route.

Gender, risk, and pre-emption: regulating mobility through trafficking "prevention" in the Western Balkans

State agencies and NGOs in the region have engaged with countering trafficking since the early 1990s. As nations of the Western Balkans emerged as countries of source, transit and destination for victims of trafficking

(Nikolić-Ristanović et al. 2004; Segrave et al. 2009), feminist organisations such as *La Strada International* strongly supported anti-trafficking initiatives in Albania, Serbia, Croatia, FYR Macedonia, and Kosovo (see Andrijasevic 2007; Milivojevic and Pickering 2013; Vullnetari and King 2014). Local NGOs and government agencies have been recipients of '[a] great deal of money… since the late 1990s', most of which has been spent on criminal justice responses and the prevention of trafficking (Surtees and de Kerchove 2014, p. 65). A proliferation of information campaigns that, under the premise of preventing trafficking, discouraged potential migrants from crossing borders is well documented in the trafficking literature (Boswell 2003; Sharma 2003; Andrijasevic 2007; Nieuwenhuys and Pécoud 2007; Pécoud 2010). The goal of ending trafficking and exploitation has commonly been pursued through graphic, violent, and gendered representation of women's vulnerable and sexualised bodies (Andrijasevic 2007) but also through restrictive border control measures. As such, the EU has long been urging FYR Macedonia, Serbia, Kosovo, and Croatia to reinforce their borders in order to combat extra-legal migration and human trafficking as a cross-border criminal activity. As I demonstrate below, prevention campaigns and punitive bordering strategies climaxed during the migrant "crisis".

While women constituted around 14 per cent of transiting non-citizens in the Western Balkans migration route in 2015 (IOM 2015), their presence in public discourse, media, and policy debates has been limited and linked almost exclusively to the risk of trafficking (Galonja and Jovanović 2011). The international community, regional agencies, foreign and local governments, and independent experts all seem to agree that trafficking is *the* key risk factor for women and children on their way to Western Europe (Krstić 2012; Morača 2014; European Parliament 2016; Women's Refugee Commission 2016; Brunovskis and Surtees 2017). Indeed, Serbia's *Strategy for Prevention and Combating Trafficking in People 2014–2020* identified migrant women and children migrants as especially vulnerable to trafficking (Rudić 2014). NGOs in the region shared this concern. As argued by Serbian anti-trafficking NGO ATINA, '[m]igrants fleeing war and insecurities and looking for better life find themselves with limited options … [They] are exposed to high risk of trafficking in people. Especially vulnerable are unaccompanied women and underage children' (ATINA 2013). While only one victim of trafficking was identified among non-citizens that transited Serbia in the period 2013–2015 (Rudić 2014; Jelačić Kojić 2016), this figure was deemed to be 'not an accurate reflection given the risks and exploitation large number of refugees and migrants face every day' (Jelačić Kojić 2016, p. 23). The haste with which men, women, and children travel through the region, as well as the magnitude of migration flows, it was argued, prevents identification of exploitation within the migrant population (Jelačić Kojić 2016; Women's Refugee Commission 2016). The victims, thus, were perhaps hard to find, but they were certainly out there.

Exposure to violence and exploitation

My research confirms findings by Brunovskis and Surtees (2017) that women non-citizens transiting through the Western Balkans during the migrant "crisis" have been linked to sexual violence and (mostly sexual) exploitation in countries of origin, transit, and destination. Overall vulnerability of women migrants has been singled out as an important starting point when discussing their mobility:

> [Women] tell us about their home country and the trip. These are horrific stories. ... Many lost at least one family member. ... Rape is common, especially for women from Congo; many are pregnant as a consequence. ... *[W]omen are more vulnerable [than men].* (participant 3, INGO; my emphasis)

The risk of violence and abuse remain with women for the duration of the journey. Authorities assisting migrants in the region flag sexual violence in countries of transit as a common experience for women, particularly if they travel on their own. While the majority of women transit the Western Balkans travel with family members or in groups, the overall consensus of professionals in the region is that the number of single women on the road is growing (participant 3, INGO; participant 5, GA, Serbia; participant 6, NGO, Serbia; participant 14, NGO, Croatia; participant 15, NGO, Croatia; see also Freedman 2016). This population is identified as especially at risk of exploitation, including trafficking (participant 5, GA, Serbia; participant 15, NGO, Croatia):

> We monitor all women, but in particular those who travel alone. Firstly, because they are alone, especially if they are young, so we immediately think forced prostitution, we are worried about that. ... We follow them more closely if they are without fathers, husbands. (participant 19, INGO)

A lack of masculine protection, thus, increases women's vulnerability. Sexual exploitation and assaults happen either in the sex industry in countries of transit or at the hands of smugglers, particularly when women's journeys are temporarily interrupted. In their recent research in the Western Balkans, Burnovskis and Surtees (2017, p. 19) argue that exploitation and victimisation of women migrants happens when they run out of resources or when migratory routes are temporarily or permanently closed. My research confirms this notion as professionals working with women argue that they are forced to 'make compromises' in order to facilitate or enable their voyages:

> Young women are extremely vulnerable to trafficking. Some of them are probably already trafficked. ... *They make compromises to keep moving*

forward. When you are alone, when you are a woman, in a place like Greece or Serbia where sexual services are requested in exchange for smuggling, ... they are forced to engage in prostitution... and that is a fertile ground for traffickers. (participant 2, NGO, Serbia; my emphasis)

The gendered nature of trafficking debate in the region is apparent as unaccompanied young men in transit do not raise the same level of concern (Brunovskis and Surtees 2017, p. 24). Men are trusted to look after themselves, even when they are young adults. Stereotypical narratives of masculinity that identify men as active participants in the migration process while linking women's mobility to risk and vulnerability were prominent in my research. To counter risks and potential exploitation, according to respondents I spoke with and according to previous research in the region, unaccompanied women actively seek or are appointed male "protectors":

Some women told us they know women forced to prostitution. Pimps say, 'you have to work, or you are dead. You have no papers'. They even tell us about women being killed in Greece. I think they were from Nigeria. ... Women told us about rape and sexual violence that happened on the Greece-Macedonia border. They need someone on the road, a guy, who will look after them. They tell us, 'he is not really my brother, but he is my brother, I travel with him'. (participant 6, NGO, Serbia)

When women from Somalia travel alone ... the smuggler appoints someone to be their brother and look after them. You don't pay for this, it is a protection of your own. ... When we go to the toilet, a man from Somalia comes with us. When someone from another country helps us, there is always someone from Somalia as well. When we sleep we are always between two guys from Somalia. ('O', cited in Morača 2014, p. 43)

A notion of naïve, innocent victims of trafficking that dominated the trafficking debate in the 1990s and early 2000s (see Doezema 2000; Andrijasevic 2007; Segrave et al. 2009; Lee 2011) seems to extend to the whole population of migrant women in times of increased mobility. Their vulnerability has arguably been furthered by their passivity, lack of education, exposure to smuggling networks, and "illegality" in countries of transit:

They are at risk as they cross borders illegally, they stay [in countries of transit] illegally, they travel with smugglers, with criminals.... They are also not educated or have limited education ... don't speak English, don't have many choices so they rely on people who can trick them. (participant 19, INGO)

Having this mind, it was not surprising that underpinning government agencies and NGOs during the "crisis" was the premise that women on the move need to be rescued, before the victimisation occurs.

Identification, rescue, and prevention

When women are faced with such adversity, it is a responsibility of the state and civil society to provide protection and rescue for potential victims. My research confirmed that authorities and agencies assisting migrants in the Western Balkans created a list of "indicators" that assists first responders, NGOs, and government agencies in identifying women at risk. Women's stories were carefully screened for possible sings of exposure to trafficking, either in countries of origin or while on the road. Interestingly, as I was told by a legal aid worker from Croatia, such signs might include the aforementioned masculine "protection". A male companion, thus, could easily be a woman's guardian but could also be a potential trafficker:

> An indicator [for trafficking] can be how she came [to Croatia]. If she says 'I came here with two men that are not my relatives and I didn't give them any money [for the trip]' or something like that – the alarm bells start to ring. (participant 15, NGO, Croatia)

As in my previous research on trafficking (Milivojevic and Pickering 2008; Segrave et al. 2009) and the works of several critical feminist scholars (Andrijasevic 2007; Ham et al. 2013; Pickering and Ham 2014), women's potential or actual engagement in the sex industry was a red flag for agencies that work with asylum seekers. They promptly reported such suspicion, largely based on women's appearance or demeanour, in order to "prevent" women's forthcoming victimisation:

> There are women from Eritrea who travel alone and want to be hairdressers or babysitters. There are cases where we suspect that women have been or still are engaged in prostitution. *You can tell when you look at them.* ... We as a state agency watch and listen to this population and everything we see or hear we pass on [to the authorities]. ... Police and other agencies come to [asylum centres] from time to time to talk to certain people. ... All the info we have – we pass on. (participant 5, GA, Serbia; my emphasis)

> The way they behave, the way they dress, those little things... might spark a suspicion [about women's involvement in sex work]. Then we report it to the police and Red Cross. (participant 15, NGO, Croatia)

Yet, as I mentioned at the beginning of this chapter, identification of victims in countries of transit is difficult and rare (see also McAdam 2013; Segrave et al. 2018). Experts working with the women I talked to identified only a handful of cases of potential trafficking, none of which were pursued, let alone prosecuted. This flawed process, however, prompted agencies to look *into the future* in order to locate *potential,* not likely risk of, trafficking. The prospect of what *could happen* to women once they got to the country of destination emerged as rationale for an intervention. As Korićanac et al. (2013, p. 12) note,

> asylum seekers use the same routes as traffickers, they often have no papers, have limited funds, often have limited information about what to expect in the country of destination, don't know the language and cannot go back to the country of origin.

Thus, preventing exploitation at the end of women's journeys legitimised restrictive measures imposed on them in transit. Again, a notion of the vulnerable, naïve, young female victim dominated the narrative, as has been the case in counter-trafficking debates in the 1990s and 2000s:

> Girls say, 'I want to be a babysitter, I want to go to school', similar to what women from Serbia talked about fifteen years ago. ... We see the same delusions again. When we work on prevention ... we give them information about trafficking and how to recognise it. ... They have unrealistic goals. When we say to them, 'things might not be like that' they don't want to hear it. ... They want to go to paradise, as they really think Europe is a paradise. (participant 2, NGO, Serbia)

> Women often have unrealistic expectations, like, 'I'll be a doctor when I get there'. You can't be a doctor if you are 23, and you have no education. And you really think you can be a doctor in Norway? [laughs] Many [women] think they will be hairdressers, babysitters, work in supermarkets. ... They think it will be easy. (participant 6, NGO Serbia)

> They know there is such a thing as trafficking... but don't think it can happen to them. So, we try to explain to them they are potential victims too. ... We tell them how to recognise the signs whether they are trafficked already or might be trafficked in the future. (participant 19, INGO)

As Vullnetari and King (2014) note, the anti-prostitution and anti-immigration agenda set up by the international counter-trafficking movement further limits women's mobility by advising them to stay at home (or in countries of transit) if they wish to be safe. A harsh reality of migration has been extrapolated in campaigns to educate the ignorant and rescue them from victimisation (Andrijasevic 2007; Nieuwenhuys and Pecoud 2007). Importantly, as noted by Korićanac et al. (2013, p. 18), such campaigns often create fear. Women non-citizens transiting the Western Balkans have been "educated" about the risks of victimisation and advised to come forward if they have been subjected to exploitation. Similar to broader anti-trafficking prevention campaigns, these education sessions reinforce the notion of "home" as a safe place (Andrijasevic 2007), even if "home" is a centre for asylum seekers in Serbia or Croatia. Education campaigns and interventions by NGOs and law enforcement specifically target women who travel alone (participant 2, NGO, Serbia; participant 3, INGO; participant 6, NGO, Serbia).

A key issue identified by several service providers in the region is that it is 'hard to fight trafficking as [women] don't stay here; they are simply in transit' (participant 2, NGO, Serbia; participant 15, NGO, Croatia). As one government representative from Serbia pointed out, women simply want to 'rest, heal, feed, get some clothes, get money and move on' (participant 5, GA, Serbia). Nevertheless, even if women reject psychological help or other assistance, agencies don't give up; they 'give them more time [to make up their mind] and continue to offer psychological help' (participant 3, INGO). Those identified as at risk of trafficking are also proactively approached by psychologists, social workers, police, and government anti-trafficking agencies; advised about risks they might face if they keep going; and ultimately instructed to rethink their journeys:

> We try to demystify the destination for them. We don't want to scare them but want to stress that trafficking exists everywhere. The place they are going to, regardless of how progressive and rich it might be, could also be a place where they will become victims. … They all use smugglers… and we try to explain to them that smugglers are often connected with traffickers, or maybe are traffickers themselves. (participant 19, INGO)

> Prevention of trafficking [is done] through informing women about dangers, giving them info about organisations in countries of destination [that can help], we do workshops, we find them – and give them everything women and young people might need. (participant 2, NGO, Serbia)

Andrijasevic (2007) and Weitzer (2007) suggested a decade ago that anti-trafficking campaigns tailored for women specifically target the risk of sex trafficking. My participants confirm that women are almost exclusively warned about trafficking for the purpose of sexual exploitation, while men are (sporadically) educated about labour trafficking:

> You have to shake them up a bit, to sober them up a bit, that the fact they are young and pretty is a risk that someone will force them into sex industry. … With men we sometimes talk about labour exploitation, that they can be drug mules, [victims of] trafficking in body parts, as that is more relevant for them, more likely to happen. (participant 19, INGO)

Counsellors also closely observe women who do not participate in anti-trafficking sessions; they often talk to women's legal advisors to discuss the case and ensure they are not at risk (participant 19, INGO). Finally, if identified as potential victims of trafficking women are offered a victim status in the country of transit (participant 19, INGO; participant 15, NGO, Croatia). Those identified as at risk of trafficking are also encouraged by law enforcement to apply for asylum, as identified in previous research in the region:

> There were 8 Somali women, with 2, 3 kids. They were not familiar with the right to asylum. Given that they were definitely potential victims, as they sold their property in Somalia, and their husbands were all killed, we told them about asylum and gave them asylum papers, even though they did not ask for them. We explained the concept for them and they applied [for asylum], of course. (Police officer, Sremska Mitrovica, Serbia, cited in Morača 2014, p. 58)

Yet, for women border crossers, "home" – whether in country of origin or in transit – is not a safe place; it is a place where war, violence, uncertainty, and poverty are the pervasive reality of women's lives. Crucially, women on the move will under no circumstances willingly interrupt their journeys to claim victim status, especially not when they are so close to their desired destinations. Nonetheless, while mobility of men has been regulated through the concoction of solid, liquid, and cloudy borders in the region, women's migration projects have been managed through both traditional and "humanitarian" strategies aimed at preventing potential victimisation in countries of destination.

A brief note on trafficking and technology: the absence of evidence and the need for future research

Given the importance of trafficking in mobility management, it is no surprise that technology has long been investigated as a potential facilitator for, and a site to combat, human trafficking (Milivojevic 2012; Musto and boyd 2014; European Parliament 2016). Constructed largely on speculative accounts and shoddy research, the risks of technology-enabled trafficking practices have been frequently pointed out by policy-makers, law enforcement agencies, and academics, all while 'the extent to which online technologies are used in both sex and labor trafficking is unclear, and the current approach to the question is lacking' (Latonero 2011, p. iv). The link between trafficking and technology has been amplified in recent times, with claims that '[t]he whole trafficking chain is facilitated by digital technologies' (European Parliament 2016, p. 6). The illusive fantasy of what I call e-trafficking (Milivojevic 2012) portrays women as the easy prey of online predators, pimps, and traffickers that use a range of hi-tech platforms (smartphones, social media, online advertising sites, and the like) to enable and facilitate exploitation. Importantly, technology itself 'has been constructed as a new (and extreme) form of violence, so much so that sweeping and somewhat apocalyptic claims … have prompted supra-national international organisations and state governments into action' (Milivojevic and Segrave 2017, p. 30). A series of reports, working papers, and other policy documents have been written in order to tackle the "problem" of e-trafficking, followed by a range of potential strategies that can utilise technological advancements in combating the issue (especially in areas of crime prevention).

Countering trafficking via technology has been particularly prominent in countries of origin and transit. Social media has been identified as a fertile ground where awareness raising strategies can be deployed. As such, national and international organisations and governments have been using social media to warn potential victims – would-be migrants – of the dangers of trafficking (Milivojevic 2012; Gong 2015; European Parliament 2016). The message is clear: stay at home and/or double check your future employer before going overseas. The focus is on "education" of (in particular young) women from the Global South that scrutinises and often dismisses their entrepreneurial mobility projects (see Mendel and Sharapov 2016 for the context of Ukraine). Surveillance of potential victims and offenders, state interventions in the digital sphere, and unconditional cooperation with law enforcement in investigating these crimes are perceived as necessary measures to "protect" women from becoming victims of trafficking (Musto and boyd 2014; Milivojevic and Segrave 2017). While these developments have been built on limited evidence, in the absence of evidence there is a strong, gendered, and moralising argument that, yet again, advocates for the rescue of innocent victims (Milivojevic and Segrave 2017).

However, the reality is that we know very little about whether and to what extent technology has been used to facilitate and prevent human trafficking. Unfortunately, this research captured only traces of cloudy borders deployed in the Western Balkans to regulate the flow of women non-citizens. While my research offers sporadic evidence that 'border police use social networks … in preventing cross-border crime, but not in a systematic way' (participant 33, GA, FYR Macedonia), and while claims that 'human trafficking can be prevented via new technologies' (participant 35, NGO, FYR Macedonia) have been chronicled in this study, the need for more comprehensive research on this topic in the Western Balkans and the Global South more broadly is apparent. There is a limited understanding of how security technologies regulate women's mobility but also of how women themselves use technology to enable their migratory journeys and the implications of counter-trafficking policies on their mobility and agency. While I touch on some of these themes here and in the final chapter, they remain largely uncharted in this volume.

Countering borders: agency, mobility, and survival

Juxtaposed with accounts of risk and future victimisation are stories of vulnerability, survival, perseverance, and – above all – agency. Jane Freedman (2016) has recently chronicled the coping strategies of women migrants in the Mediterranean, some of whom potentially tracked the Western Balkans migratory route. Against the odds, women in the region battled not only memories and experiences of violence in countries of origin but also hazards they encountered in transit:

> We had a complaint from a woman from Nigeria. She was in a detention facility and was harassed by two men. She complained to the guards and social workers, but no one helped her. When we raised this with the asylum authority they simply denied it, they blamed the victim. Officials said, 'why didn't she do this or that'. So even if they want to … prevent sexual and gender-based violence … the mechanisms [to do so] are not in place. (participant 10, NGO, Hungary)

Analogous to previously recorded testimonies of women migrants and asylum seekers in Serbia (APC/CZA 2012), my research confirms that the journeys of women transiting the region are not linear but delayed and intercepted. While they were not identified as potential or actual victims of trafficking, and while the government agencies and NGOs I spoke with identified only a handful of potential victims they worked with during the migrant "crisis", limited opportunities for transnational mobility pressured many women to appoint "agents".[1] People assisting women in the region also confirmed the vital role that smugglers play in enabling mobility. Still, women's journeys were often interrupted, if only temporarily, by illness, pregnancy, or weather conditions, or simply because they needed to rest:

> A woman from Afghanistan … her child was very sick. … She was here for a month. Everyone helped her, for free, and the child survived, but the husband couldn't come [to see them]. When he finally came, it was one of the most emotional moments [for us]. She was like a new person, with make-up on, glowing. They left after a week and called us from Germany. That was a good story. (participant 1, NGO Serbia)

> There are women in the centre, but not here, at the border. … It is so cold in the "jungle",[2] it's almost as cold as it is outside. They have to be in the "jungle" for several days [in order to cross the border]. Can you imagine a pregnant woman here, right? I mean, it is different in summer. It is Ok. Well, it's not Ok, it's never Ok to sleep outside. But at least they won't freeze. They are not used to this weather. We had a woman a few days ago in slippers! [laughs] I mean, seriously, what are you doing?! (participant 24, NGO Serbia)

> My impression is that women with families stay [in the region] a bit longer. They stay in asylum centres. I'm not sure if this is because they need to get the money, or they want to give their kids a rest. (participant 3, INGO)

Women I talked to and others on the Western Balkans migration route stumble, albeit temporarily, at the gates of Fortress Europe. "Zainab" from Iraq remembered a young woman from Africa with a seven-month-old baby. Police caught this woman at the Serbia-Hungary border and brought her back to the asylum centre in Bogovađa. 'That must be hard', Zainab said, 'with the baby'. "Delaram", a woman from Afghanistan, left her home country five years ago, contrary to her husband's wishes. She made him leave Afghanistan too. They spent five years in Turkey, unable to cross the Turkey-Greece border. Delaram's husband was at the time of my research in Switzerland, while she was stuck in Serbia with children. As she explained, 'the situation [on the road] is always perfect for a man, not for a woman'. When asked about her experience of crossing borders, Khandan from Iran quietly said, '[i]t was scary. You know I still have bad dreams, every night. I woke up I cry. And I call my father. He is in Iran. He says that I should let go of Iran. Iran is bad'.

Yet women are often the ones who show agency and initiative on the road, even in precarious situations. As the below quotes indicate, they quickly adapt to new surroundings and do what they need to do to survive, even if this means disobeying traditional gender roles:

> I approached a group of women and men from Afghanistan in the "jungle". They were just about to cross the [Serbia-Hungary] border. One woman was clearly pregnant. When I approached them, they got scared and hid in the bush. I pointed out that I brought them some water. Two women approached me and took water bottles, while men stayed behind. That was odd, given they were from Afghanistan. They didn't say a word. They answered my questions with 'thank you'. … The next day they were gone. (participant 24, NGO, Serbia)

> There was a family… a father, a mother, and two sons. A father, a husband who was a breadwinner in Turkey, was all of the sudden not a breadwinner anymore. … He was not doing well, psychologically. His wife was now doing it all, she studied Croatian, she did everything with her sons, and they found jobs. They said he was driving them mad, he was very stubborn, and was really angry with them all. So, in a way mum was taking on dad's role. (participant 14, NGO, Croatia)

Pickering and Cochrane's (2013) ground-breaking work demonstrates that pregnant women are more likely to die at border frontiers. Pregnancy and motherhood, however, did not derail the journeys of women during the migrant "crisis", as testified by the professionals I spoke with. They shared stories of many pregnant women and mothers that trekked through FRY Macedonia, Serbia, Kosovo, and Croatia, often on foot. Faced with countless difficulties, they simply kept going:

> [W]e had several women that gave birth here, and women that were heavily pregnant. ... One Somali woman, she was heavily pregnant when she left, she fled the hospital. (participant 3, INGO)

> A woman from Syria was four months pregnant. ... She travelled with her partner and another couple. ... They slept at the railway station. ... A police officer told them if they stay one more day ... he would beat them up with a baton. She was pregnant! ... When police came back they let her sleep there. ... I once saw a woman; she was from Afghanistan and eight months pregnant. She kept going. (participant 24, NGO, Serbia)

> There was a woman on her own, with three kids. They came all the way from Somalia. All of the sudden she disappeared. She was granted asylum, we were supposed to get her an apartment, but she disappeared within three days. She kept going, obviously. (participant 13, GA, Croatia)

> Having kids on the road is very difficult. Kids see people fall overboard, they travel in cramped spaces, walk for miles. ... Nowadays most women travel with kids, they don't leave them behind. (participant 6, NGO, Serbia) (Figure 5.1)

Khandan's cross-border journey was also not halted by pregnancy; she was at the time I talked to her expecting her third child but was unlikely to stay in Serbia for childbirth. Women's agency, often challenged in the public discourse, was pervasive in my research. They kept going, and the intersection of victimisation and survival seemed to further enable their migration journeys, as seen in the following case study):

> We had a woman from Somalia. She ran away, her dad got killed, something really bad also happened to her mum. When she was 16, [her family] wanted to marry her. She ran away, as she didn't want to marry this old guy. Her dad supported [her], so they killed him. That is a common scenario. It rarely happens that you marry someone you like, and someone who is not going to abuse you. Even if it happens, you still have no future. They tell us, 'our lives are ruined, but we are doing this for our kids, to give them a chance'. ... She walked for weeks, in the middle of winter, you have to feel for her. ... A very small number of women come back [to Serbia]. They mostly make it. She did too. (participant 3, INGO)

Women I spoke with were not approached by government agencies or NGOs to discuss potential exposure and vulnerability to trafficking. This might be because most of them travelled with families or with other women.

Figure 5.1 A child's mitten, hand-made by a woman in Bogovađa centre for asylum seekers, Serbia.

Photo: Sanja Milivojevic.

As such, while counter-trafficking interventions in countries of transit in the region have had limited impact on mobility of women in my research, their potential effect on the length and scope of women's journeys needs to be investigated, especially in a time of increased migration pressures. It is also important to note that this research captured a very small fraction of women border crossers in the Bogovađa centre for asylum seekers in Serbia. This limitation should be taken into consideration when discussing the results and findings presented here. I return to this important point in Chapter 7.

Conclusion

Freedom of movement is a fundamental human right. Yet, as I demonstrate in this and previous chapters, given that globalisation is 'a composite of processes that generate patterns of exclusion, pockets of wealth, and sites of violence' (Giles and Hyndman 2004, p. 302), this right has ceased to be universal for both men and women border crossers. Border hardening encompasses a range of interventions at physical, internal, and digital borders that categorise people on the move and regulate mobility flows. Offshoring of border control to countries of origin and transit is of the utmost importance in creating the "cordon sanitaire" of EUrope (Morrison and Crosland 2000, p. 47). As demonstrated in this chapter, this transfer creates new sites of border enforcement in the Global South that specifically target women border crossers.

Anti-trafficking efforts have long 'been linked to receiving countries' immigration priorities' (Nwogu 2014, p. 50). The developed world spent millions of dollars of taxpayers' money to combat and reduce extra-legal migration under the guise of fighting trafficking; in the past two decades, the EU 'has been a major donor for anti-trafficking initiatives both from NGOs and other stakeholders in the filed' (Hoff 2014, p. 113). As Hoff (2014, p. 114) points out, many EU anti-trafficking initiatives have been closely linked to migration and asylum, with one programme spending over EUR 3.5 million in 2011 alone 'on anti-trafficking grants and contracts for organisations operating outside the European Union'. Anti-trafficking and anti-smuggling efforts, thus, 'are intertwined for the same purpose of reducing outward migration' (Nwogu 2014, p. 52).

Yet border lockdowns limit women's legal options and shift migratory patterns towards riskier, less accessible places, and expose them to human smugglers. Their journeys are more likely to be interrupted by personal and financial difficulties as well as sexual and physical violence. Their reliance on people smugglers can potentially make them more vulnerable to exploitation and abuse, including trafficking. However, policy developments that follow the EU expansion to Southeast Europe further limit women's mobility through tough law and order policies to counter trafficking and smuggling. Trafficking as a 'transgressive practice that calls into question the sovereign performance' of nation-states across the Global North became 'an ideal site at which [control over their borders] can be legitimized and practiced' (Berman 2003, p. 52). In this context, narratives of actual and potential, pre-emptive victimisation (which might happen to women if they commence or continue their journeys) overshadows their agency and the ability to migrate (Mahdavi 2014, p. 13). The notion of agency-deprived actual or potential victims of trafficking in need of rescue calls for an interventionist approach that can, and indeed does, harm women border crossers. A robust scholarship in the trafficking literature successfully demonstrates how damaging anti-trafficking interventions can be for the rights and mobility of trafficked women (or those perceived to be vulnerable to trafficking). Sassen (2000), Kempadoo and Doezema (1998), Berman (2003), Weitzer (2007), Lee (2011), Segrave et al. (2009, 2018), and others expose the fact that law and order response and criminalisation of trafficking do little to stop this exploitative practice or to protect women from exploitation. What they do manage, however, is to further restrict women's mobility.

By deploying solid, liquid, and cloudy borders against non-citizens in transit, nations at the fringes of EUrope fulfil their roles as regulators of mobility. Women, however, are further regulated through humanitarian/ rescue pre-emptive interventions that aim to deter them from completing their journeys. If they travel alone and/or with children, women migrants are assessed as particularly vulnerable, stopped, questioned, and warned about dangers that await them if they proceed. Yet again, defenceless, young, naïve women from the Global South are perceived as in need of salvation, especially if they are suspected to be (purported or genuine) sex workers. Subsequently, women are 'scared and immobilized' (Korićanac et al. 2013, p. 18), while current interventions 'risk not so much solving the problem of trafficking but rather ending the right of asylum' (Morrison and Crosland 2000, p. 5). As I argued elsewhere with Segrave and Pickering, practices of profiling and identifying risk and potential victimisation 'intersect with expectations that are gendered, racialised and based on numerous stereotypes' (Segrave et al. 2018, p. 37). While my research did not fully capture the impact of such concerns on women migrants in the Western Balkans, it suggests that such pre-emptive strategies are in place. Further research on the topic that will analyse the effects of such policies is both essential and urgent.

Mobility is an exclusive right for those who occupy the higher tiers of the 'hierarchy of mobility' (Bauman 1998); trafficked women, women asylum seekers, and low-skilled women from the Global South are not, and are un-likely to be, members of that elite club. Nevertheless, as this research suggests, women have been crossing, and will continue to cross, borders. Similar to the interventions outlined in Chapters 3 and 4, the purpose of bordering practices is not to immobilise but to govern women non-citizens. Traditional border control mechanisms accompanied by counter-trafficking pre-emptive interventions result in a balance of women that will access labour markets and asylum systems in the West. Importantly, the inaccessibility of legal migra-tion routes leads women into the willing and able black market of migration service providers who charge significant funds to enable immigration. In doing so, they can put women (and men) at the risk of debt bondage and/ or other exploitative practices in transit or upon arrival (Segrave et al. 2009; Chacón 2010; Lee 2011).

Finally, as Lambert et al. (2003, p. 166) argue,

> [i]t is no longer acceptable (if it ever has been) to ponder questions of hu-man rights apart from issues of experience or attempts at narration by and with those who are always talked about but never found within esteemed legal and political commentary.

Voices of women on the move can tell us a lot about courage, survival, vulnerability, resistance, and hope. Their non-linear and often troubled journeys confirm women's exposure to many hurdles while on the road. Indeed, the very fact that they have reached the Western Balkans 'is a proof of their resilience and determination' (APC/CZA 2013a, p. 11). Women don't move as fast as men; they often change their migratory plans but do not give up, even when pregnant or accompanied by children. They are exposed to victimisation but manage to stay afloat. Women show agency and determination; what motivates them is a desire for a better life, for themselves, their families, and – above all – their children. Mobility control measures, whether traditional or "humanitarian", can perhaps succeed in striking the right balance of women that make it by keeping them on the road longer. While we continue to monitor and critique such interventions, an important question that we, as critical criminologists and feminists, have to keep asking is: at what cost? In the following chapter I examine counter-security technologies and the role technology plays in enabling mobility of men and women non-citizens, creating active memory of migration, and instigating social change.

Notes

1 A jargon for smugglers.
2 A jargon for improvised dwellings that people on the move use in countries of transit.

Chapter 6

"Stealing the fire", 2.0 style?

Counter-security technology, mobility, and de-securitisation of migration[1]

First of all, why are people in a migration having cell phones? It's sort of strange. Who's paying for those cell phones? Where are they coming from? Who are they calling? These are people — can you imagine, many, many, many cell phones. Where do they get cell phones? Who pays their monthly bill? (President of the US Donald Trump, at a campaign rally in Mesa, Arizona, December 2015, cited in Tashman 2015)

Quickly the boat became full of water and started to sink. I rang the Greek coastguard and started shouting 'help us, help us' but they couldn't really hear me. ... So I sent a WhatsApp message giving my GPS and asking them to help us. I also sent my family a message with my GPS and explained the situation but said 'don't worry, even though the weather is bad, we'll make it across'. (A Syrian refugee, cited in Kozlowska 2015)

Introduction

At the beginning of the 21st century, Jürgen Habermas (2001, p. 67) argued that contemporary borders are 'internally operated "floodgates", meant to regulate the currents so that only the desired influxes (or outflows) are permitted'. Contemporary bordering practices challenge the right of citizens to leave the territory of nation-states (as I demonstrate in Chapter 4 of this volume) and control the right to entry of non-citizens (see Chapters 3 and 5; also Mau et al. 2012; Council of Europe 2013). Borders in all their multiplicity are checkpoints of segregation and pushback for those assessed as dangerous and/or risky, points of entry for desired mobile populations, and purgatory for the majority of illegalised non-citizens (grey-listers of transnational mobility). In the previous chapters I charted both policy and theoretical shifts that have recently occurred, in which the focus of border scholarship is not on geographical borders *per se* but on the multiplicity of borders and bordering practices as a 'complex array of overlapping socio-political spatial processes' (Cooper and Perkins 2015, p. 14) in countries of origin, transit, and destination. The process of border deterritorialisation – a detachment of borders from the sovereign territory of nation-states – has resulted in a spatial (physical) and digital expansion of bordering practices.

Borders are now enforced within and beyond states' territorial limits by a range of state and non-state actors outside the traditional border enforcement apparatus, such as hospitals, schools, welfare agencies, and universities (see Mau et al. 2012; Pickering and Weber 2013; Aliverti 2015; Cooper and Perkins 2015). As I demonstrate throughout the book, the mobility regulatory mechanisms in countries of origin and transit have been growing apace: it is here, as Mau et al. (2012, p. 100) argue, that 'potential migrants encounter several stages of control on behalf of their destination country' (see also Andrijasevic 2010; Milivojevic 2018a). During the recent refugee "crisis", as I elaborate in Chapters 3, 4, and 5, states on the Western Balkans migration route have emerged as buffer zones in which thousands of people illegalised through bordering policies and practices (Bauder 2013) have been temporarily housed, immobilised, and slowly filtered through a complex techno-social migration apparatus.

Parallel to the process of the spatial re-distribution of bordering practices is their expansion in a digital world, in which states deploy a range of technological advancements to facilitate, manage, and regulate global mobility flows. Technological innovations have been positioned in countries of origin and transit, widely heralded as essential tools in the securitisation of migrants – a contemporary 'global security problem' (Bigo 2001). As I document in Chapter 3, security technologies have been particularly valuable in regulating the migration flows of non-citizens in times of increased mobility pressures. Yet, to quote Habermas (1970, p. 87) again, 'there is an immanent connection between the technology known to us and the structure of purposive-rational action'. Technology, thus, serves not only as a mobility regulator but also as an enabler, a potential key tool in the de-securitisation and re-humanisation of migrants.

I developed the central theoretical contribution of this chapter by drawing on the scholarship of Stefania Milan (2013), in particular her book *Social Movements and Their Technologies*. Milan holds that groups and individuals, like the mythical Prometheus who stole the fire from the Greek Gods and gave it to the people in order to enable the progress of humankind, can "steal the fire" from the elites, state agencies, and other narrative setters. We can do so by reclaiming technology to 'convey [our] own messages, bypassing the filters of commercial and state gatekeepers' (Milan 2013, p. 1). Milan argues that in order to do so, groups and individuals need to create autonomous means of communication: innovative platforms such as non-commercial Internet service providers or community radio stations that will be immune to gatekeepers' interventions. Drawing on this original idea, in this chapter I argue that border crossers increasingly reclaim technology in order to facilitate their migratory projects and challenge the narrative of the "dangerous migrant". However, I differ from Milan insofar that I argue that this process in the context of transborder mobility largely occurs on existing (mainstream) technological platforms, such as social media and smartphone technology. By reclaiming technology through the creation and distribution of information pertinent to their migratory journeys, people on the move contribute to the "digital knowledge commons" – decentralised databases of information created and shared by people via the Internet and social media (Wonders et al. 2012) that can potentially transform narratives around migration. Images, videos, and personal stories captured by mobile phones and shared on social media can arguably create social consciousness, if not a social movement on the issue. Yet to date there has been limited engagement pertinent to the use of technology for resistance and social change, and the potential impact of these processes on the lives of border crossers and official accounts of migration.

In this chapter I analyse a range of counter-security technologies and practices of reclaiming technology by migrants in the Western Balkans. In particular, I focus on re-appropriating technology to enable mobility (micro or the individual level), advance social memory (mezzo or the community level), and de-securitise and re-humanise border crossers (macro or the structural level). Through the analysis of the technology-migration nexus, this chapter highlights the theoretical significance and potential ramifications of "stealing the fire" processes for border criminology as well as the likely limitations of such inquiry. This chapter contains more comprehensive theoretical content than other chapters in the book. There are two reasons for this: first, contrary to the use of security technologies in regulating mobility, its use for other purposes such as enabling mobility of border crossers has been largely ignored in academia. Second, this chapter is an extended version of the paper I published elsewhere that aimed to further theory on the issue (Milivojevic 2018b). Thus, in the first part of this chapter I review existing literature and analyse media reports and interviews from my research in the Western Balkans. In the final section of the chapter I theorise the role technology can play in changing the way we think and talk about illegalised migration and mobility. The purpose of this chapter is both to complete the analysis on security technologies in the Western Balkans and to serve as a starting point for fostering research and future thinking on this important topic in border criminologies.

Mobility, smartphone technology, and social media nexus in the Western Balkans

As I investigated in detail in Chapter 2, policing of global mobility within informed space and the use of technology in border control have been subjects of academic inquiry for quite some time. Scholars mostly ventured into this area of academic inquiry to document the use of technology to observe and control mobile populations.[2] Rarely did academic attention focus on the use of technology as a site of resistance and/or social change (Newell et al. 2016; for notable exceptions see Rovisco 2015; Gillespie et al. 2016). This lack of inquiry is somewhat surprising, given the coverage of the technology-migration nexus and 'smartphone-wielding migrants' (Gillespie et al. 2016, p. 23) in the media but also its exposure in popular culture (Ortega 2011; Craigie 2014).

Technology, I argue, has the potential to mobilise the public by countering securitisation narratives about illegalised migration and facilitate migrants' cross-border journeys. It can also be a formidable tool for challenging dominant accounts on migration by enabling those who are considered dangerous to speak (Aradau 2004). Storytelling 'is often a powerful way to politicise borders and challenge sovereign power' (Kinnvall and Svensson 2015, p. 8). Giving voice to border crossers has arguably never been easier: smartphones and social media are indeed valuable tools for conveying migrants' perspectives and enabling their voyages in the 21st century.

Technology as a mobility enabler: information gathering and dissemination in a pursuit for mobility

Mobile phones and social media play an important role in the facilitation of international migration (Schaub 2012; Dekker and Engbersen 2013). According to the UNHCR, 'refugees can easily spend a third of their disposable income on staying connected' (*The Economist* 11 February 2017; see also UNHCR 2016). While there is a "digital divide" (Dekker and Engbersen 2013; Zijlstra and van Liempt 2017) – an uneven distribution of technology between countries and social groups of illegalised migrants – smartphones are often seen as 'more important than food or shelter' (Gillespie et al. 2016, p. 11). The 'death of distance' (Cairncross 1997) in a modern world was cemented with the development of web-based instant messaging and video chat applications, such as Skype, WhatsApp, Viber, Google Allo, Facebook Messenger, Telegram, Signal, WeChat, and others.

My research in the Western Balkans corroborates the notion that access to these platforms is essential for people on the road. As I chronicled during my visit to the Bogovađa asylum centre in Serbia, a majority of the men and women I talked to suggested that they visit the only Internet café in the Bogovađa village as often as possible, given that the centre's wireless network was available for staff use only (field notes, 10 October 2013). "Amooz", an asylum seeker from Afghanistan that I spoke to frequently during my visits to the centre, commented that 'some [migrants] in the centre are rich. They pay 150 dinars (about EUR 1.1) per hour for the Internet, and they go on for hours. They all go to the Internet café' (field notes, 10 October 2013). To overcome many hurdles on their way, people in transit increasingly rely on mobile technology and social media, 'with food and water … an essential, a must-have tool for migrants, refugees travelling through to Austria, or Germany' (Lee 2015). Indeed, as one participant from Serbia pointed out, 'they constantly look at their phones, phones ring all the time' (participant 24, NGO, Serbia).

Staying in touch with family, friends, other border crossers, and smugglers via online channels is essential as a lack of information can mean the end of the journey[3] or even death for those on the move (Gillespie et al. 2016). Many professionals I spoke with in Serbia, Croatia, Kosovo, and FYR Macedonia pointed out the role that technology plays in illegalised migrants' connection with family and fellow travellers at home or while in transit:

> They are in contact with people ahead of them, who tell them about the conditions, what to expect. Or you have a split family – some are in Serbia, the rest in Greece or Macedonia. And they tell you, I'm going to Skype my boyfriend, and he will send me the money [to keep going]. (participant 6, NGO, Serbia)

> Migrants are well organised. They know which [sections of] borders are porous, which way they should go, both women and men. They come in big groups, so they see where the gaps are. When they leave, they leave in groups. They are well informed and networked. There are leaders that pop up from the crowd, the ones who lead the way. ... The leaders know everything, who is where, whether they [manage to] cross the border, where they want to go. At first it is quite astonishing [to find out] how organised they are. (participant 3, INGO)

Mobile and smartphone use is not without risks. They are increasingly under police surveillance (Gundhus 2005; Aas et al. 2009; Schaub 2012; Gillespie et al. 2016; Oltermann 2016) and can potentially make people vulnerable to exploitation and trafficking (Newell et al. 2016; see also Chapter 5 of this volume). Nevertheless, research to date suggests an extensive use of smartphones by this population (Gillespie et al. 2016; Zijlstra and van Liempt 2017).[4] Technology, as my study in the Western Balkans confirms, provides more credible information, especially when it comes to finding assistance on the road and crossing physical borders:

> They have information; we don't need to advertise [our services]. They have their own world, and they are connected; they talk on Skype, [use] the Internet, Yahoo. They are well informed. ... A few of them [were locked up in a jail for illegalised migrants] and asked to talk to us. When questioned how they found out about our NGO, a guy said: 'everyone in Greece knows where to go, and what to do'. So, the connection is there. Even if they want to go to Australia, they would know how to do it. People talk. Those in front send information to the ones trailing behind, and the Internet enables that. We do not have posters in asylum centres, but they find us, no problem. (participant 2, NGO, Serbia)

> It is a well-developed network; they have a plan where they are heading, and how to get there. ... They know exactly where to go in Subotica, where other illegals wait to cross the [Serbia-Hungary] border. They know

which [asylum] centres are good, and the ones that should be avoided. ... A guy told us he knew when he was in Greece... so at that point he still had to go through Macedonia and Serbia... but he knew that he should come to Banja Koviljača [asylum centre]. Maybe he didn't quite know that Banja Koviljača is in Serbia, he perhaps had no idea what the name of the country is, but he knew where to come. (participant 19, INGO)

While the majority of the men and women I talked to were on their way to a set destination, some had to change their plan while on the road. Technology was vital in attaining mobility and ensuring the success of their illegalised journeys:

I come to Turkey and stayed three months there to go to Australia. But at that moment so many boats had problems, boats crashed. My dad called and [he] said: 'please do not go, change your plan'. So, I said I go to [England], and he said no, no! And I said I just want to go somewhere. I think I'll stay in Germany. (Khandan, Iran)

Platforms with end-to-end encryption, such as WhatsApp, are particularly popular to the extent that a map of a trip from Turkey to Germany has been widely shared on WhatsApp, with prices for smugglers and transport clearly marked on the map (Gillespie et al. 2016, p. 47). Importantly, smartphone technology potentially makes migrants less reliant on smugglers (Zijlstra and van Liempt 2017; see also Price 2015; Khalaf 2016). As one participant in my research suggested, '[t]hey spend a lot of time studying Google maps. They take notes and write things down. They are on it' (participant 3, INGO). Online maps are particularly helpful in covering short distances, such as trekking across FYR Macedonia:

[To go through] Macedonia with a smuggler is approximately EUR 600. So, they look on the Google maps and it looks flat, easy to cross. They go on foot to try to save the money. (participant 6, NGO, Serbia)

Media reports in the region also confirm border crossers' good command of digital maps and GPS navigation. As one of them confirmed to Serbian media, '[w]e use GPS to get to Germany. It is simple' (Ðaković 2015, p. 23). Two Internet cafés in the Banja Koviljača asylum centre in Serbia are constantly filled with border crossers 'studying Google maps. Upon closer inspection, we see that these are the maps of borders in Slovenia, Austria, Slovakia' (Todorović 2011). It is the same in Bogovađa. The only Internet café in the village is

[a]sylum free only from 1pm to 3pm, which is lunch time in the Centre [for asylum seekers]. ... The rest of the time you can barely breathe because it is so crowded, and smoke is thick. This is where they charge

their phones, talk to their families on Skype, and study Google Maps. (Rudić 2012)

Less reliance on smugglers is important, given that encounters with "agents" can be adverse. While smugglers are still considered an essential tool in securing the success of clandestine migratory journeys, the outcome is not always what people have in mind or what the actual agreement between smugglers and border crossers was:

> Most of them think Croatia is Italy. They say, we sat in a truck, paid for the trip to Italy, and [smugglers] opened the door and said - you are in Italy, all the while they were in Croatia. ... [Migrants] talk openly about smugglers, most of them are honest, they say: 'this is what happened'. They talk about how much they paid [for smugglers] and complain, like 'we paid a lot of money and they tricked us'. (participant 15, NGO, Croatia)

> Ok, some of them are, I mean, they need to brush up on their geography. An "agent" took 1,000 EUR [from a migrant] in Subotica and promised to take him to Italy. I was like, Ok, you have no idea where Italy is; it is so far away from Subotica! He dumped them in the middle of nowhere and said: 'border is 100 m away'. Police arrived after ten minutes and picked them up. They were in Macedonia. (participant 24, NGO, Serbia)

> A few months ago [police] intercepted a group of people in southern Serbia. ... I told them, Ok, you are travelling with smugglers, and thus far you haven't had a bad experience, but this doesn't mean that you won't in the future. I think that is very important. Smugglers are a part of their lives, migrants they rely on them a lot. Often, they are the only people who can take them to Europe. They have to work with smugglers. It is important for migrants to know what to pay attention to, how they can protect themselves from that criminal world. (participant 19, INGO)

Women in the Bogovađa asylum centre confirmed they all use "agents". But, as Delaram from Afghanistan told me in no uncertain terms, 'yes [we used smugglers] but all the smuggler, should kill him. Kill all'. Men and women in transit often have a lot to say about their complex relationship with smugglers, as the reality of smuggler-migrant encounters is far from straightforward.

In addition to obtaining information about migration routes and assistance on the road, technology fulfils another very important function: communication with illegalised migrants' support networks – families, friends, lawyers, and supporters. Social media, as Dekker and Engbersen (2013, p. 403) argue, 'have created a deterritorialized social space that facilitates communication among geographically dispersed people in migrant networks'. Tensions between restrictive migration policies imposed by states and social media as enablers of mobility are neatly conceptualised in the following quote:

The use of the social networks is a new challenge and a new question; to-day, [people] seek to use social networks ... to get information they need. Citizens have the need for information [that will enable their] freedom of movement, but on the other side is the state, which through its structures is quite closed. (participant 32, IO)

Thus, by creating content on social media platforms, people on the move effec-tively forge a path for potentially safer (or less precarious) passage for others (see Zijlstra and van Liempt 2017, p. 177). The digital divide when it comes to social media is seemingly non-existent among non-citizens transiting the Western Balkans as '[t]hey are technologically savvy. ... Facebook, they are all on it, they all use it, old or young - doesn't matter' (participant 19, INGO). By using these platforms men and women preserve anonymity, remain unobservable (Broeders and Engberson 2007, p. 1594), and ensure uninterrupted access to information:

[T]hey all use social media. Not to communicate to us, but to talk to each other. They are always on Facebook. ... They talk to family, friends, they really use it a lot. The first question is always: is there Internet here? In-ternet, Internet, that is the most important thing. (participant 3, INGO)

Media reports corroborate that transiting non-citizens in the Western Bal-kans use social media, in particular Facebook, to 'crowdsource every leg of their journey – sharing tips, maps and contacts in public and private groups established across the site' (Cunningham 2015). They reclaim technology by crafting unique means of communication in existing digital spaces and by leaving a digital trail – an active memory of their voyages that serves a variety of purposes. One such purpose is to capture the complexities of migrants' covert endeavours and convey a message of despair and survival through tes-timonies of abusive bordering practices, a message that is increasingly diffi-cult to silence.

Technology as active memory: recording and countering bordering practices in countries of transit

The journeys of illegalised migrants are by nature clandestine, hidden from the public eye. While those involved more often than not actively pursue secrecy, they extensively use mobile technology to document their precari-ous journeys. Smartphones, as Gillespie et al. (2016, p. 9) note, 'are a living, expanding photo album and an archive that documents the digital passage to Europe'. Digital scrapbooking is an important part of the journey of people I talked to at the Bogovađa asylum centre in Serbia. Khandan showed me her smartphone, which had hundreds of photos and videos of her family's journey through Greece, FYR Macedonia, and Serbia. Featured in the photos and videos were the cattle wagons in which they travelled through Greece, places where the family rested and hid from police, and happy and not so happy memories from the 14-hour on-foot trip across Macedonia she took with her children. The journey itself was so scary for Khandan that she had frequent nightmares about it. She used her smartphone to record the whole journey:

> Khandan: 'I took pictures. Everything [is] on my mobile. … Where we stayed, when trains [slowed down], this guy said [jump] on the train. We jumped. And in five hours we should jump [out]. [Zainab] was inside. We were [on the] same train! She says, she stayed from six [in the] morning until 3 [in the] afternoon. She [slept] inside. I said, you [are] lucky. She took [the] train from [The]ssaloniki. I walked [for 14 hours]. [laughter] I said bravo for me.'
> SM: 'Was this a passenger train?'
> Khandan: 'No, no. No passenger train.'
> Khandan's husband: 'Yes, yes, passenger train, ticket!' [laugher]
> SM: 'This video is excellent.'
> Khandan: 'Yes. [It was] 12 people [in the group]. The family. In Skopje, [it was] perfect. I have pictures and videos. The whole thing.'
> SM: 'Looks like you were having a good time on a train.'
> Khandan: 'Yes. We play. Sand. Kids play.'
> Khandan: [showing more pictures] 'Skopje, camp.'
> SM: 'This looks like a prison.'
> Khandan: 'Yes, like prison. But we [could] go out. Nobody [knew] we [were] inside. No security…. Very dirty room. Move on and you see more [pictures]. This boy was from Syria. … He is now in Austria. Vienna.'
> SM: 'You look very tired [in a photo].'
> Khandan: 'Because we walked 14 hours. I was pregnant. Yes, I'm pregnant now. Three months.'

Khandan told me that one day she would like to have an exhibition of these digital memories so that people can better understand the complexity of her journey.

An important function of these digital libraries is that they can create active sites of resistance by documenting abusive bordering practices in countries of transit and posting them on the digital knowledge commons. A report published in 2015 by Amnesty International documented widespread abuses of illegalised migrants in FYR Macedonia, Serbia, and Hungary, claiming that

> refugees are routinely subjected to unlawful push-backs and ill-treatment by Border Police. They might be arbitrarily detained by the authorities. Their irregular status also makes them vulnerable to financial exploitation by law enforcement officers, who misuse their authority to demand bribes. (Amnesty International 2015a, p. 5)

Kamal Zadran, a 20-year-old English teacher from Afghanistan, one of many asylum seekers stranded in the region after the closure of the Western Balkans route, testified that Croatian police beat up and sent a large group of migrants back to Serbia. He claimed to have 'a phone full of pictures of friends with bloody gashes on their heads resulting from [police] beatings' (Cupolo 2016). Indeed, as the following quotes confirm, such treatment of people on the move is common, in particular as they transit through Turkey, Greece, and FYR Macedonia:

> Yes, they complain about police a lot. In particular that police ask for money. Sort of, give us the money and we won't deport you. They go to a local supermarket, and police waits for them there and ask for money. (participant 24, NGO, Serbia)

> You know, [we all have] the same problem. The person they catch, [they ask] where are you coming from, they shout, and ... sometimes. .... In the Macedonia, they didn't [do this] to my family, you know, but they hit them, hit some boys. I saw that. They [were] very upset. (Khandan, Iran)

While recording and sharing abuses by border police, guards, militia, or smugglers can have serious repercussions for migrants (Gillespie et al. 2016), citizen-witnessing of border violence can make them feel safer and assist in achieving accountability for human rights violations (Newell et al. 2016). Social media can also serve as a platform where such testimonies can be shared anonymously. A good example of this is the case of Hungarian television camerawoman Petra László, who was filmed kicking and tripping up men and women on the Serbia-Hungary border on 8 September 2015. After the footage went "viral" on social media, the journalist was dismissed from her job, subjected to public ridicule on Facebook, and ultimately found guilty and convicted of breaching the peace (Dearden 2017). Similarly, footage of beating of Serbian state television (RTS) team at the same location in September 2015 prompted the Hungarian government to issue an official apology for the incident (Đurović 2015). Online platforms, such as the EyeWitness for Atrocities (http://www.eyewitnessproject.org/), which collects, verifies, and secures eyewitness' evidence admissible in trials, or the Australian Border Deaths Database (http://artsonline.monash.edu.au/thebordercrossingobservatory/publications/australian-border-deaths-database/), which records deaths associated with Australia's borders, are a good starting point in achieving accountability. The catalogue of human rights violations captured by border crossers and shared on social media could further assist in holding those responsible to account in a court of law and in the public discourse, and in creating a change on a macro (structural) level, to which I now turn.

Technology as a tool for de-securitisation and re-humanisation: countering official border narratives

Securitisation of migration as a discursive practice brings the issue of supposedly risky, dangerous border crossers into the political arena and justifies extraordinary interventions, which often include violation of human rights, in order to mitigate the risk. Underpinning this narrative is the notion of migrants as a credible threat that endangers the survival of the nation or, more specifically, 'its capacity to control the method of shaping [society's] wealth' (Huysmans 2006, p. 49). Securitisation is a self-referential process; to use Guild's analogy of a balloon – the more air your blow into it, the larger the issue becomes (Guild 2009; see also Gerard 2014). As such, securitisation has transformed the issue of migration and mobility from "normal" to "extraordinary" and border politics from "normal" to "exceptional" (see Aradau 2004 regarding the development of a successful securitisation narrative). Accounts about migration 'are submerged in images, such as flood or invasion, representing a mass that endangers' (Huysmans 2006, p. 58). The success of border securitisation measures is largely built on a dehumanised concept of a dangerous "Other" – decorporealised digital spectres of people on the move who, with the assistance of technology, represent nothing more than 'mere identificatory biodata' (Pugliese 2013, p. 592). Reduced to a ghostly, human-like shape on a thermal imaging security camera or a simple hit in the database, men, women, and children are bare targets for security-driven border enforcers (see Chapter 3 of this volume).

The securitisation of migration valorises the internal security of the nation/community, its cultural identity, and the concept of the welfare state (Gerard 2014). Legal claims about the rights of the mobile population are largely absent from the public discourse or if present are silenced by the logic of security and the preservation of the nation, its culture, and wealth. Thus, in order to de-securitise the issue, abandon the politics of exceptional measures, and reinstate the 'democratic politics of slow procedures which can be contested' (Aradau 2004, p. 393), we ought to re-corporalise and re-humanise its objects and expose the abuses and violations committed in the name of such policies. However, it is not just records of abuses and harms that have the potential to re-humanise: it is migrants' experiences, stories of survival, photos of families and friends hugging and smiling at the shores of the Mediterranean, and jokes they share along the way that can recreate a "normal refugee" – one that is here for a good reason and is not abusing our hospitality (see Chimni 1998).

Researchers of immigration detention have extensively documented migrants' voices, as expressed through testimonials and art, and their potential for countering official border narratives (see Bosworth 2014). Such an inquiry should extend to the whole field of migration and mobility. While Isin and Ruppert (2015, p. 136) argue that technology is not necessarily counter-hegemonic, its potential to contest if not override official accounts warrants our attention. The 2015 World Press Photo competition-winning image, "Hope for a New Life", by Australian photographer Warren Richardson pictures a man handing his baby under a barbwire fence somewhere along the Serbia-Hungary border. *The Mapping Journey Project* by Bouchra Khalili captures stories of eight migrants via a long shot of a hand with a marker, drawing their journey into the unknown (Khalili 2017). These artistic endeavours by allies, similar to the celebrated photograph of Aylan Kurdi, a boy whose body washed up on the beach near Bodrum, Turkey, and an image of a shell-shocked five-year old, Omran Daqneesh, covered in blood in Aleppo, partially altered public discourse (see Bulos and King 2016; El-Enany 2016). In the case of Aylan Kurdi, his lifeless body on a remote Mediterranean beach spread to the screens of almost 20 million people across the world in the space of 12 hours, featuring in approximately 30,000 tweets (D'Orazio 2015). After it went "viral", this photographic evidence of brutal and deadly bordering practices evoked empathy, prompting a debate on a humanitarian, rather than security-driven, approach to the issue of migration. It commenced 'a new regime of visuality, meaning-making through images coupled with the power of social media and their new role in publishing and associated changes in political agency' (Gourinova 2015, p. 5; see also Burns 2015; Stević and Car 2016). Photos of torment and loss shifted the rhetoric, albeit perhaps temporarily, with thousands of people tweeting about "refugees", not "migrants" (D'Orazio 2015, p. 11).

Stories by border crossers themselves shared on social media have the potential to tell, perhaps even more powerfully, their tales of suffering, pain, survival, and hope (see Ghonim 2012 for the impact of images shared on social media in the context of the Egyptian revolution). A Twitter Periscope app that broadcasted live the passage of a group of Syrian refugees from the Mediterranean to Germany was played over 90,000 times by the end of their journey (Dredge 2015). Similarly, personal testimonies captured via disposable cameras and posted on Twitter via the #RefugeeCameras hashtag conveyed to the wide audience accounts of anguish and courage but most importantly portrayed border crossers as '"already a part of" the community which seeks to construct them as the threatening Other' (Glover 2011, p. 81). In the following section I analyse "stealing the fire" processes in mobility management and their relevance for border criminology.

Theorising the technology-migration nexus and its role in transforming borders from below

Smartphones and social media are potentially mainstream platforms of resistance. In 2016, an estimated 62.9 per cent of the world population already owned a mobile phone. It is predicted that the number will grow to 67 per cent in 2019 (Statista 2017a), especially in the Global South (Kemp 2017). Social media is seemingly unstoppable too: Facebook alone has almost two billion active monthly users globally (Statista 2017b). The sheer penetration rate of these technological innovations and their constant advancement require a closer look at their impact while avoiding traps of technological determinism. Technology does not have an independent causal power to drive human history (Reed 2014); nevertheless, it is an important player in the development of a globalised world and, as such, requires much greater attention than it has currently been given in border criminology. Huub Dijstelbloem (2017) has recently called for more research in the area of '"counter-surveillance" deployed by non-state actors to highlight emergencies or contest claims that governments make'. My research in the Western Balkans has focussed, among other things, on such quests.

In this chapter I mapped the use of technology in challenging social, economic, and political borders. I investigated the role that smartphones and social media play in constructing social memory (and social consciousness) of abusive bordering practices, challenging predominant accounts of migration, de-securitising and re-humanising mobility, and attaining freedom of movement. I theorised the potential transformation of borders from below as migrants transiting the Western Balkans reclaim technology to enable safe passage, create counter-narratives of migration, and contribute to the new "digital knowledge commons" – a collaborative and decentralised digital body of knowledge that can potentially shift restrictive migration policies. The chapter also highlighted the importance of studying the technology-mobility nexus and greater theoretical engagement *vis-à-vis* the use of technology as a tool for social change as migration continues to play a pivotal role in political and public debates across the globe.

As I suggest, borders are increasingly reshaped by technology. There are three potential levels of transformation: a micro level, which refers to the ability of technology to advance mobility projects; a mezzo level, in which technology is used as a platform to document the journeys and human rights abuses; and a macro level, where technology can assist us in the de-securitisation and re-humanisation of illegalised migrants. Undoubtedly, technology can enable safer journeys and provide access to more credible migration-related information (and make men and women on the move potentially less dependent on smugglers). Smartphones and social media, however, are not simply a lifeline for border crossers but also a likely game-changer in political and social discourse on migration in Europe and beyond. The fundamental power struggle today 'is the battle for the construction of meaning in the minds of people' (Castells 2012, p. 5). In the era of Web 2.0, in which we are both knowledge producers and consumers, stories captured by smartphones and shared on social media can generate a counter-narrative to the security-driven anti-migration sentiments. Indeed, as Milan (2013, p. 2) states, technology 'is not an end in itself; it is a means to a political end'. Nowadays, it is us – technology users who draw our own maps; they are 'no longer imparted to us by a trained cadre of experts' (Crampton and Krygier, cited in Zijstra and van Liempt 2017, p. 182). "Stealing the fire" through the process of creating, recording, sharing, and consuming information happens in mainstream digital spaces, 'powerful site[s] for new forms of public participation and civic engagement' (Wonders et al. 2012, p. 7).

Social impact theory suggests that people's experiences and actions are influenced by multiplicative functions of strength (factors such as intellect, wealth, or the status of a person make them more or less influential), immediacy (the distance between the source and the target of influence), and the number of influences that one is subjected to (how many sources of influences are out there, impacting on us – see Seltzer et al. 2013). In the age of social media, as argued by Chang et al. (2018, p. 283), 'it is easier than ever for individuals to be influenced by the real, implied, or imagined presence or actions of others'. In the new digital commons and in particular on social media, information value is not linked to traditional sources of influence, such as the government agencies or the media; instead, value is in 'personal bonds of trust and interdependence' between the social media user and the source of information (Wonders et al. 2012, p. 8; see also Castells 2014).

As users, we endlessly engage with snippets of information from our networks and identify what it is important to know. We value information based on where information comes from. Moreover, immediacy between the influencer and the social media user, and a number of posts shared by people we trust on social media, can potentially have a greater value than the information we access in the traditional media. As such, emotion-charged reports that originate from those that experience, rather than those claiming to be official interpreters of, the event, shared by our community of friends and networks, can indeed be singled out as a more trustworthy and/or more honest account of mobility. "Stealing the fire" in this context means breaking the monopoly of the official truth-telling actors of migration (state agencies, media, and supra-national organisations) through mass self-communication in the digital knowledge commons. In times of increased mobility pressures, this process is more important than ever.

A decade ago Huysmans (2006) argued that the vulnerability of migrants, their life stories, and how they link to global and local structural inequalities could indeed result in the de-securitisation of migration and accountability for human rights violations. Such knowledge, produced by migrants, is an extension of 'a continuous ethical and moral project of cosmopolitanism', one that 'makes the individual the agent par excellence endowed with rights and claims' (Benhabib, cited in Alvarez 2014, p. 183). While I agree with Aradau (2004) that this counter-narrative has to penetrate the institutions from which security narratives originate, I believe that other non-institutional battlegrounds are equally important in order to generate social change. It is in the new digital commons, and in particular on social media, that knowledge is captured and disseminated by those most affected by contemporary border regimes. Deconstructing the "threat" and exposing what is done in the name of security is crucial in this process. Technology, I argue, provides a means to potentially "steal the fire" from the experts' 'regime of truth' (Bigo 2002, p. 66) and is a key platform for the re-humanisation of border crossers and deconstruction of the idea of migrants as a collective dangerous force (Huysmans 2006, p. 56).

Undoubtedly, we need to be cautious here: counter-narratives can, and indeed most likely will, be met with resistance. While it was beyond the scope of this chapter to highlight potential responses by nation-states that might create "no technology" zones, restrict access to communication technologies, or expose illegalised non-citizens to a range of surveillance strategies, these issues should be the focus of border criminologists in the future. Unequal availability of technology for diverse groups of migrant populations[5], limited or no access to charging stations, and partial coverage of mobile telephony towers are also points of concern, and they too should be the focus of future research. Moreover, misinterpretation and de-legitimisation of migrants' experiences[6] is a further concern. As Poletta (2006, p. 3) argues, for disadvantaged groups storytelling and narratives carry both risks and benefits. The risk of not being believed, being pitied, and being subjected to vilification on social media is all too real. There are also risks associated with presenting migrants as victims who need to be rescued, often through security-based surveillance measures. A prospect that web-based border "slacktivisim" (where a limited time is dedicated to important social issues, with little or no effect) will fail to yield social change is also tangible as migration and mobility narratives are driven by powerful political and economic forces. Network social movements can and indeed do fall short of expectations – as witnessed in the aftermath of the Arab Spring, the Occupy Wall Street, or KONY 2012 movements (see Schumann 2015). Finally, one of the key conundrums is that there is no consensus in the literature on the potential of technology to foster social change and democracy as smartphones and social media are neoliberal and commercial platforms, and, as such, are increasingly governed (see Dean 2009; Milan 2013). As Milan (2013, p. 1) warns, technology is 'owned and controlled by media and telecoms corporations whose agenda focuses on profit and corporate interests rather than participation, empowerment, and social justice'. Communicative capitalism merges democracy and capitalism, and ultimately traps its contemporary subjects/consumers (Dean 2009, p. 22). Certainly, autonomous and independent systems of communication, as advocated by Milan, ought to be a subject of future research, especially given the recent Cambridge Analytica/Facebook scandal. Nevertheless, I concur with Castells (2012, p. 2) that Internet social networks, including mainstream social media, are (still?) fairly resilient to regulations of governments and corporations. As this chapter suggests, the re-appropriation of technology already happens on these mainstream platforms and, as such, should be examined in more detail, together with its potential to deliver change on an individual, community, and structural level. The big questions are to what extent, for how long, and is it enough?

Counter-security technologies indisputably create and redistribute power. They enable migrant populations to complete their journeys, expose and document abuses, and shift narratives and public opinion. Through the use of technology, we bring to life a diversity of biographies, personal stories that can lead to a more inclusive approach to migration (Huysmans 2006, p. 58). Sharing border crossers' personal stories, photographs, and voices in the new digital knowledge commons can transform bordering strategies by dismantling security narratives that give them legitimacy. While, as Castells (2012, pp. 236–7) notes, networked social movements initially have a limited impact on policy, they can eventually change the minds of people. In order to 'turn powerlessness into empowerment' (Castells 2012, p. 45) technology has to merge with the "offline" world and create hybrid public spaces where information will be shared and consumed, narratives will be challenged, and accountability will be achieved. Such a quest for social change is even more important, given that '[t]his refugee crisis is unlike any before it. It's the *first* of its kind in a digital age' (BBC 2016; emphasis added). It is for all these reasons that border criminology can no longer ignore the role and impact of counter-security technologies, and I hope this chapter will foster further scholarly engagements with this important topic. In the final chapter I bring together key points of inquiry presented in this book and suggest where we ought to go from here.

Notes

1 This chapter is a modified and extended version of an article published in *Theoretical Criminology* as a part of the Special Edition on Transforming borders from below (2019). I thank Sage Journals for granting me permission to use it in the book.

2 See, for example, Briskman (2013) on technology in immigration detention, Broeders and Engbersen (2007) on the digitalisation of borders in Europe, Newell et al. (2016) on the US-Mexico border, and Andersson (2016) on EU's offshoring surveillance strategies in North Africa.

3 A recent example was an attempt by Hungarian authorities to lure people into a train that was going to a refugee camp by announcing that the train was going to Austria and Germany. Thanks to the information distributed via mobile phones many migrants avoided being detained (Price 2015).

4 Approximately 86 per cent of young Syrian refugees in the Zaatari refugee camp in Jordan own a mobile phone, while more than 50 per cent use the Internet at least once a day (Koons 2015).

5 The importance of smartphones and social media is now recognised by the technology sector and NGOs who work tirelessly to bridge the "digital divide" and eliminate inequalities when it comes to access to technology (Ram 2015; UNHCR 2016).

6 A "children overboard" incident in which the Australian Immigration Minister falsely accused migrants on unauthorised vessel SIEV 4 of threatening to throw their children overboard being just one example of this.

Chapter 7

Conclusion

Security technologies, mobility, and countering bordering practices in the Global South

A recent collection by Leanne Weber (2015a) engaged with the topic of re-thinking border control in a globalised world. In it, prominent border schol-ars questioned and pondered the future of borders in a world that moves so quickly we can hardly keep up with the news headlines. Instead, every morning we are presented with a one-minute summary of the news in almost all major newspapers and TV portals. Yet the world in motion has arguably never been more static for many: all the while global populations have con-stantly been categorised according to their hierarchy of mobility. Weber and others imagined the world with or without borders in a thought experiment that should make us think about our role as border scholars in understanding, mapping, and countering borders of the future.

An ongoing pursuit of security and pre-empting risk in the risk society seem to make a borderless world, or at least a world where borders might be more permeable, a rather bleak prospect. As the condition of 'being protected from threats' (Zedner 2009, p. 14), security is most sought after in the area of migra-tion management. In fact, it is mobility *itself* that has become the key security concern (Popescu 2015). The state's preoccupation with border protection and mobility of citizens and non-citizens is unlikely to fade in the near future. Proliferation and multiplication of physical, internal, and digital borders creates a fault line that separates green- from grey- and black-listers of transnational mobility. This fault line is located at the physical barriers that divide the Global North and the Global South, and beyond. Certainly, as this book demonstrates, borders in the traditional sense are still vital cogs in the mobility machine. Contemporary borders are complex political, philosophical, socio-legal con-structs: sometimes they are visible, like barbwire fences on Hungary's borders with Serbia and Croatia; often, however, they are almost impossible to detect. Borders, it seems, have never been more multifaceted when it comes to their location and character. They move in and out, extending to countries of origin and transit via policies, databases, drones, education campaigns and racial pro-filing practices, and a range of other border security technologies.

Anticipation of future risks that are *probable* or *likely* to happen in the future (as opposed to *credible* risks) has been a centrepiece of policy-making in the

Global North in the 21st century. Worst-case scenarios seems to be the focus of key stakeholders in EUrope, the US, Australia, and elsewhere. And while migration and mobility has been at the top of the list of risks for quite some time, the Global North was undoubtedly caught off-guard by the influx of illegalised non-citizens in the mid-2010s. A temporary collapse of border regimes in countries of destination for migrants and asylum seekers fleeing Iraq, Afghanistan, and other conflict zones placed countries of origin and transit under unprecedented pressure. They were tasked with the job of regaining control over ever-growing mobility flows. Non-EU "allies" (Serbia, Kosovo, and FYR Macedonia) and new member states (Croatia) have been put in the spotlight, which quickly turned the region, troubled by its recent past, into the unexpected and unlikely warden of the EU border regime. Crucially, the ultimate objective of the migration machine is unequivocal: well-controlled, secured (European Partnership 2018), and *seamless* borders. The two juxtaposed processes of border fortification and fluidity are concurrent, while the purpose of security technologies is to assist in reclaiming control over mobility. On the other hand, counter-security technologies have the potential to aid illegalised migrants in crossing borders and change the way we *think* and *do* migration control. Technology acts not only as a mobility regulator but also as an enabler. As such, it can be an important tool in the de-securitisation and re-humanisation of migrants.

Border Policing and Security Technologies focussed on four key themes: **the nature and formation of borders**, their **location**, **performance**, and **impact**. The book examined a range of techno-social interactions deployed to detect, categorise, filter, or immobilise mobile populations in the Western Balkans. It outlined the establishment and developments of the migration machine in the region prior to, during, and after the migrant "crisis" of the 2010s by focussing on three categories of border crossers: non-citizens transiting the region, citizens of the Western Balkans seeking asylum in the EU, and women. Importantly, the book also mapped the development of counter-security technologies that have the potential to enable mobility and create social change. Charting physical, internal, and digital borders, and the overall process of the proliferation and externalisation of borders and bordering practices in the Western Balkans were at the core of this volume. In the final section of the book, I would like to revisit key arguments raised in previous chapters.

Exploring borders and bordering practices in the Western Balkans

Nature, structure, scope, and location of borders

This book detailed a system of divergent borders and the bifurcated process of re-bordering in the region – one that targets citizens seeking asylum in the West and one that targets non-citizens in transit. In addition, I detailed "humanitarian" borders targeting women. Some of these borders were self-imposed by the nations of the Western Balkans. More often, they were developed under pressure (or under guidance and financial support) from the EU and its member states. As such, the borders of EUrope were externalised to the region, and their function was to create "dams" and regulate mobility, especially in times of increased mobility pressures. Like a giant sieve, borders in the region created a *purgatory* for non-citizens and citizens, and classified, blocked, and filtered border crossers. Such purgatory, as evidenced in the book, had many sites of enforcement – from physical borders between Serbia and Hungary or FYR Macedonia and Greece, and practices of racial profiling against "bogus" asylum seekers to anti-trafficking interventions targeting women transiting the region. The *Europeanisation* of the Western Balkans through legal, policy, and democratic conditionality was particularly evident in the area of migration management. Security assemblage that aims to stratify mobility flows and strike the right balance of wanted/needed/useful border crossers on behalf of the Global North was in full swing during the "crisis". Buffer zones of social segregation that targeted citizens and non-citizens were ubiquitous, while ongoing conditionality when it comes to border management resulted in states' constant pursuit of the EU standards and policy requirements.

As I argued in Chapter 3, border regimes in the region changed significantly prior to, during, and after the migrant crisis, inspired and directed by the administration in Brussels, Berlin, and other centres of power in the EU. I detailed this change in the borders' nature and structure, and their transformation from permeable to semi-permeable and finally to a border shutdown. A techno-social machine for social sorting impacted profoundly on and extended to border crossings, airports, asylum centres, and public discourses in the region. In the phase of *limited engagement* nation-states on the Western Balkans migration route effectively suspended their migration and asylum systems, as seen by the non-engagement of government agencies and law enforcement in countries of transit. Indeed, agencies in charge of registering non-citizens in Serbia and FYR Macedonia have (actively and passively) encouraged people to leave the region as soon as possible. A "mockery of a system" inspired by a lack of pressure from the EU but also the xenophobia, Islamophobia, and racism of local populations enabled thousands of border crossers to reach the West. As the pressure by the Union and its member states grew, and following media campaigns that focussed on the racialised criminal "Other", solid and cloudy borders were promptly reinstated in the region. This resulted in *non-entrée* and border shutdown policies, in which former enemies (such as Kosovo and Serbia, and Serbia and Croatia) emerged as partners in mobility management in the region. In Chapter 4, I documented how countries of origin and in particular their border guards "do borders" on behalf of destination countries. I mapped how the growing number of "bogus" asylum seekers prompted a change in border regime in Serbia, Kosovo, and FYR Macedonia that infringed upon the right to mobility and the right to seek asylum of thousands of people from the region.

Borders in the region, thus, have been anything but static. Physical, internal, and digital borders were deployed as needed, and re-bordering followed trends in mobility of non-citizens, citizens, and women border crossers. Borders expanded, multiplied, and spread following migratory pressures in the region and political developments in the EU and beyond. Throughout this volume I argued that these pre-frontier controls had a clear aim: to compensate for the perceived vulnerability of the EU through the identification, assessment, and control of people outside of its territory in times of the "crisis". The "emergency politics" was deployed to regulate the amplified mobility of people from the Global South. Borders were continuously renewed and enabled, embodied in physical borders, digital spaces, territories of other sovereign states, and the bodies of the people who attempted to cross them.

Performance of solid, liquid, and cloudy borders

McCulloch and Pickering (2012, pp. 1–2) noted that '[d]espite the efforts of states to intensify and rigidify the borders that surround them, borders are fluid, shifting, and contradictory physical and discursive spaces'. This book mapped the interplay and performance of borders on the Western Balkans migration route that regulated mobility and, even in times of border closure, enabled people to reach the West. Borders, thus, were never completely shut. The demand for low-skilled labour acted as a driver for streaming migrants through the regulatory mechanisms of borders. After all, the immobility of black- and the assessment of grey-listers of transnational mobility was, and still is, borders' real purpose. Establishing the *right number* of the *right people* who will be allowed to access labour markets and/or asylum systems in the West is their ultimate goal, and the combination and fine-tuning of solid, liquid, and cloudy borders is, as demonstrated in this book, the strategy to reach it.

Solid borders, such as fences, pushbacks, and violence along physical and internal borders, were omnipresent in the Western Balkans prior to, during, and after the "crisis". As their purpose is to create barriers that block and remove the dangerous or unwanted "Other" (both citizens and non-citizens), they served and continue to serve as membranes that immobilise or temporarily restrict people until their usefulness in the labour markets or asylum systems of the West is thoroughly evaluated. In previous chapters I mapped the expansion, timeline, and origin and *modus operandi* of solid borders in the region. In Chapter 4, for example, I outlined how the threat of the suspension of visa-free regime by the EU and its member states resulted in the reinstating of solid borders in the region through legal reforms, education campaigns, and practices of racial profiling and pushbacks along the physical borders of

Serbia, FYR Macedonia, and Kosovo. The targets of such practices were racially different would-be migrants or – in the case of Kosovo – a majority of its population. Liquid borders, as 'rivers full of locks' (Bigo 2014, p. 213), were also the key mechanism in articulating human mobility in the region. Designed and inspired by the Global North, these borders were essential in regulating mobility of non-citizens, citizens, and women. They were the backbone of bordering strategies in all three streams of migratory flows, serving to strike the right balance of people that would be able to pass through the region in order to ensure both the economic growth and the supremacy of EUrope. From letting "genuine" refugees make their way through the Western Balkans migration route to special interventions that, while targeting some citizens, enabled others to cross borders, borders were constantly calibrated and re-calibrated during the "crisis".

Finally, cloudy borders deployed and defended in the digital sphere were the last yet vital cog in this growing migration machine. Computer systems, databases, servers, and hi-tech hardware were fine-tuned mechanisms for the articulation of mobility but also the most difficult to observe and analyse. In this book I managed to capture only a small fraction of cloudy borders that targeted transiting non-citizens. Possible causes for this lack of evidence could be that those aimed at local populations were perhaps too obscured and/or not as developed as those targeting non-citizens. When it comes to "bogus" asylum seekers and women in transit, such borders remained elusive. Nevertheless, there is no doubt that this mixture of borders was instrumental in mobility management during and after the migrant "crisis". While liquid borders dominated in Phase 1, solid borders that included violence, pushbacks, and the erection of fences, and cloudy borders that included a range of techno-social innovations reinstated "order" and governance over mobility in the region at the peak of the "crisis".

Impact of security and counter-security technologies

As I demonstrate in the book, people on the move are constantly classified and reclassified through bordering practices. Black-listing follows a security logic and excludes known threats. Most of the mobile population, however, were catalogued as grey-listers and subjected to data analysis, risk profiling, and assessment. During the "crisis" the Western Balkan region was transformed into a buffer zone, a labour reserve (Cross 2013) where filtering and (more or less) temporary immobilisation took place. Many tentacles of the migration machine in the region blocked, delayed, filtered, categorised, and re-categorised people on the move, effectively creating a manageable flow of migrants. The equilibrium of people who were allowed to cross – those assessed as useful in the labour markets or as genuine asylum seekers who would validate the purportedly humanitarian nature of the asylum system of the West – was reached in countries of origin and transit. This outcome was achieved through the cooperation of nations that were in a conflict less than 20 years ago; they were reunited, if not reconciled, in order to accomplish this important task. I will return to this central point in a moment.

Border policing and security technologies, wherever they might be deployed, are arguably becoming more violent. This book captured testimonies of violence, pushbacks, and exploitation that are the direct outcome of border securitisation. While perhaps not as graphic as the sites of shipwrecks in Lampedusa or bodies scattered on Mediterranean beaches, the region's "collateral damage" was arguably equally tragic and dramatic. Underpinning purported willingness to tolerate human tragedy and casualties in the region was the racism and xenophobia of the local population, and humanitarian "rescue" narratives that target women border crossers. The negative and at the same time inevitable impacts of these processes, such as violence and border pushbacks, racial profiling, and governing mobility based on the race and ethnicity of border crossers, were, it seems, a price that candidate and potential candidate states were willing to pay to get political points for the big prize – EU membership. The Global North, on the other hand, was not only tolerating but arguably instigating and promoting such harmful practices.

Yet, as I argue in Chapter 6, countries of origin and transit such as those in the Western Balkans were also spaces where border struggles took place and where mobile bodies reclaimed technology in order to enhance their migratory projects, record abusive bordering practices, and potentially create counter-narratives of migration. "Stealing the fire" already happens on existing technology platforms, such as smartphones and social media. This topic and its potential in enabling mobility, achieving accountability, and countering security narratives in the public and policy discourse around migration needs to be investigated by criminologists and social scientists more broadly. The potential of counter-security technologies in the de-securitisation of migration is, while to some extent carved out in this volume, largely unexplored in the literature. Stories by people who have been crossed by borders (Cisneros 2013) shared on social media have the potential to transfer their suffering, pain, survival, and hope to broader audiences. "Stealing the fire" in this context can potentially mean breaking the monopoly of the official truth-telling actors of migration through mass self-communication in the digital knowledge commons.

Impact, however, goes further than mobility of border crossers or narratives around mobility. My research in the Western Balkans outlined the EU's effect on the region's legal, political, and mobility frameworks. External pressures located in mechanisms for accession to the EU and regional agreements (such as the *acquis*, the *GAMM*, the *Roadmaps*, the IBM, the *Thessaloniki Agenda*, and the *Ohrid Process*) leave the geographically and politically anaemic states of the Western Balkans under a significant spotlight, with a limited space to manoeuvre. These rule exporting practices enabled the region to play a key role in ensuring that mobility is properly governed. In addition, a range of financial assistance programmes, such as IPA and IPA II, underpinned the multiplication of borders in the region, which, through restraining and filtering strategies, simultaneously enabled and disabled the passage of border crossers on behalf of the Global North.

Finally, joining the "ring of friends" has arguably commenced the process of the de-balkanisation and Europeanisation of the region that was accelerated and amplified during the migrant "crisis". Through successful mobility management the states of the Western Balkans have commenced their readmission 'into the self-anointed circle of genuine and proper Europe-ness' (De Genova 2017a, p. 20). As I demonstrate in the book, this remote migration management on behalf of Europe set the region on the pathway to reversing the process of balkanisation and one step closer to EU membership. Former enemies cooperated in mobility control, as evidenced in the case of Serbia and Croatia in Chapter 3, and Kosovo and Serbia in Chapter 4. This is significant, given the region's troubled history, but can also be a new spark that can potentially rekindle the animosities and grievances of the past. Racial profiling and religious or nationality-driven interventions and practices in a region where ethnicity, race, and religion have caused so much suffering are negligent at best. However, the outcry over such practices fell mostly on the states and governments of the Western Balkans. And while EUrope's requests for unrestricted freedom of movement without discrimination does exist on paper, these interventions, although committed by nations of the region, were inspired and orchestrated by those that benefit from such practices.

A way forward

This book commenced the process of mapping and evaluating borders and the migration machine in the Western Balkans. It is important to note yet again that the research that underpins this book and the book itself have many limitations in terms of scope, access, gatekeepers, methodology, sample, and analysis. As such, this volume should be read as the first step 'into an unofficial future' (Carlen 2017, p. 19). It is a contribution that sheds some (albeit partial) light on borders and bordering practices in a region that has, for too long, been bypassed by scholars. It was not my intention to capture borders and bordering practices in the region in its their complexity. Indeed, a range of topics has been only lightly touched upon in this volume, such as the role of security technologies in enabling and preventing human trafficking. However fragmented, the accounts collected here suggest that the complexity of illegalised migrants' experiences in the Global South requires our careful exploration. The voices of women and men migrating through and from the region can tell us about courage, survival, vulnerability, resistance, and hope. These and the many other topics I only skimmed in this volume should be addressed in the future. I have no doubt that more comprehensive research in terms of scope but also depth of inquiry is likely to follow very soon. My goal in *Border Policing and Security Technologies* was first and foremost to start the debate on a range of topics, one of which is the role of countries of origin and transit in migration management, a role that can no longer be ignored. My intention was also to shift the discussion around accountability for what occurs in countries of origin and transit to those that benefit most from re-bordering processes across the developing world. While this approach is certainly not novel in academia, the more we talk about human rights violations and accountability for such practices, the more likely the prospect of social change will be in the future.

While in Chapter 1 I did acknowledge some of the challenges I faced in doing this research, and while it took me many years to get to this point, the importance of this region and many other under-researched locations in the developing world for our understanding and engaging with mobility management requires our full and unequivocal attention. Indeed, everything is political in the Western Balkans, including mobility. Access is by no means guaranteed. Gatekeepers are often uncooperative and non-transparent. Yet the region's role as a "parking lot", "buffer zone", and "labour reserve" for people who have been (temporarily or permanently) immobilised is unlikely to fade in the near future. The Western Balkan's strategic importance in what is considered to be a renewal of the migrant "crisis" in Europe is beyond doubt. Future research will certainly fill the gaps when it comes to the nature, structure, and impact of security technologies across the globe. Indeed, we cannot fully comprehend what happens in Brussels, Paris, or Calais if we ignore developments in Belgrade, Skopje, or Zagreb. Importantly, if we continue to ignore the Western Balkans and other under-researched regions on the fringes, we will fail to uphold the human rights of people on the move and assist policy-makers in creating effective polices and laws that will ensure such protection.

This book is, no doubt, one of many future expeditions that map, analyse, and critique security and counter-security technologies in the Global South. As explorers have been doing for centuries, at the beginning of a journey into the unknown border scholars that investigate these important issues should not be afraid of the voyage or what change or painful discoveries such a voyage might bring. They ought to review what we know already, read the signs and signposts, gather the troops, and start the engine.

Bibliography

Aas K F 2005 "Getting Ahead of the Game": Border Technologies and the Chang-ing Space of Governance, in Zureik E and Salter M (eds) *Global Surveillance and Policing: Borders, Security, Identity*, Routledge, London and New York, pp. 194–214.

Aas K F 2007 *Globalization and Crime*, Sage, London.

Aas K F 2011 "Crimmigrant" Bodies and Bona Fide Travellers: Surveillance, Citizen-ship and Global Governance, *Theoretical Criminology*, vol. 15, no. 3, pp. 331–346.

Aas K F 2012 (In)Security-at-a-Distance: Rescaling Justice, Risk and Warfare in a Transnational Age, *Global Crime*, vol. 13, no. 4, pp. 235–253.

Aas K F 2013 The Ordered and Bordered Society: Migration Control, Citizenship, and the Northern Penal State, in Aas K F and Bosworth M (eds) *Borders of Punish-ment: Migration, Citizenship, and Social Exclusion*, Oxford University Press, Oxford, pp. 21–39.

Aas K F, Gundus H and Lomell H 2009 Introduction: Technologies of Insecurity, in Aas K, Gundus H and Lomell H (eds) *Technologies of Insecurity: The Surveillance of Everyday Life*, Routledge-Cavendish, Abingdon, pp. 1–17.

ABC News 2014 Ukraine Crisis: European Security Watchdog Says It Will Use Drones to Monitor Russia-Ukraine Ceasefire, 12 September, available at www.abc.net.au/news/2014-09-12/osce-will-use-drones-to-monitor-russia-ukraine-border/5738786, accessed 16 January 2018.

Adey P 2004 Secured and Sorted Mobilities: Examples from the Airport, *Surveillance and Society*, vol. 1, no. 4, pp. 500–519.

Adey P 2006 'Divided We Move': The Dromologics of Airport Security and Surveil-lance, in Monahan T (ed) *Surveillance and Society: Technological Politics and Everyday Life*, Routledge, New York, pp. 195–208.

Adey P 2009 *Mobility*, Routledge, Abingdon and New York.

Agamben G 2004 Bodies Without Words: Against the Biopolitical Tattoo, *German Law Journal*, vol. 5, no. 2, pp. 168–169.

Akee R, Basu A, Chau N and Khamis M 2010 Ethnic Fragmentation, Conflict, Dis-placed Persons and Human Trafficking: An Empirical Analysis, in Epstein G S and Gang I N (eds) *Migration and Culture, Frontiers of Economics and Globalization, Vol. 8*, Emerald Group Publishing, Bingley, pp. 691–716.

Aliverti A 2013 *Crimes of Mobility: Criminal Law and the Regulation of Immigration*, Routledge, London and New York.

Aliverti A 2015 Enlisting the Public in the Policing of Immigration, *British Journal of Criminology*, vol. 55, no. 2, pp. 215–230.

Alvarez J 2014 (Re)Imagining Migration, *Peace Review*, vol. 26, no. 2, pp. 178–184.

Amnesty International 2015a Europe's Borderlands: Violations Against Refugees and Migrants in Macedonia, Serbia and Hungary, available at www.amnesty.org/en/documents/eur70/1579/2015/en/, accessed 16 October 2017.

Amnesty International 2015b Macedonia: Thousands Trapped and at Risk of Violence as Borders Sealed, available at www.amnesty.org/en/latest/news/2015/08/macedonia-thousands-trapped-and-at-risk-of-violence-as-border-sealed/, accessed 17 June 2018.

Amoore L 2009 Lines of Sight: On the Visualization of Unknown Futures, *Citizenship Studies*, vol. 13, no. 1, pp. 17–30.

Amoore L 2013 *The Politics of Possibility: Risk and Security Beyond Probability*, Duke University Press, Durham and London.

Amoore L, Marmura S and Salter M 2008 Editorial: Smart Borders and Mobilities: Spaces, Zones, Enclosures, *Surveillance & Society*, vol. 5, no. 2, pp. 96–101.

Andersson R 2016 Hardwiring the Frontier? The Politics of Security Technology in Europe's 'Fight Against Illegal Migration', *Security Dialogue* vol. 47, no. 1, pp. 22–39.

Andrijasevic R 2007 Beautiful Dead Bodies: Gender, Migration and Representation in Anti-Trafficking Campaigns, *Feminist Review*, vol. 86, pp. 24–44.

Andrijasevic R 2010 From Exception to Excess: Detention and Deportation Across the Mediterranean Space, in de Genova N and Peutz N (eds) *The Deportation Regime: Sovereignty, Space, and the Freedom of Movement*, Duke University Press, Durham and London, pp. 147–165.

Angelos J 2011 From Serbia to Germany – and Back: Wave of Roma Rejected as Asylum Seekers, Spiegel Online International, 26 May, available at www.spiegel.de/international/germany/from-serbia-to-germany-and-back-wave-of-roma-rejected-as-asylum-seekers-a-764630.html, accessed 1 March 2018.

Apap J, Cullen P and Medved F 2002 Counteracting Human Trafficking: Protecting the Victims of Trafficking, Centre for European Studies, available at www.childtrafficking.org/pdf/user/counteracting_human_trafficking_protecting_victims.pdf, accessed 2 February 2018.

APC/CZA 2012 *Azilne priče*, Centar za zaštitu i pomoć tražiocima azila – APC/CZA, Beograd.

APC/CZA 2013a *Analiza – tražioci azila u Srbiji i srpski azilanti u Evropi*, APC/CZA, Beograd.

APC/CZA 2013b *Tražioci azila i iregularni migranti u Srbiji, fenomen, potrebe, problemi, očekivanja, profil*, APC/CZA, Beograd.

Aradau C 2004 Security and the Democratic Scene: Desecuritization and Emancipation. *Journal of International Relations and Development* vol. 7, no. 4, pp. 388–413.

Askola H 2011 Roma, Free Movement and Gendered Exclusion in the Enlarged European Union, in FitzGerald S (ed) *Regulating the International Movement of Women: From Protection to Control*, Routledge, New York, pp. 48–66.

ATINA 2013 Otvaranje dijaloga u lokalnim zajednicama između migranata i građana o međusobnoj toleranciji i nenasilju, available at http://atina.org.rs/dijalozi_lokalne.html, accessed 2 February 2018.

B92 2010 Prva srpska bespilotna letelica, 1 May, available at www.b92.net/info/vesti/index.php?yyyy=2010&mm=05&dd=01&nav_id=428205, accessed 8 December 2016.

B92 2011 Interior Minister Announces Stricter Border Controls, 8 May, available at www.b92.net/eng/news/politics.php?yyyy=2011&mm=05&dd=08&nav_id=74223, accessed 21 June 2018.

B92 2012 Lažni azilanti postali profesija, 18 October, available at www.b92.net/info/vesti/index.php?yyyy=2012&mm=10&dd=18&nav_category=1262&nav_id=652773, accessed 24 March 2018.

B92 2018 Serbia Could Host 'Camps for Expelled Migrants', 15 June, available at www.b92.net/eng/news/world.php?yyyy=2018&mm=06&dd=15&nav_id=104410, accessed 17 June 2018.

Balch A and Geddes A 2011 The Development of the EU Migration and Asylum Regime, in Dijstelbloem H and Meijer A (eds) *Migration and the New Technological Borders of Europe*, Palgrave Macmillan, Basingstoke and New York, pp. 22–39.

Balibar É 2002 *Politics and the Other Scene*, London, Verso.

Barker V 2015 Border Protests: The Role of Civil Society in Transforming Border Control, in Weber L (ed) *Rethinking Border Control for a Globalizing World*, Routledge, London and New York, pp. 133–152.

Basham V and Vaughan-Williams N 2013 Gender, Race and Border Security Practices: A Profane Reading of "Muscular Liberalism", *The British Journal of Politics and International Relations*, vol. 15, pp. 509–527.

Bauböck R 2015 Rethinking Borders as Membranes, in Weber L (ed) *Rethinking Border Control for a Globalizing World*, Routledge, London and New York, pp. 169–178.

Bauder H 2013 Why We Should Use the Term Illegalized Immigrant, RCIS Research Brief no. 2013/1, available at http://ffm-online.org/wp-content/uploads/2013/08/RCIS_RB_Bauder_No_2013_1.pdf, accessed 19 November 2017.

Bauman Z 1998 *Globalization: The Human Consequences*, Columbia University Press, New York.

Bauman Z 1999 The Self in a Consumer Society, *The Hedgehog Review*, Fall, vol. 1, pp. 35–40.

Bauman Z 2000 *Liquid Modernity*, Polity Press, Cambridge.

Bauman Z 2011 *Collateral Damage: Social Inequalities in a Global Age*, Polity Press, Cambridge.

BBC 2016 Your Phone Is Now a Refugee Phone [watch on a mobile], BBC media action YouTube channel, available at www.youtube.com/watch?v=m1BLsySgsHM accessed 20 October 2017.

Belgrade Centre for Human Rights, Macedonian Young Lawyers Association and Oxfam 2017 *A Dangerous "Game": The Pushbacks of Migrants, Including Refugees, at Europe's Border* – A Joint Agency Briefing Paper, Oxfam International.

Bellanova R and Duez D 2012 A Different View on the "Making" of European Security: The EU Passenger Name Record System as Socio-Technical Assemblage, *European Foreign Affairs Review*, vol. 17, no. 5, pp. 109–124.

Bellanova R and Duez D 2016 The Making (Sense) Of EUROSUR: How to Control the Sea Borders?, in Bossong R and Carpaccio H (eds) *EU Borders and Shifting Internal Security-Technology, Externalization and Accountability*, Springer, Heidelberg, pp. 23–44.

Bell M and Ward G 2000 Comparing Temporary Mobility with Permanent Migration, *Tourism Geographies*, vol. 2, no. 1, pp. 87–107.

Beogradski Centar za Ljudska Prava 2016 *Pravo na azil u Republici Srbiji 2015*, Beogradski Centar za Ljudska Prava, Beograd.

Berman J 2003 (Un)popular Strangers and Crises (un)bounded: Discourses of Sex-Trafficking, the European Political Community and the Panicked State of the Modern State, *European Journal of International Relations*, vol. 9, no. 1, pp. 37–86.

Berman J 2010 Biopolitical Management, Economic Calculation and "Trafficked Women", *International Migration*, vol. 48, no. 4, pp. 84–113.

Beznec B, Speer M and Stojić-Mitrović M 2016 Governing the Balkan Route: Macedonia, Serbia and the European Border Regime, Research Paper Series of Rosa Luxemburg Stiftung Southeast Europe, Belgrade.

Bigo D 2001 Migration and Security, in Guiradon V and Joppke C (eds) *Controlling a New Migration World*, Routledge, London, pp. 121–149.

Bigo D 2002 Security and Immigration: Toward a Critique of the Governmentality of Unease, *Alternatives: Global, Local, Political*, vol. 27, no. 1, pp. 63–92.

Bigo D 2014 The (in)securitization Practices of the Three Universes of EU Border Control: Military/Navy – Border Guards/Police – Database Analysts, *Security Dialogue*, vol. 45, pp. 209–225.

Bigo D 2015 Death in the Mediterranean Sea: The Results of Three Fields of Action of European Union Border Controls, in Jansen Y, Celikates R and de Bloois J (eds) *The Irregularizaiton of Migration in Contemporary Europe*, Rowman and Littlefield, London and New York, pp. 55–70.

Bigo D and Guild E 2005 Policing at a Distance: Schengen Visa Policies, in Bigo D and Guild E (eds) *Controlling Frontiers: Free Movement into and Within Europe*, Ashgate, Aldershot, pp. 233–263.

Bieber F 2012 The Western Balkans are Dead – Long Live the Balkans! Democratization and the Limits of the EU, in Džihić V and Hamilton D (eds) *Unfinished Business: The Western Balkans and the International Community*, Brookings Institution Press, Washington, pp. 3–10.

Blic 2011 Srpska bespilotna letelica, 27 June, available at www.blic.rs/Vesti/Drustvo/262372/Srpska-bespilotna-letelica, accessed 8 December 2016.

Blic 2013 Lažni azilanti drmaju bezvizni režim, 20 December, available at www.blic.rs/vesti/politika/lazni-azilanti-drmaju-bezvizni-rezim/7hwxkxn, accessed 9 April 2018.

Blic 2015 Stoltenberg: Teroristi bi kao migranti mogli da stignu u Evropu, 18 May, available at www.blic.rs/Vesti/Svet/559973/Stoltenberg-Teroristi-bi-kao-migranti-mogli-da-stignu-u-Evropu, accessed 8 April 2018.

Blic 2015 Reke migranata: Vozovi na Đevđeliji puni ljudi koji nadiru prema Srbiji, 12 August, available at www.blic.rs/Vesti/Drustvo/582253/REKE-MIGRANATA-Vozovi-na-Djevdjeliji-puni-ljudi-koji-nadiru-prema-Srbiji, accessed 9 March 2018.

Blic 2015 Godina kada su migranti pokorili Evropu, 26 August, available at www.blic.rs/Vesti/Svet/585832/Godina-kada-su-migranti-pokorili-Evropu, accessed 8 April 2018.

Blic 2015 SRBIJA BAZA ZA TERORISTE Nikolić: Neki migranti imaju borbeno iskustvo, 29 July, available at www.blic.rs/vesti/hronika/srbija-baza-za-teroriste-nikolic-neki-migranti-imaju-borbeno-iskustvo/4rbl2nc, accessed 9 April 2018.

Blic 2015 Vučić: Srbija će primiti jedan broj migranata, 'evropskiji' smo od Evrope, 31 August, available at www.blic.rs/Vesti/Politika/587052/Vucic-Srbija-ce-primiti-jedan-broj-migranata-evropskiji-smo-od-Evrope, accessed 8 April 2018.

Boer, M den and Goudappel F 2007 How Secure Is Our Privacy in Seceurope? European Security Through Surveillance, in McGarity N, Davis F and Williams G (eds) *Surveillance, Counter-Terrorism and Comparative Constitutionalism*, Routledge, London and New York, pp. 73–92.

Bojić S 2017 Slepilo za nijanse, *Deutsche Welle Serbia*, available at www.dw.com/sr/slepilo-za-nijanse/a-39956069, accessed 21 March 2018.

Bonifazi C and Mamolo M 2004 Past and Current Trends of Balkan Migrations, *Espace, Populations, Societies*, no. 3, pp. 519–531.

Bossong R and Carappico H 2016 The Multidimensional Nature and Dynamic Transformation of European Borders and Internal Security, in Bossong R and Carrapico H (eds) *EU Borders and Shifting Internal Security: Technology, Externalization and Accountability*, Springer, Cham, Heidelberg, New York, Dordrecht, London, pp. 1–22.

Boswell C 2003 The 'External Dimension' of EU Immigration and Asylum Policy, *International Affairs*, vol. 79, no. 3, pp. 619–638.

Boswell C and Geddes A 2011 *Migration and Mobility in the European Union*, Palgrave Macmillan, Basingstoke and New York

Bosworth M 2008 Border Control and the Limits of the Sovereign State, *Social and Legal Studies*, vol. 17, no. 2, pp. 199–215.

Bosworth M 2014 *Inside Immigration Detention*, Oxford University Press, Oxford.

Bosworth M, Franko K and Pickering S 2018 Punishment, Globalization and Migration Control: 'Get Them the Hell Out of Here', *Punishment and Society*, vol. 20, no. 1, pp. 34–53.

Bourne M, Johnson H and Lisle D 2015 Laboratizing the Border: The Production, Translation and Anticipation of Security Technologies, *Security Dialogue*, vol. 46, no. 4, pp. 307–325.

Boyne R 2000 Post-Panopticism, *Economy and Society*, vol. 29, pp. 285–307.

Briskman L 2013 Technology, Control, and Surveillance in Australia's Immigration Detention Centres, *Refuge: Canada's Journal on Refugees*, vol. 29, pp. 9–19.

Broeders D 2007 The New Digital Borders of Europe: EU Databases and the Surveillance of Irregular Migrants, *International Sociology*, vol. 22, no. 1, pp. 71–92.

Broeders D 2009 *Breaking Down Anonymity: Digital Surveillance of Irregular Migrants in Germany and the Netherlands*, Amsterdam University Press, Amsterdam.

Broeders D 2011 A European 'Border' Surveillance System under Construction, in Dijstelbloem H and Meijer A (eds) *Migration and the New Technological Borders of Europe*, Palgrave Macmillan, Basingstoke and New York, pp. 40–67.

Broeders D and Engbersen G 2007 The Fight Against Illegal Immigration: Identification Policies and Immigrants' Counter Strategies, *American Behavioral Scientist*, vol. 50, no. 12, pp. 1592–1609.

Broeders D and Hampshire J 2013 Dreaming of Seamless Borders: ICTs and the Pre-Emptive Governance of Mobility in Europe, *Journal of Ethnic and Migration Studies*, vol. 39, no. 8, pp. 1201–1218.

Brouwer E 2008 *Digital Borders and Real Rights: Effective Remedies for Third-Country Nationals in the Schengen Information System*, Martinus Nijhoff Publishers, Leiden.

Brouwer J, van der Woude M and van der Leun J 2017a Border Policing, Procedural Justice and Belonging: The Legitimacy of (cr)immigration Controls in Border Areas, *British Journal of Criminology*, vol. 58, no. 3, pp. 624–643.

Brouwer J, van der Woude M and van der Leun J 2017b Framing Migration and the Process of Crimmigration: A Systematic Analysis of the Media Representation of

Unauthorised Immigrants in the Netherlands, *European Journal of Criminology*, vol. 14, no. 1, pp. 100–119.

Brunovskis A and Surtees R 2017 *Vulnerability and Exploitation Along the Balkan Route: Identifying Victims of Human Trafficking in Serbia*, Fafo, Oslo.

Bruns B, Happ D and Zichner H 2016 Introduction, in Bruns B, Happ D and Zichner H (eds) *European Neighbourhood Policy: Geopolitics between Integration and Security*, Palgrave Macmillan, London, pp. 1–22.

Brzakoska Bazerkoska J 2016 The European Union and (frozen) Conflicts in Its Neighbourhood: The SAP and the ENP Compared, in Gstöhl S (ed) *The European Neighbourhood Policy in a Comparative Perspective: Models, Challenges, Lessons*, Routledge, London and New York, pp. 235–255.

Bulos N and King L 2016 Image Captures Plight of Syria Kids; Video of a Boy Pulled from the Rubble of His Home Brings Grief and Outrage Worldwide, *Los Angeles Times*, 19 August, A3.

Burns A 2015 Discussion and Action: Political and Personal Responses to the Aylan Kurdi Images, in Vis F and Gourinova O (eds) *The Iconic Image on Social Media: A Rapid Research Response to the Death of Aylan Kurdi*, Visual Social Media Lab, December 2015, available at https://research.gold.ac.uk/14624/1/KURDI%20 REPORT.pdf, accessed 24 April 2018.

Bump P 2013 The Border Patrol Wants to Arm Drones, *The Wire*, 2 July, available at www.theatlantic.com/national/archive/2013/07/border-patrol-arm-drones/ 313656/, accessed 8 December 2016.

Buzan B and Wæver O 2003 *Regions and Powers: The Structure of International Security*, Cambridge University Press, Cambridge.

Buzan B, Wæver O and Jaap de Wilde J 1998 *Security: A New Framework for Analysis*, Lynne Rienner Publishers, Boulder.

Bytyci F and Than K 2015 Dramatic Surge in Kosovars Crossing Illegally into EU, available at www.reuters.com/article/2015/02/04/us-kosovo-eu-migrants-idUSKBN0L811120150204, accessed 2 March 2018.

Cadier D 2013 Is the European Neighbourhood Policy a Substitute for Enlargement? *The Crisis of EU enlargement*, LSE IDEAS Report, available at www.lse.ac.uk/ IDEAS/publications/reports/pdf/SR018/Cadier_D.pdf, accessed 9 May 2018.

Cairncross F 1997 *The Death of Distance: How the Communication Revolution is Changing Our Lives*, Harvard Business School Press, Boston.

Calic M-J 2019 *A History of Yugoslavia*, Purdue University Press, West Lafayette.

Cani B 2015 Kosovski Albanci bez šansi za azil, *Deutsche Welle Serbian*, available at www.dw.de/kosovski-albanci-bez-%C5%A1ansi-za-azil/a-18244886, accessed 2 March 2018.

Carlen P 2017 Doing Imaginative Criminology, in Jacobsen M and Walklate S (eds) *Liquid Criminology: Doing Imaginative Criminological Research*, Routledge, London and New York, pp. 17–30.

Casas-Cortes M, Cobarrubias S and Pickles J 2016 'Good Neighbours Make Good Fences': Seahorse Operations, Border Externalization and Extra-Territoriality, *European Union and Regional Studies*, vol. 23, no. 3, pp. 231–251.

Casier T 2008 The New Neighbours of the European Union: The Compelling Logic of Enlargement? in DeBardleben J (ed) *The Boundaries of EU Enlargement: Finding a Place for Neighbours*, Palgrave Macmillan, Basingstoke, pp. 19–32.

Castells M 2012 *Networks of Outrage and Hope: Social Movements in the Internet Age*, Polity Press, Cambridge.

Castells M 2014 *Communication Power*, Oxford University Press, Oxford.

Castles S 2003 The International Politics of Forced Migration, *Development*, vol. 46, no. 3, pp. 11–20.

Celador G and Juncos A 2012 The EU and Border Management in the Western Balkans: Preparing for European Integration or Safeguarding EU External Borders? *Southeast European and Black Sea Studies*, vol. 12, no. 2, pp. 201–220.

Ceyhan A 2008 Technologization of Security: Management of Uncertainty and Risk in the Age of Biometrics, *Surveillance & Society*, vol. 5, no. 2, pp. 102–123.

Chachipe 2012 Srbija: Vizna liberalizacija po svaku cenu? in Jeremic V (ed) *Od migracije do deportacije: Prilozi kritičkoj analizi politike prema romskim migrantima i migrantkinjama u Evropi*, Pekograf, Beograd, pp. 73–94.

Chacón J 2010 Tensions and Trade-Offs: Protecting Trafficking Victims in the Era of Immigration Enforcement, *University of Pennsylvania Law Review*, vol. 158, no. 6, pp. 1609–1653.

Chang J-H, Zhu Y-Q, Wang S-H and Li Y-J 2018 Would You Change Your Mind? An Empirical Study of Social Impact Theory on Facebook, *Telematics and Informatics*, vol. 35, pp. 282–292.

Cherkezova S 2014 Potential Romani Migrants from the Western Balkans, in Guild E (ed) *Going Nowhere? Western Balkan Roma and EU Visa Liberalisation*, Special issue of the *Roma Rights: Journal of the European Roma Rights Centre*, European Roma Rights Centre, Budapest, pp. 5–13.

Chimni B S 1998 The Geopolitics of Refugee Studies: A View from the South, *Journal of Refugee Studies*, vol. 11, no. 4, pp. 350–374.

Chuang J 2014 Exploitation Creep and the Unmaking of Human Trafficking Law, *American Journal of International Law*, vol. 108, no. 4, pp. 609–649.

Chudoska Blazhevska I and Flores Juberías C 2016 Macedonia in the 2015 Refugee Crisis, *Balkania*, no. 7, pp. 217–244.

Cisneros J D 2013 *The Border Crossed Us: Rhetoric of Borders, Citizenship, and Latina/o Identity*, The University of Alabama Press, Tuscaloosa.

Cocco, E 2017 Where is the European Frontier? The Balkan Migration Crisis and Its Impact on Relations between the EU and the Western Balkans, *European View*, vol. 16, pp. 293–302.

Cohen L 2008 The Europeanization of 'Defective Democracies' in the Western Balkans: Pre-accession Challenges to Democratic Consolidation, in DeBardleben J (ed) *The Boundaries of EU Enlargement: Finding a Place for Neighbours*, Palgrave Macmillan, Basingstoke, pp. 205–221.

Cohen R 1991 East-West and European Migration in a Global Context, *New Community*, vol. 18, no. 1, pp. 9–26.

Collantes-Celador G and Juncos A 2012 The EU and Border Management in the Western Balkans: Preparing for European Integration or Safeguarding EU External Borders? *Southeast European and Black Sea Studies*, vol. 12, no. 2, pp. 201–220.

Collett E 2007 The 'Global Approach to Migration': Rhetoric or Reality? Policy Brief, European Policy Centre, available at www.isn.ethz.ch/Digital-Library/Publications/Detail/?ots591=0c54e3b3-1e9c-be1e-2c24-a6a8c7060233&lng=en&id=45563, accessed 3 December 2017.

Commissioner for Human Rights of the Council of Europe 2013 The Right to Leave a Country: Issue Paper, October 2013, Council of Europe, available at www.coe.int/t/commissioner/source/prems/prems150813_GBR_1700_The RightToLeaveACountry_web.pdf, accessed 9 March 2018.

Connor P 2015 Asylum Seeker Demography: Young and Male, available at www.pewglobal.org/2016/08/02/4-asylum-seeker-demography-young-and-male/, accessed 18 January 2018.

Cooper A and Perkins C 2015 Mobile Borders/Bordering Mobilities: Status Functions, Contemporary State Bordering Practices and Implications for Resistance and Intervention, in Kinnvall C and Svensson T (eds) *Governing Borders and Security: The Politics of Connectivity and Dispersal*, Routledge, London and New York, pp. 14–31.

Cornelisse G 2015 State Borders, Human Mobility and Social Equality: From Blueprints to Pathways, in Weber L (ed) *Rethinking Border Control for a Globalizing World*, Routledge, London and New York, pp. 80–97.

Cote-Boucher K 2008 The Diffuse Border: Intelligence-Sharing, Control and Confinement along Canada's 'Smart Border', *Surveillance & Society*, vol. 5, no. 2, pp. 142–165.

Council of Europe 2013 The Right to Leave a Country, Issue Paper by the Council of Europe Commissioner for Human Rights, available at www.commissioner.coe.int, accessed 4 July 2017.

Craigie H 2014 Beyond Humanitarianism: Border Songs and the Politics of Migration, *NACLA Report on the Americas*, vol. 47, no. 1, pp. 76–77.

Cross H 2013 *Migrants, Borders and Global Capitalism: West African Labour Mobility and EU Borders*, Routledge, London and New York.

Csernatoni R 2018 Constructing the EU's High-Tech Borders: FRONTEX and Dual-Use Drones for Border Management, *European Security*, vol. 27, no. 2, pp. 175–200.

Cunningham E 2015 Facebook is the New Travel Guide for Iraqis Headed to Europe, *The Washington Post*, 16 September, available at www.washingtonpost.com/world/facebook-is-the-new-travel-guide-for-iraqis-headed-to-europe/2015/09/16/c4142d16-566f-11e5-9f54-1ea23f6e02f3_story.html?utm_term=.a071b71e4735, accessed 7 July 2017.

Cupolo D 2013 Drone Use Soars in Latin America, Remains Largely Unregulated, available at http://upsidedownworld.org/main/international-archives-60/4615-drone-use-soars-in-latin-america-remains-widely-unregulated-, accessed 22 November 2017.

Cupolo D 2016 Train to Nowhere: Refugees in Serbia Stranded on E.U. Border, Refugees Deeply, available at www.newsdeeply.com/refugees/articles/2016/12/21/train-to-nowhere-refugees-in-serbia-stranded-on-e-u-border, accessed 24 April 2018.

Dauvergne C 2004 Sovereignty, Migration, and the Rule of Law in Global Times, *The Modern Law Review*, vol. 67, no. 4, pp. 588–615.

Danas 2015 Popović: EU čini sve da migranti ostanu u Srbiji, 24 August, available at www.danas.rs/danasrs/politika/popovic_eu_cini_sve_da_migranti_ostanu_u_srbiji.56.html?news_id=306909, accessed 8 April 2018.

Dauvergne C 2007 Security and Migration Law in a Less Brave New World, *Social and Legal Studies*, vol. 16, no. 4, pp. 533–549.

Dean J 2009 *Democracy and Other Neoliberal Fantasies: Communicative Capitalism and Left Politics*, Duke University Press, Durham and London.

Dearden L 2017 Hungarian Camerawoman Avoids Jail after Being Filmed Tripping Up and Kicking Refugees. *Independent*, 13 January, available at www.independent.co.uk/news/world/europe/hungarian-camerawoman-petra-laszlo-trips-fleeing-refugee-kicking-filmed-video-convicted-sentencing-a7525136.html, accessed 6 July 2017.

de Borja Lasheras F, Tcherneva V and Wesslau F 2016 Return to Instability: How migration and great power politics threaten the Western Balkans, European Council on Foreign Relations Policy Brief, ECFR/163, March 2016.

De Clercq R 2007 Final Conclusions and Recommendations of the Chair, available at https://gfmd.org/docs?search_api_views_fulltext=Final+Conclusions+and+Recommendations+of+the+Chair, accessed 22 March 2018.

De Genova N 2010 The Deportation Regime: Sovereignty, Space, and the Freedom of Movement, in De Genova N and Peutz N (eds) *The Deportation Regime: Sovereignty, Space, and the Freedom of Movement*, Duke University Press, Durham, pp. 33–65.

De Genova N 2017a Introduction: The Borders of "Europe" and the European Question, in De Genova N (ed) *The Borders of Europe: Autonomy of Migration, Tactics of Bordering*, Duke University Press, Durham and London, pp. 1–35.

De Genova N 2017b The Migrant "Crisis" as Racial Crisis: Do Black Lives Matter in Europe? *Ethnic and Racial Studies*, August 2017, pp. 1–18.

Dekker R and Engbersen G 2013 How Social Media Transform Migrant Networks and Facilitate Migration, *Global Networks*, vol. 14, no. 4, pp. 401–418.

Dijstelbloem H 2017 Migration Tracking Is a Mess, *Nature*, available at www.nature.com.ez.library.latrobe.edu.au/news/migration-tracking-is-a-mess-1.21542, accessed 16 October 2017.

Dijstelbloem, H and Broeders, D 2015 Border Surveillance, Mobility Management and the Shaping of Non-Publics in Europe, *European Journal of Social Theory*, vol. 18, no. 1, pp. 21–38.

Dijstelbloem H, Meijer A and Besters M 2011 The Migration Machine, in Dijstelbloem H and Meijer A (eds) *Migration and the New Technological Borders of Europe*, Palgrave Macmillan, Basingstoke and New York, pp. 1–21.

Dijstelbloem H, van Reekum R and Schinkel W 2017 Surveillance at Sea: The Transactional Politics of Border Control in the Aegean, *Security Dialogue*, vol. 48, no. 3, pp. 224–240.

Dimitriadi A 2016 The Interrelationship between Trafficking and Irregular Migration, in Carrera S and Guild E (eds) *Irregular Migration, Trafficking and Smuggling of Human Beings: Policy Dilemmas in the EU*, Centre for European Policy Studies, Brussels, pp. 64–69.

Doezema J 2000 Loose Women or Lost Women: The Re-Emergence of the Myth of "White Slavery" in Contemporary Discourses of Trafficking in Women, *Gender Issues*, vol. 18, no. 1, pp. 23–50.

Donev D, Onceva S and Gligorov I 2002 Refugee Crisis in Macedonia During the Kosovo Conflict in 1999, *Croatian Medical Journal*, vol. 43, pp. 184–189.

Donnan H and Wilson T 1999 *Borders: Frontiers of Identity, Nation and State*, Berg Publishers, Oxford.

D'Orazio F 2015 Journey of an Image: From a Beach in Bodrum to Twenty Million Screens Across the World, in Vis F and Gourinova O (eds) *The Iconic Image on Social Media: A Rapid Research Response to the Death of Aylan Kurdi*, Visual Social Media Lab, December 2015, available at https://research.gold.ac.uk/14624/1/KURDI%20REPORT.pdf, accessed 24 April 2018.

Dredge S 2015 How Live Video on Periscope Helped 'Get Inside' the Syrian Refugees Story. *The Guardian*, 13 September, available at www.theguardian.com/media/2015/sep/13/periscope-app-syrian-refugees-bild, accessed 10 July 2017.

Đaković T 2015 Vozovi nade, vlakovi tuge, *NIN*, 24 September 2015.

Đorđević B 2009 The European Policy on the Management of Migration Flows and Serbia Role's Within It, *Western Balkan Security Observer*, January, pp. 78–91.

Đurović J 2015 Suzavac, batine i jauci, *Vreme*, 24 September 2015.

EASO 2015 *Asylum Applicants from the Western Balkans: A Comparative Analysis of Trends, Push-Pull Factors and Responses – Update*, European Asylum Support Office, Luxembourg.

Edwards A 2007 Traffic in Human Beings: At the Intersection of Criminal Justice, Human Rights, Asylum/Migration and Labor, *Denver Journal of International Law and Policy*, vol. 36, no. 1, pp. 9–53.

Ejdus F 2018 Professional Practices of Security Community Building: Theoretical Introduction, in Stojanović-Gajić S and Ejdus F (eds) *Security Community Practices in the Western Balkans*, Routledge, Abingdon and New York, pp. 1–12.

El-Enany N 2016 Aylan Kurdi: The Human Refugee, *Law Critique*, vol. 27, pp. 13–15.

Elsie R and Destani B T 2015 *Tajar Zavalani: History of Albania*, Center for Albanian Studies, London.

ERSTE Stiftung and ESI 2013 Saving Visa-Free Travel: Visa, Asylum and the EU Roadmap Policy, Berlin and Brussels, available at www.esiweb.org/pdf/esi_document_id_132.pdf, accessed 7 March 2018.

ESI 2018 The Visa Roadmaps, available at www.esiweb.org/index.php?lang=en&id=352, accessed 25 February 2018.

eu-LISA 2014 VIS to Start Operations in the Western Balkans and Turkey, available at www.eulisa.europa.eu/Newsroom/PressRelease/Pages/VIS-to-start-operations-in-the-Western-Balkans-and-Turkey.aspx, accessed 24 February 2018.

EUROPA 2013 'Smart Borders': Enhancing Mobility and Security, available at http://europa.eu/rapid/press-release_IP-13-162_en.htm, accessed 2 December 2016.

EUROPA 2016 EURODAC System, available at http://europa.eu/legislation_summaries/justice_freedom_security/free_movement_of_persons_asylum_immigration/l33081_en.htm, accessed 4 December 2017.

European Commission 2008a Visa Liberalisation with Serbia: Road Map, available at www.esiweb.org/pdf/White%20List%20Project%20Paper%20-%20Roadmap%20Serbia.pdf, accessed 22 November 2017.

European Commission 2008b Communication from the Commission to the European Parliament, the Council, the European Economic and Social Committee and the Committee of the Regions: Examining the Creation of a European Border Surveillance System (EUROSUR), European Commission, Brussels.

European Commission 2011 Communication from the Commission to the European Parliament, the Council, the Economic and Social Committee and the Committee of the Regions: The Global Approach to Migration and Mobility, Brussels, 18 November 2011.

European Commission 2015a Report from the Commission to the European Parliament and the Council: Fifth Report on the Post-Visa Liberalisation Monitoring for the Western Balkan Countries in accordance with the Commission Statement of 8 November 2010, Brussels, available at http://ec.europa.eu/dgs/home-affairs/what-is-new/news/news/docs/20150225_5th_post-visa_liberalisation_report_with_western_balkan_countries_en.pdf, accessed 1 March 2018.

European Commission 2015b Communication from the Commission to the European Parliament, the Council, the European Economic and Social Committee and the Committee of the Regions – A European Agenda on Migration, available at https://ec.europa.eu/home-affairs/sites/homeaffairs/files/what-we-do/policies/european-agenda-migration/background-information/docs/communication_on_the_european_agenda_on_migration_en.pdf, accessed 25 June 2018.

European Commission 2017a Serbia- Financial Assistance under IPA II, available at https://ec.europa.eu/neighbourhood-enlargement/instruments/funding-by-country/serbia_en, accessed 12 February 2018.

European Commission 2017b The Former Yugoslav Republic of Macedonia- Financial Assistance under IPA II, available at https://ec.europa.eu/neighbourhood-enlargement/instruments/funding-by-country/former-yugoslav-republic-of-macedonia_en, accessed 12 February 2018.

European Commission 2017c Report from the Commission to the European Parliament and the Council: First Report under the Visa Suspension Mechanism, 20 December, Brussels, available at https://ec.europa.eu/home-affairs/sites/homeaffairs/files/what-is-new/news/20171220_first_report_under_suspension_mechanism_en.pdf, accessed 7 March 2018.

European Commission 2018a Border Crossing, available at http://ec.europa.eu/dgs/home-affairs/what-we-do/policies/borders-and-visas/border-crossing/index_en.htm, accessed 20 May 2018.

European Commission 2018b Visa Information System, available at https://ec.europa.eu/home-affairs/what-we-do/policies/borders-and-visas/visa-information-system_en, accessed 20 May 2018.

European Commission 2018c Global Approach to Migration and Mobility, available at https://ec.europa.eu/home-affairs/what-we-do/policies/international-affairs/global-approach-to-migration_en, accessed 19 May 2018.

European Commission 2018d Eurosur, available at https://ec.europa.eu/home-affairs/what-we-do/policies/borders-and-visas/border-crossing/eurosur_en, accessed 20 May 2018.

European Parliament 2013 EU Border Surveillance: MEPs Approve EUROSUR Operating Rules, available at www.europarl.europa.eu/news/en/news-room/20131007IPR21624/eu-border-surveillance-meps-approve-eurosur-operating-rules, accessed 15 December 2017.

European Parliament 2016 The Gender Dimension of Human Trafficking, available at www.europarl.europa.eu/RegData/etudes/BRIE/2016/577950/EPRS_BRI(2016)577950_EN.pdf, accessed 18 June 2018.

European Partnership 2018 European Partnership: Integrated Border Management Capacity Building Project, available at www.eap-ibm-capacitybuilding.eu/en/about/ibm, accessed 26 February 2018.

Feldman G 2012 The Migration Apparatus: Security, Labor, and Policymaking in the European Union, Stanford University Press, Stanford.

Ferreira N and Kostakopolou D 2016 The Roma and European Union Citizenship, in Ferreira N and Kostakopolou D (eds) *The Human Face of the European Union: Are EU Law and Policy Humane Enough?* Cambridge University Press, Cambridge, pp. 206–234.

Ferrell J 2009 Kill Method: A Provocation, *Journal of Theoretical and Philosophical Criminology* vol. 1, no. 1, pp. 1– 22.

Ferzek K 2015 Talas izbeglica kao naručen za Orbana, *Deutsche Welle Serbian*, available at www.dw.de/talas-izbeglica-kao-naru%C4%8Den-za-orbana/a-18257667, accessed 2 March 2018.

Fitz-Gibbon K 2017 Gaining Access and Managing Gatekeepers: Undertaking Criminological Research with Those "within" the System, in Jacobsen M and Walklate S (eds) *Liquid Criminology: Doing Imaginative Criminological Research*, Routledge, London and New York, pp. 173–187.

Flessenkemper T and Bütow T 2011 Building and Removing Visa Walls: On European Integration of the Western Balkans, *Security and Peace*, vol. 29, no. 3, pp. 162–168.

Freedman J 2007 *Gendering the International Asylum and Refugee Debate*, Palgrave Macmillan, New York.

Freedman J 2010 Protecting Women Asylum Seekers and Refugees: From International Norms to National Protection? *International Migration*, vol. 48, no. 1, pp. 175–198.

Freedman J 2016 Engendering Security at the Borders of Europe: Women Migrants and Mediterranean "Crisis", *Journal of Refugee Studies*, vol. 29, no. 4, pp. 568–582.

Frelick B, Kysel I and Podkul J 2016 The Impact of Externalization of Migration Control on the Rights of Asylum Seekers and Other Migrants, *Journal on Migration and Human Security*, vol. 4, no. 4, pp. 190–220.

Friedrich Ebert Stiftung 2015 The Kosovo Torrent to EU: People, Reasons and Ways, Friedrich Ebert Stiftung, Prishtina.

Frontex 2013 *Annual Risk Analysis 2013*, available at http://frontex.europa.eu/assets/Publications/Risk_Analysis/Annual_Risk_Analysis_2013.pdf, accessed 1 February 2018.

Frontex 2016 *Western Balkans: Annual Risk Analysis 2016*, Frontex, Warsaw.

Frontex 2017a Western Balkan Route, available at http://Frontex.europa.eu/trends-and-routes/western-balkan-route/, accessed 10 July 2017.

Frontex 2017b A Year in Review: First 12 Months of the European Border and Coast Guard Agency, available at http://frontex.europa.eu/assets/Publications/General/A_Year_in_Review.pdf, accessed 19 February 2018.

Frontex 2018a Roles and Responsibilities, available at https://frontex.europa.eu/operations/roles-responsibilities/, accessed 18 May 2018.

Frontex 2018b Western Balkan Route, available at http://frontex.europa.eu/trends-and-routes/western-balkan-route/, accessed 13 February 2018.

Frontex 2018c Rapid Intervention, available at https://frontex.europa.eu/operations/rapid-intervention/, accessed 29 June 2018.

Frontex 2018d Western Balkans Annual Risk Analysis, available at https://frontex.europa.eu/publications/wb-ara-2018-eW3T1c, accessed 24 January 2019.

Galonja A and Jovanović S 2011 *Zaštita žrtava i prevencija trgovine ljudima*, Zajednički program UNHCR, UNOCD i IOM za borbu protiv trgovine ljudima u Srbiji, Beograd.

Gashi A and Haxhikadrija A 2012 Social Impact of Emigration and Rural-Urban Migration in Central and Eastern Europe: Final Country Report Kosovo, European Commission and GVG.

Geddes A and Scholten P 2016 *The Politics of Migration and Immigration in Europe*, Sage, Los Angeles, London, New Delhi.

Geiger M 2013 The Transformation of Migration Politics: From Migration Control to Disciplining Mobility, in Geiger M and Pécoud A (eds) *Disciplining the Transnational Mobility of People*, Palgrave Macmillan, Basingstoke, pp. 15–40.

Geiger M 2016 Identity Check: Smart Borders and Migration Management as Touchstones for EU-Readiness and – Belonging, in Amelina A, Horvath K and Meeus B (eds) *An Anthropology of Migration and Social Transformation: European Perspectives*, Springer, Heildelberg, New York, Dordrecht, London, pp. 135–149.

Gerard A 2014 *The Securitization of Migration and Refugee Women*, Routledge, Abington and New York.

Gerard A and Pickering S 2012 The Crime and Punishment of Somali Women's Extra-Legal Arrival in Malta, *British Journal of Criminology*, vol. 52, pp. 514–533.

Ghonim W 2012 *Revolution 2.0: The Power of the People Is Greater than the People in Power*, Fourth Estate, London.

Giandomenico J 2015 *Transformative Power Challenged: EU Membership Conditionality in the Western Balkans Revisited*, Uppsala Universitet, Uppsala.

Gil-Bazo M 2006 The Practice of Mediterranean States in the Context of the European Union's Justice and Home Affairs External Dimension. The Safe Third Country Concept Revisited, *International Journal of Refugee Law*, vol. 18, no. 3–4, pp. 571–600.

Giles W and Hyndman J 2004 *Sites of Violence: Gender and Conflict Zones*, University of California Press, Berkeley.

Gillespie M, Ampofo L, Cheesman M, Faith B, Illiadou E, Issa A, Osseiran S and Skleparis D 2016 Mapping Refugee Media Journeys: Smartphones and Social Media Networks – Research Report, The Open University/France Médias Monde.

Glover R 2011 The Theorist and the Practitioner: Linking the Securitization of Migration to Activist Counter-Narratives, *Geopolitics, History, and International Relations*, vol. 3, no. 1, pp. 77–102.

Gong R 2015 Indignation, Inspiration, and Interaction on the Internet: Emotion Work Online in the Anti-Human Trafficking Movement, *Journal of Technology in Human Services*, vol. 33, no. 1, pp. 87–103.

Gourinova O 2015 Introduction, in Vis F and Gourinova O (eds) *The Iconic Image on Social Media: A Rapid Research Response to the Death of Aylan Kurdi*, Visual Social Media Lab, December 2015, available at https://research.gold.ac.uk/14624/1/KURDI%20REPORT.pdf, accessed 24 April 2018.

Gozdziak, E 2015 Data Matters: Issues and Challenges for Research on Trafficking, in Dragiewitz M (ed) *Global Human Trafficking: Critical Issues and Contexts*, Routledge, Abingdon and New York, pp. 23–38.

Greider A 2017 Outsourcing Migration Management: The Role of the Western Balkans in the European Refugee Crisis. Migration Policy Institute, available at www.migrationpolicy.org/article/outsourcing-migration-management-western-balkans-europes-refugee-crisis, accessed 17 October 2017.

Grupa 484 and Nexus 2012 Iregularno može biti regularno – migracije sa juga Srbije, Grupa 484 and Nexus, Beograd.

Guild E 2009 *Security and Migration in the 21st Century*, Polity Press, Cambridge.

Guild E, Carrera S and Geyer F 2008 The Commission's New Border Package: Does It Take Us One Step Closer to a "Cyber-Fortress" Europe? Centre for European Policy Studies Policy Brief, available at www.ceps.be/book/commissions-new-border-package-does-it-take-us-one-step-closer-cyber-fortress-europe, accessed 2 December 2016.

Gundhus H 2005 'Catching' and 'Targeting': Risk-Based Policing, Local Culture and Gendered Practices, *Journal of Scandinavian Studies in Criminology and Crime Prevention*, vol. 6, no. 2, pp. 128–146.

Habermas J 1970 *Toward a Rational Society: Student Protest, Science, and Politics*, Beacon Press, Boston.

Habermas J 2001 *The Postnational Constellation. Political Essays*, MIT Press, Cambridge.

Haggerty K and Ericson R 2000 The Surveillant Assemblage, *British Journal of Sociology*, vol. 51, no. 4, pp. 605–622.

Ham J, Segrave M and Pickering S 2013 In the Eyes of the Beholder: Border Enforcement, Suspect Travelers and Trafficking Victims, *Anti-Trafficking Review*, vol. 2, pp. 51–66.

Hayes B and Vermeulen M 2012 Borderline: The EU's New Border Surveillance Initiative, Henrich Böll Foundation, available at www.boell.de/sites/default/files/DRV_120523_BORDERLINE_-_Border_Surveillance.pdf, accessed 22 March 2018.

Hayes B, Jones C and Toepfer E 2014 EURODRONES Inc, Statewatch, available at www.statewatch.org/news/2014/feb/sw-tni-eurodrones-inc-feb-2014.pdf, accessed 9 December 2016.

Hennebry J, Grass W and McLaughlin J 2016 Women Migrant Workers' Journey Through the Margins: Labour, Migration and Trafficking, European Union and UN Women, available at www.unwomen.org/-/media/headquarters/attachments/sections/library/publications/2017/women-migrant-workers-journey.pdf?la=en&vs=4009, accessed 12 August 2018.

Hess S and Kasparek B 2017 Under Control? Or Border (as) Conflict: Reflections on the European Border Regime, *Social Inclusion*, vol. 5, no. 3, pp. 58–68.

Heuser H 2014 Blitzverfahren – German Asylum Procedures for Roma from Western Balkan Countries, European Roma Rights Centre (ed) *Going Nowhere? Western Balkan Roma and EU Visa Liberalisation*, European Roma Rights Centre, Budapest, pp. 71–78.

Hills A 2004 *Border Security in the Balkans: Europe's Gatekeepers*, Oxford University Press, Oxford.

Hills A 2006 Control, Protection and Negligence: Border Security in the Western Balkans, in Pickering S and Weber L (eds) *Borders, Mobility and Technologies of Control*, Springer, the Netherlands, pp. 123–148.

Hoff S 2014 Where Is the Funding for Anti-Trafficking Work? A Look at Donor Funds, Policies and Practices in Europe, *Anti-Trafficking Review*, vol. 3, pp. 109–132.

House of Lords Select Committee on International Relations 2018 The UK and the Future of the Western Balkans, available at https://publications.parliament.uk/pa/ld201719/ldselect/ldintrel/53/53.pdf, accessed 17 June 2018.

Hudson B 2003 *Justice in Risk Society*, Sage, London, Thousand Oaks and New Delhi.

Huysmans J 2006 *The Politics of Insecurity: Fear, Migration and Asylum in the EU*, Routledge, London and New York.

Hyndman J and Mountz A 2008 Another Brick in the Wall? Neo-Refoulement and the Externalization of Asylum in Australia and Europe, *Government and Opposition*, vol. 43, no. 2, pp. 259–269.

Ikuteyijo L 2014 The Impact of European Union Migration Policies on Irregular Migration in Sub-Saharan Africa, in Walton-Roberts M and Hennebry J (eds) *Territoriality and Migration in the E.U. Neighbourhood: Spilling over the Wall*, Springer, Dordrecht, pp. 97–110.

Infantino F 2016 *Outsourcing Border Control: Politics and Practice of Contracted Visa Policy in Morocco*, Palgrave Macmillan, New York.

IOM 2008 *World Migration Report: Managing Labour Mobility in the Evolving Global Economy*, IOM, Geneva.

IOM 2015 European Migration Crisis (Western Balkans) Situation Report, available at www.iom.int/sites/default/files/situation_reports/file/European-Migration-Crisis-Western-Balkans-Situation-Report-11Sep2015.pdf, accessed 25 June 2018.

IOM 2016 Key Migration Terms, available at www.iom.int/key-migration-terms, accessed 27 October 2016.

Isin E and Ruppert E 2015 *Being Digital Citizens*, Rowman & Littlefield International, London.

Jakesevic R and Tatalovic S 2016 Securitization (and desecuritization) of the European Refugee Crisis: Croatia in the Regional Context, *Teorija in Praksa*, vol. 53, no. 5, pp. 1246–1278.

Jelačić Kojić M 2016 Migranti i migrantkinje u iregularnom statusu u Republici Srbiji – Aktuelna pitanja i perspektive, Grupa 484, ASTRA and AŽC, Beograd.

Jutarnji List 2015 Među migrantima stižu teroristi Islamske Države: Stručnjak za sigurnost tvrdi: opasnost stiže kroz Makedoniju i Srbiju, 8 July 2015, available at www.jutarnji.hr/medu-migrantima-stizu-teroristi-islamske-drzave-strucnjak-za-sigurnost-tvrdi--opasnost-stize-kroz-makedoniju-i-srbiju/1379156/, accessed 9 April 2018.

Kacarska S 2015 Losing the Rights along the Way: The EU-Western Balkans Visa Liberalisation, *European Politics and Society*, vol. 16, no. 3, pp. 363–378.

Kalm S 2010 Liberalizing Movements? The Political Rationality of Global Migration Management, in Geiger M and Pécoud A (eds) *The Politics of International Migration Management*, Palgrave, Basingstoke and New York, pp. 21–44.

Kaplan D 2003 *Ricoeur's Critical Theory*, State University of New York Press, Albany.

Kapur R 2016 Cross-border Movements and the Law: Renegotiating the Boundaries of Difference, in Kempadoo K, Sanghera J and Pattanaik B (eds) *Trafficking and Prostitution Reconsidered: New Perspectives on Migration, Sex Work, and Human Rights*, Routledge, London and New York, pp. 25–42.

Kasparek B and Speer M 2015 Of Hope. Hungary and the long Summer of Migration, available at www.bordermonitoring.eu/ungarn/2015/09/of-hope-en, accessed 9 May 2018.

Kaufmann V 2002 *Re-Thinking Mobility: Contemporary Sociology*, Ashgate, Aldershot.

Kemp S 2017 Digital in 2017: Global Overview, available at https://wearesocial.com/special-reports/digital-in-2017-global-overview, accessed 20 November 2017.

Kempadoo K and Doezema J 1998 *Global Sex Workers: Rights, Resistance, and Redefinition*, Routledge, New York.

Kempadoo K, Sahgera J and Pattanaik B 2005 *Trafficking and Prostitution Reconsidered: New Perspectives on Migration, Sex Work and Human Rights*, Paradigm Publishers, Boulder.

Kenk V, Križaj J, Štruc V and Dobrišek S 2013 Smart Surveillance Technologies in Border Control, *European Journal of Law and Technology*, available at http://ejlt.org/article/view/230/378, accessed 8 December 2016.

Khalaf R 2016 Technology Comes to the Rescue in Migrant Crisis. *Financial Times*, 24 February, available at www.ft.com/content/a731a50a-da29-11e5-a72f-1e7744c66818?mhq5j=e2, accessed 10 July 2017.

Khalili B 2017 The Mapping Journey Project: Video Installation. 2008–2011, available at www.bouchrakhalili.com/the-mapping-journey-project/, accessed 16 October 2017.

Khosravi S 2010 *'Illegal' Traveller: An Auto-Ethnography of Borders*, Palgrave Macmillan, Hampshire.

Kilibarda P and Kovačević N 2016 *Aida Asylum Information Database: Country Report Serbia*, Beogradski Centar za Ljudska Prava, Belgrade.

Kinnvall C and Svensson T 2015 Introduction: Bordering Securities in a Global World, in Kinnvall C and Svensson T (eds) *Governing Borders and Security: The politics of connectivity and dispersal*, Routledge, London and New York, pp. 1–13.

Kmak M 2015 Between Citizen and Bogus Asylum Seeker: Management of Migration in the EU Through the Technology of Morality, *Social Identities*, vol. 21, no. 4, pp. 395–409.

Korićanac I, Petronijević V and Ćirić D 2013 *Tražioci azila iz Srbije: migracije, siromaštvo i rizici od trgovine ljudima*, Grupa 484, available at http://grupa484.org.rs/publikacije/trazioci-azila-iz-srbije-migracije-siromastvo-i-rizici-od-trgovine-ljudima/, accessed 2 February 2018.

Komel M 2015 Splitting Eurobalkanism: Europeanisation of the Balkans, Balkanisation of Europe – A Short Psychoanalytical Observation, in Zimmerman T and Jakir A (eds) *Europe and the Balkans: Decades of "Europeanization"?*, Königshausen and Neumann, Magdeburg, pp. 81–86.

Koons S 2015 IST Researchers Explore Technology Use in Syrian Refugee Camp. Penn State News, available at http://news.psu.edu/story/350156/2015/03/26/research/ist-researchers-explore-technology-use-syrian-refugee-camp, accessed 20 October 2017.

Koser K 2000 Asylum Policies, Trafficking and Vulnerability, *International Migration*, vol. 38, no. 3, pp. 91–111.

Koser K 2001 New Approaches to Asylum? *International Migration*, vol. 39, no. 6, pp. 85–100.

Koslowski R 2001 Personal Security and State Sovereignty in a Uniting Europe, in Guiraudon V and Joppke C (eds) *Controlling a New Migration World*, Routledge, Abington and New York, pp. 99–120.

Koslowski R 2004 New Technologies of Border Control in an Enlarged Europe, available at www.wilsoncenter.org/publication/299-new-technologies-border-control-enlarged-europe, accessed 2 December 2016.

Kozlowska H 2015 The Most Crucial Item that Migrants and Refugees Carry Is a Smartphone. Quartz, available at https://qz.com/500062/the-most-crucial-item-that-migrants-and-refugees-carry-is-a-smartphone/, accessed 21 November 2017.

Krasteva A 2015 Mobile Balkans: Temporality, Types, Trends, *Glasnik Etnografskog Muzeja SANU*, vol. LXIII, no. 3, pp. 515–536.

Krstić I 2012 *Zastita prava migranata u Republici Srbiji: Priručnik za državne službenike i službenike u javnim samoupravama*, IOM, Beograd.

Kurir 2015 (VIDEO I FOTO) NAJEZDA NA BALKAN: Hiljadu migranata u Đevđeliji čeka voz za Srbiju, 14 August, available at www.kurir.rs/region/makedonija/video-najezda-na-balkan-hiljadu-migranata-u-devdeliji-ceka-voz-za-srbiju-clanak-1894175, accessed 9 April 2018.

Kuzmanovski B 2018 Makedonija pred istorijskom odlukom, Radio Slobdna Evropa, 31 July 2018, available at www.slobodnaevropa.org/a/makedonija-pred-istorijskom-odlukom/29400934.html, accessed 4 August 2018.

Lahav G and Guiraudon V 2000 Comparative Perspectives on Border Control: Away from the Border and Outside the State, in Andreas P and Snyder T (eds) *The Wall Around the West: State Borders and Immigration Controls in North America and Europe*, Rowman and Littlefield Publishers, Lanham, Boulder, New York, Oxford, pp. 55–77.

Lambert C, Pickering S and Alder C 2003 *Critical Chatter: Women and Human Rights in South East Asia*, Carolina Academic Press, Durham.

Lange S 2016 The Western Balkans: Back in the EU Spotlight, Brief Issue, European Union Institute for Security Studies, no. 9, March 2016.

Latonero M 2011 Human Trafficking Online: The Role of Social Networking Sites and Online Classifieds, University of Southern California, available at http://technologyandtrafficking.usc.edu/files/2011/09/HumanTrafficking_FINAL.pdf, accessed 18 January 2018.

Latonero M, Musto J, Boyd Z, Boyle E, Bissel A, Gibson K and Kim J 2012 The Rise of Mobile and the Diffusion of Technology-Facilitated Trafficking, University of Southern Carolina, available at http://technologyandtrafficking.usc.edu/files/2012/11/Tech_Trafficking_2012_SUMMARY.pdf, accessed 13 August 2018.

Lazaridis G 2001 Trafficking and Prostitution: The Growing Exploitation of Migrant Women in Greece, *European Journal of Women's Studies*, vol. 8, no. 1, pp. 67–102.

Lazarova I 2016 Razor-Wired. Stranded Migrants in Macedonia, Awarded theses 2015–2016, European Regional Master's Programme in Democracy and Human Rights in South East Europe, available at https://dspace.eiuc.org/bitstream/handle/20.500.11825/255/Lazarova_GC_S-E_Europe%28ERMA%29_15-16.pdf?sequence=1&isAllowed=y, accessed 26 February 2018.

Lee M 2011 *Trafficking and Global Crime Control*, Sage, Los Angeles, London, New Delhi, Singapore, Washington DC.

Lee G 2015 The 'Vital' Role of Mobile Phones for Refugees and Migrants, Video Report, *BBC News*, 7 September, available at www.bbc.co.uk/news/av/world-europe-34171687/the-vital-role-of-mobile-phones-for-refugees-and-migrants, accessed 14 July 2017.

Leko J 2017 Migration Regimes and the Translation of Human Rights: On the Struggles for Recognition of Romani Migrants in Germany, *Social Inclusion*, vol. 5, no. 3, pp. 77–88.

Levi M and Wall D 2004 Technologies, Security, and Privacy in the Post 9–11 European Information Society, *Journal of Law and Society*, vol. 31, no. 2, pp. 194–220.

Lilyanova V 2016 The Western Balkans: Frontline of the Migrant Crisis, European Parliamentary Research Service, available at www.europarl.europa.eu/RegData/

etudes/BRIE/2016/573949/EPRS_BRI(2016)573949_EN.pdf,   accessed   15
February 2018.

Livingstone E 2016 Angela Merkel Drops 'We Can Do It' Slogan, *Politico*, available at www.politico.eu/article/angela-merkel-drops-the-we-can-do-it-slogan-catchphrase-migration-refugees/, accessed 3 November 2018.

Loader I 2002 Policing, Securitization and Democratization in Europe, *Criminal Justice*, vol. 2, no. 2, pp. 125–153.

Loescher G 2001 *The UNHCR and World Politics*, Oxford University Press, Oxford.

Lukić V 2016 Understanding Transit Asylum Migration: Evidence from Serbia, *International Migration*, vol. 54, no. 4, pp. 31–43.

Lukić Z 2013 Idu na Zapad da prezime, *Novi Magazin*, no. 120, 15 August 2013.

Lyon D 2003a Surveillance as Social Sorting: Computer Codes and Mobile Bodies, in Lyon D (ed) *Surveillance as Social Sorting: Privacy, Risk and Digital Discrimination*, Routledge, London, pp. 13–30.

Lyon D 2003b *Surveillance after September 11*, Polity Press, Oxford.

Lyon D 2005 The Border Is Everywhere: ID Cards, Surveillance and the Other, in Zureik E and Salter M (eds) *Global Surveillance and Policing: Borders, Security, Identity*, Willan Publishing, Cullompton, pp. 66–82.

Lyon D 2007a *Surveillance Studies: An Overview*, Polity Press, Cambridge.

Lyon D 2007b Surveillance, Power and Everyday Life, in Mansell R, Avgerou C, Quah D and Silverstone R (eds) *The Oxford Handbook of Information and Communication Technologies*, Oxford University Press, Oxford, pp. 449–467.

Mahdavi P 2014 *From Trafficking to Terror: Constructing a Global Social Problem*, Routledge, New York.

Mahmut T and Bikovski Z 2014 Macedonia – Creating a Padlocked Cage for Roma Called "Measures for Asylum Seekers", in European Roma Rights Centre (ed) *Going Nowhere? Western Balkan Roma and EU Visa Liberalisation*, European Roma Rights Centre, Budapest, pp. 23–25.

Malaj V and de Rubertis S 2017 Determinants of Migration and the Gravity Model of Migration – Application on Western Balkan Emigration Flows, *Migration Letters*, vol. 14, no. 2, pp. 204–220.

Malecki M 2014 The New Europe: Freedom Against Aliens and Minorities, in Walton-Roberts M and Hennebry J (eds) *Territoriality and Migration in the E.U. Neighbourhood: Spilling over the Wall*, Springer, Dordrecht, pp. 111–124.

Malloch M and Stanley E 2005 The Detention of Asylum Seekers in the UK: Representing Risk, Managing the Dangerous, *Punishment and Society*, vol. 7, no. 1, pp. 53–71.

Marchand M 2008 The Violence of Development and the Migration/Insecurities Nexus: Labour Migration in a North American Context, *Third World Quarterly*, vol. 29, no. 7, pp. 1375–1388.

Martin M 2013 'Trust in Frontex': The 2013 Work Programme, Statewatch, available at www.statewatch.org/analyses/no-219-fsrontex-work-programmes.pdf, accessed 8 December 2016.

Martin L 2017 The Deployment of Drone Technology in Border Surveillance, between Techno-Securitization and Challenges to Privacy and Data Protection, in Friedewald M, Burgess J, Cas J, van Lieshout M, Bellanova R and Peissl, W (eds) *Surveillance, Privacy and Security: Citizens' Perspectives*, Routledge, London, pp. 107–122.

Mau S, Brabandt H, Laube L and Roos C 2012 *Liberal States and the Freedom of Movement: Selective Borders, Unequal Mobility*, Palgrave Macmillan, Basingstoke and New York.

McAdam M 2013 Who's Who at the Border? A Rights-Based Approach to Identifying Human Trafficking at International Borders, *Anti-Trafficking Review*, vol. 2, pp. 33–49.

McCulloch J and Pickering S 2012 Introduction, in McCulloch J and Pickering S (eds) *Borders and Crime: Pre-Crime, Mobility and Serious Harm in an Age of Globalization*, Palgrave Macmillan, London and New York, pp. 1–14.

McCulloch J and Wilson D 2016 *Pre-Crime: Pre-Emption, Precaution and the Future*, Routledge, London and New York.

McGuire M 2012 *Technology, Crime and Justice*, Routledge, London and New York.

McNamara F 2013 Member State Responsibility for Migration Control within Third States – Externalisation Revisited, *European Journal of Migration and Law*, vol. 15, pp. 319–335.

Medić V 2015 Za tri dana više od četiri hiljade uhapšenih migranata, *RTS*, 9 February 2015, available at www.rts.rs/page/stories/sr/story/135/Hronika/1824109/Za+tri+dana+vi%C5%A1e+od+%C4%8Detiri+hiljade++uhap%C5%A1enih+migranata.html accessed 2 March 2018.

Mendel J and Sharapov K 2016 Human Trafficking and Online Networks: Policy, Analysis, and Ignorance, *Antipode*, vol. 48, no. 3, pp. 665–684.

Mezzadra S and Neilson B 2013 *Borders as Method, or, the Multiplication of Labor*, Duke University Press, Durham and London.

Michalowski R 2015 Security and Peace in the US–Mexico Borderlands, in Weber L (ed) *Rethinking Border Control for a Globalizing World*, Routledge, London and New York, pp. 44–63.

Migszol 2016 Out of Sight, Out of Mind? Violence Continues on the Anniversary of the Hungarian-Serbian Border Closure, 15 September, available at www.migszol.com/blog/out-of-sight-out-of-mind-violence-continues-on-the-anniversary-of-the-hungarian-serbian-border-closure, accessed 22 June 2018.

Milan S 2013 *Social Movements and Their Technologies: Wiring Social Change*, Palgrave Macmillan, Basingstoke and New York.

Milivojevic S 2012 The State, Virtual Borders and E-Trafficking: Between Fact and Fiction, in McCulloch J and Pickering S (eds), *Borders and Crime: Pre-Crime, Mobility and Serious Harm in the Age of Globalization*, Palgrave MacMillan, Basingstoke and New York, pp. 72–90.

Milivojevic S 2013 Borders, Technology and Mobility: Cyber-Fortress Europe and Its Emerging Southeast Frontier, *Australian Journal of Human Rights,* vol. 19, no. 3, pp. 99–120.

Milivojevic S 2016 Re-Bordering the Peripheral Global North and Global South: Game of Drones, Immobilising Mobile Bodies and Decentring Perspectives on Drones in Border Policing, in Zavrsnik A (ed) *Drones and Unmanned Aerial Systems: Legal and Social Implications for Security and Surveillance*, Springer, Cham, Heidelberg, New York, Dordrecht, London, pp. 83–100.

Milivojevic S 2018a Race, Gender and Border Control in the Western Balkans, in Bosworth M, Parmar A and Vasquez Y (eds) *Race, Criminal Justice and Migration Control: Enforcing the Boundaries of Belonging*, Oxford University Press, Oxford, pp. 78–92.

Milivojevic S 2018b 'Stealing the Fire' 2.0 Style? Technology, The Pursuit for Mobility, Social Memory and De-Securitization of Migration, *Theoretical Criminology,* first published 20 October, pp. 1–17.

Milivojevic S and Pickering, S 2008 Football and Sex: The 2006 FIFA World Cup and Sex Trafficking, *Temida,* vol. 11, no. 2, pp. 21–48.

Milivojevic S and Pickering S 2013 Trafficking in People, 20 Years on: Sex, Migration and Crime in the Global Anti-Trafficking Discourse and the Rise of the "Global Trafficking Complex", *Current Issues in Criminal Justice,* vol. 25, no. 2, pp. 585–604.

Milivojevic S and Segrave M 2017 Gendered Exploitation in the Digital Border Crossing?: An Analysis of the Human Trafficking and Information-Technology Nexus, in Segrave M and Vitis L (eds) *Gender, Technology and Violence,* Routledge, London and New York, pp. 28–44.

Milivojevic S, Segrave M and Pickering S 2017 The Limits of Migration-Related Human Rights: Connecting Exploitation to Immobility, in Weber L, Fishwick E and Marmo M (eds) *The Routledge International Handbook on Criminology and Human Rights,* Routledge, London and New York, pp. 291–300.

Miller J, Copes H and Hochstetler A 2015 The History and Evolution of Qualitative Criminology, in Copes H and Miller J (eds) *The Routledge Handbook of Qualitative Criminology,* Routledge, London and New York, pp. 3–21.

Ministarstvo za ljudska i manjinska prava 2010 Strategija za unapređivanje položaja Roma u Republici Srbiji, available at www.inkluzija.gov.rs/wp-content/uploads/2010/03/Strategija-SR-web-FINAL.pdf, accessed 2 March 2018.

Mitsilegas V 2015 Rethinking Border Control from the Perspective of the Individual, in Weber L (ed) *Rethinking Border Control for a Globalizing World,* Routledge, London and New York, pp. 15–31.

Monahan T 2006 Questioning Surveillance and Security, in Monahan T (ed) *Surveillance An Security: Technological Politics and Power in Everyday Life,* Routledge, London and New York, pp. 1–23.

Morača T 2014 Migrantkinje i migrant u lokalnim zajednicama u Srbiji, ATINA, available at http://atina.org.rs/biblioteka/publikacije/Migranti%20i%20migrant kinje%20u%20lokalnim%20zajednicama%20u%20Srbiji.finalno.pdf, accessed 2 February 2018.

Morehouse C and Blomfield M 2011 *Irregular Migration in Europe,* Transatlantic Council on Migration, Washington DC, Migration Policy Institute.

Morrison J and Crosland B 2000 *The Trafficking and Smuggling of Refugees: The End Game in European Asylum Policy,* available at http://library.gayhomeland.org/0047/EN/EN_traffick.pdf, accessed 18 January 2018.

Mountz A and Kempin R 2016 The Spatial Logic of Migration Governance Along the Southern Frontier of the European Union, in Walton-Roberts M and Hennebry J (eds) *Territoriality and Migration in the E.U. Neighbourhood: Spilling Over the Wall,* Springer, Dordrecht, Heidelberg, New York, London, pp. 85–96.

Möllers J, Arapi-Gjini A, Herzfeld T and Xhema S 2017a Exit or Voice? The Recent Drivers of Kosovar Out-Migration, *International Migration,* vol. 55, no. 3, pp. 173–186.

Möllers J, Traikova D, Herzfeld T and Bajrami E 2017b Study on Rural Migration and Return Migration in Kosovo, Discussion Paper, Leibniz Institute of Agricultural Development in Transition Economies, No. 166, available at http://nbn-resolving.de/urn:nbn:de:gbv:3:2-76033, accessed 22 March 2018.

Muller B 2010 *Security, Risk and Biometric State*, Routledge, New York.

Murati A 2015 An Asylum Story from the Heart of Europe – What is Going on in Kosovo? *European Western Balkans*, available at http://europeanwesternbalkans. com/2015/02/12/an-asylum-story-from-the-heart-of-europe-what-is-going-on-in-kosovo/, accessed 1 March 2018.

Musto J and boyd d 2014 The Trafficking-Technology Nexus, *Social Politics*, vol. 21, no. 3, pp. 461–483.

Neal A 2009 Securitization and Risk at the EU Border: The Origins of FRONTEX, *Journal of Common Market Studies*, vol. 47, no. 2, pp. 333–356.

Nelken D 2010 Human Trafficking and Legal Culture, *Israeli Law Review*, vol. 43, no. 3, pp. 479–513.

Neocleous M 2006 Theoretical Foundations of the 'New Police Science', in Dubber M and Valverde M (eds) *The New Police Science: The Police Power in Domestic and International Governance*, Stanford University Press, Stanford, pp. 17–41.

Newell B, Gomez R and Guajardo V 2016 Information Seeking, Technology Use, and Vulnerability among Migrants at the United States-Mexico Border. *The Information Society* vol. 32, no. 3, pp. 176–191.

Nieuwenhuys C and Pecoud A 2007 Human Trafficking, Information Campaigns, and Strategies of Migration Control, *American Behavioral Scientist*, vol. 50, no. 12, pp. 1674–1695.

Nikolić-Ristanović V, Ćopić S, Simeunović-Patić B, Milivojević S and Mihić B 2004 *Trgovina ljudima u Srbiji*, OSCE, Beograd.

Norris D 2015 Mind the Gap!: The Balkans as Literary Trope, in Zimmerman T and Jakir A (eds) *Europe and the Balkans: Decades of "Europeanization"?* Königshausen and Neumann, Magdeburg, pp. 33–38.

Novak Lalić G 2013 Europeizacija hrvatskoga sustava azila: mehanizmi i instrumenti utjecaja Europske unije na javne politike i institucije, *Društvena istraživanja*, vol. 22, no. 2, pp. 237–255.

Nwogu V 2014 Anti-Trafficking Interventions in Nigeria and the Principal-Agent Aid Model, *Anti-Trafficking Review*, no. 3, pp. 41–63.

O'Connell Davidson R 2015 *Modern Slavery: The Margins of Freedom*, Palgrave Macmillan, New York.

Oltermann P 2016 German Proposal Could See Refugees' Phones Searched by Police. *The Guardian*, 11 August, available at www.theguardian.com/world/2016/aug/11/germany-security-proposals-refugees-phones-searched-suspicious-posts-social-media, accessed 10 July 2017.

Ortega V 2011 Digital Technology, Aesthetic Imperfection and Political Film-Making: Illegal Bodies in Motion, *Transnational Cinemas* vol. 2, no. 1, pp. 3–19.

OSCE 2006 Managing Borders in a "Borderless" World, OSCE Magazine, Vienna, available at www.osce.org/secretariat/19833?download=true, accessed 4 August 2018.

Pantić, M 2013 Pasoš pod mišku, pa pred ambasadu, *Novi Magazin*, no. 125, 19 September 2013.

Parker S 2015 'Unwanted Invaders': The Representation of Refugees and Asylum Seekers in the UK and Australian Print Media, *eSharp 23: Myth and Nation*, available at www.gla.ac.uk/media/media_404384_en.pdf, accessed 9 March 2018.

Parkin J 2011 The Difficult Road to the Schengen Information System II: The Legacy of "Laboratories" and the Cost for Fundamental Rights and the Rule of Law, Centre for European Policy Studies, available at http://ceps.eu, accessed 1 December 2016.

Pasplanova M 2008 Undocumented vs. Illegal Migrant: Towards Terminological Coherence, *Migraciones Internacionales*, vol. 4, no. 3, June 2008, available at www.scielo.org.mx/scielo.php?script=sci_arttext&pid=S1665-89062008000100004, accessed 22 May 2018.

Pawlak P 2014 Reducing Uncertainties in Cyberspace through Confidence and Capacity-Building Measures, in Giacomello G (ed) *Security in Cyberspace: Targeting Nations, Infrastructures, Individuals*, Bloomsbury, New York and London, pp. 39–58.

Pavlović A 2016 A Passage to Europe: Serbia and the Refugee Crisis, *Contemporary Southern Europe*, vol. 3, no. 1, pp. 59–65.

Pécoud A 2010 Informing Migrants to Manage Migration? An analysis of IOM's Information Campaigns, in Geiger M and Pécoud A (eds) *The Politics of International Migration Management*, Palgrave, Basingstoke and New York, pp. 184–201.

Pickering S 2011 *Women, Borders and Violence*, Springer, New York.

Pickering S 2013 Deadly Borders: Women and Children Seeking Asylum, *The Conversation*, 3 April, available at http://theconversation.com/deadly-borders-women-and-children-seeking-asylum-13099, accessed 2 February 2018.

Pickering S and Cochrane B 2013 Irregular Border-Crossing Deaths and Gender: Where, How and Why Women Die Crossing Borders, *Theoretical Criminology*, vol. 17, no. 1, pp. 27–48.

Pickering S and Ham J 2014 Hot Pants at the Border: Sorting Sex Work from Trafficking, *The British Journal of Criminology*, vol. 54, no. 1, pp. 2–19.

Pickering S and Weber L 2006 Borders, Mobility and Technologies of Control, in Pickering S and Weber L (eds) *Borders, Mobility and Technologies of Control*, Springer, Dordrecht, pp. 1–19.

Pickering S and Weber L 2013 Policing Transversal Borders, in Aas K and Bosworth M (eds) *The Borders of Punishment: Migration, Citizenship, and Social Exclusion*, Oxford University Press, Oxford, pp. 93–110.

Pickering S, Bosworth M and Aas K F 2014 The Criminology of Mobility, in Pickering S and Ham J (eds) *The Routledge Handbook on Crime and International Migration*, Routledge, London and New York, pp. 382–395.

Poletta F 2006 *It Was Like a Fever: Storytelling in Protest and Politics*, The University of Chicago Press, Chicago and London.

Politika 2013 Navala lažnih azilanata može da ukine bezvizni režim, 12 September, available at www.politika.rs/scc/clanak/269868/Навала-лажних-азиланата-може-да-укине-безвизни-режим, accessed 9 March 2018.

Popescu G 2011 *Bordering and Ordering the Twenty-first Century*, Rowman & Littlefield Publishers, Lanham and Plymouth.

Popescu G 2015 Controlling Mobility: Embodying Borders, in Szary A and Giraut F (eds) *Borderities and the Politics of Contemporary Mobile Borders*, Palgrave, Basingstoke and New York, pp. 100–115.

Press Online 2011 Prvi let bespilotne letelice proizvedene u Srbiji, 19 October, available at http://pressrs.ba/sr/vesti/vesti_dana/story/2387/Prvi+let+bespilotne+letelice+proizvedene+u+Srbiji.html, accessed 9 December 2016.

Price R 2015 Google Maps Is Putting Europe's Human Traffickers Out of Business. Business Insider Uk, 9 September, available at http://uk.businessinsider.com/refugee-crisis-how-syrian-migrants-use-smartphones-avoid-traffickers-2015-9, accessed 10 July 2017.

Pugliese J 2013 Technologies of Extraterritorialisation, Statist Visuality and Irregular Migrants and Refugees, *Griffith Law Review*, vol. 22, no. 3, pp. 571–597.

Raeymaekers T 2014 Europe's Bleeding Border and the Mediterranean as a Relational Space, *ACME*, vol. 13, no. 2, pp. 163–172.

Ram A 2015 Smartphones Bring Solace and Aid to Desperate Refugees, *WIRED*, available at www.wired.com/2015/12/smartphone-syrian-refugee-crisis/, accessed 20 October 2017.

Reed T 2014 *Digitized Lives: Culture, Power, and Social Change in the Internet Era*, Routledge, London and New York.

Renner S and Trauner F 2009 Creeping EU-Membership in Southeast Europe: The Dynamics of EU Rule Transfer to the Western Balkans, *Journal of European Integration* vol. 31, no. 4, pp. 449–465.

Reslow N 2012 The Role of Third Countries in EU Migration Policy: The Mobility Partnerships, *European Journal of Migration and Law*, vol. 14, no. 4, pp. 393–415.

Riegert B 2012 EU Criticizes Roma Asylum Applications, Deutsche Welle, 16 October, available at www.dw.de/eu-criticizes-roma-asylum-applications/a-16309833, accessed 2 March 2018.

Rovisco M 2015 Community Arts, New Media and the Desecuritisation of Migration and Asylum Seeker Issues in the UK, in Kinnvall C and Svensson T (eds) *Governing Borders and Security: The Politics of Connectivity and Dispersal*, Routledge, London and New York, pp. 98–115.

RTS 2011 Oštra konrola lažnih azilanata, 10 March, available at www.rts.rs/page/stories/sr/story/125/drustvo/856112/ostra-kontrola-laznih-azilanata.html, accessed 18 June 2018.

RTS 2015 Bavarske vlasti traže zaustavljanje priliva azilanata sa Kosova, available at www.rts.rs/page/stories/sr/story/10/Svet/1825381/Bavarske+vlasti+tra%C5%BEe+zaustavljanje+priliva+azilanata+sa+Kosova.html, accessed 1 March 2018.

RTV 2015 Veljović: Smanjenje lažnih azilanata prioritet, 29 October, available at http://rtv.rs/sr_lat/drustvo/veljovic-smanjenje-laznih-azilanata-prioritet_433033.html, accessed 8 April 2018.

Rudić M 2012 Čekanje zime u džungli, *Vreme*, 29 November.

Rudić M 2014 Dijalogom do tolerancije i nenasilja, *Vreme*, br. 1232, available at www.vreme.com/cms/view.php?id=1220334, accessed 17 January 2018.

Rujević N 2017 Ne trošiti pare na lažne tražioce azila, Deutsche Welle, 21 November, available at www.dw.com/sr/ne-tro%C5%A1iti-pare-na-la%C5%BEne-tra%C5%BEioce-azila/a-41453624, accessed 7 March 2018.

Sanchez G 2013 Four Corners: Human Smuggling and the Spectacle of Suffering, *The Conversation*, 19 November, available at https://theconversation.com/four-corners-human-smuggling-and-the-spectacle-of-suffering-20405, accessed 2 January 2018.

Santora M and Dimishkovski A 2018 Macedonia Moves Ahead with Name Change, Helping Its NATO Bid, *The New York Times*, 19 October, available at www.nytimes.com/2018/10/19/world/europe/macedona-greece-name.html, accessed 1 November 2018.

Sardelić J 2014 Romani Minorities and the Variety of Migration Patterns in the Post-Yugoslav Space, in European Roma Rights Centre (ed) *Going nowhere? Western Balkan Roma and EU Visa Liberalisation*, European Roma Rights Centre, Budapest, pp. 15–22.

Sassen S 1999 *Guests and Aliens*, New York Press, New York.

Sassen S 2000 Women's Burden: Counter-Geographies of Globalization and the Feminization of Survival, *Journal of International Affairs*, vol. 53, no. 2, pp. 503–524.

Sassen S 2006 *Territory, Authority, Rights: From Medieval to Global Assemblages*, Princeton University Press, Princeton.

Sassen S 2014 Anti-Immigrant Politics Along with Institutional Incorporation? in Walton-Roberts M and Hennebry J (eds) *Territoriality and Migration in the E.U. Neighbourhood: Spilling over the Wall*, Springer, Dordrecht, pp. 13–26.

Schaub M 2012 Lines Across the Desert: Mobile Phone Use and Mobility in the Context of Trans-Saharan Migration. *International Technology for Development* vol. 18, no. 2, pp. 126–144.

Scheel S 2017 'The Secret is to Look Good on Paper': Appropriating Mobility within and Against a Machine of Illegalization, in De Genova N (ed) *The Borders of Europe: Autonomy of Migration, Tactics of Bordering*, Duke University Press, Durham and London, pp. 37–63.

Schumann S 2015 *How the Internet Shapes Collective Action*, Palgrave, Basingstoke and New York.

Scott J W 2012 European Politics of Borders, Border Symbolism and Cross-Border Cooperation, in Wilson T M and Donnan H (eds) *A Companion to Border Studies*, Wiley-Blackwell, Chichester, pp. 83–99.

Segrave M 2017 *Exploited and Illegal: Unlawful Migrant Workers in Australia*, Border Crossing Observatory and Monash University, Melbourne.

Segrave M and Milivojevic S 2015 Human Trafficking: Examining Global Responses, in Barak G (ed) *The Routledge International Handbook of the Crimes of the Powerful*, Routledge, Abingdon, Oxon, pp. 132–143.

Segrave, M, Milivojevic, S and Pickering, S 2009 *Sex Trafficking: International Context and Response*, Willan Publishing, Devon.

Segrave M, Milivojevic S and Pickering S 2018 *Sex Trafficking and Modern Slavery: The Absence of Evidence*, Routledge, London and New York.

Seltzer N, Johnson A and Amira K 2013 Revisiting Dynamic Social Impact Theory: Extensions and Applications for Political Science. *International Journal of Politics, Culture, and Society* vol. 26, no. 4, pp. 349–367.

Sharma N 2003 Travel Agency: A Critique of Anti-Trafficking Campaigns, *Refuge*, vol. 21, no. 3, pp. 53–65.

Sheptycki J 1998 The Global Cops Cometh: Reflections on Transnationalization, Knowledge Work and Policing Subculture, *British Journal of Sociology*, vol. 49, no. 1, pp. 57–74.

Simurdić M 2016 Region između geografije i geopolitike- pogled iz Srbije, in Simurdić M, Teokarević J, Minić J and Đukanović D (eds) *Zapadni Balkan: Između geografije i geopolitike*, Fondacija Fridriech Ebert i Evropski pokret u Srbiji, available at http://library.fes.de/pdf-files/bueros/belgrad/12678.pdf, accessed 10 October 2016.

Sky Plus 2013 Srbija Realno, 3 December. Available at www.youtube.com/watch?v=FGVwclHxtKw, accessed 22 March 2018.

Sommo L 2011 EU Proposes Mechanism to Suspend Visa-Free Regime, Balkan Insight, available at www.balkaninsight.com/en/article/eu-proposes-mechanism-to-suspend-visa-free-regime, accessed 7 March 2018.

Srbija Danas 2018 Vučić: Mlade koji odlaze iz Srbije će zameniti migranti, 18 March, available at www.srbijadanas.net/vucic-mlade-koji-odlaze-iz-srbije-ce-zameni-migranti-video/, accessed 7 September 2018.

Staab A 2011 *European Union Explained, Second Edition: Institutions, Actors, Global Impact*, Indiana University Press, Bloomington, Indianapolis.

Statista 2017a Number of Mobile Phone Users Worldwide from 2013 to 2019 (in billions), available at www.statista.com/statistics/274774/forecast-of-mobile-phone-users-worldwide/, accessed 20 November 2017.

Statista 2017b Facebook- Statistics and Facts, available at www.statista.com/topics/751/facebook/, accessed 3 January 2018.

Stein A 2013 Turkey's Missile Programs: A Work in Progress, available at www.edam.org.tr/Media/Files/208/Turkey%20Missile%20Programs.pdf, accessed 9 December 2016.

Stević A and Car V 2016 Vizualno portretiranje izbjeglica i migranata – ikonske fotografije, available at http://unizg.academia.edu/ViktorijaCar, accessed 24 April 2018.

Stojić-Mitrović M 2014 Serbian Migration Policy Concerning Irregular Migration and Asylum in the Context of the EU Integration Process, *Issues in Ethnology and Anthropology*, vol. 9, no. 4, pp. 1105–1120.

Stumpf J 2007 The Crimmigration Crisis: Immigrants, Crime, and Sovereign State, *Lewis & Clark Law School Legal Research Paper Series*, vol. 2, pp. 1–44.

Stute D 2015 Kako smanjiti priliv izbeglica sa Kosova? available at www.dw.de/kako-smanjiti-priliv-izbeglica-sa-kosova/a-18255441, accessed 1 March 2018.

Squire V 2010 *The Contested Politics of Mobility: Borderzones and Irregularity*, Routledge, London.

Surtees R and de Kerchove F 2014 Who Funds Re/integration? Ensuring Sustainable Services for Trafficking Victims, *Anti-Trafficking Review*, no. 3, pp. 64–86.

Suilleabhain A 2013 Already Pushing Legal Boundaries, EU's Border Agency Now Seeking Drones, *Global Observatory*, 27 March, available at http://theglobalobservatory.org/analysis/465-already-pushing-legal-boundaries-eus-border-agency-now-seeks-drones.html, accessed 9 December 2016.

Sun Z, Wang P, Vuran M, Al-Rodhaan M, Al-Dhelaan A and Akyildiz I 2011 BorderSense: Border Patrol Through Advanced Wireless Sensor Networks, *Ad Hoc Networks*, vol. 9, no. 3, pp. 468–477.

Szary A and Giraut F 2015 Borderities: The Politics of Contemporary Mobile Borders, in Szary A and Giraut F (eds) *Borderities and the Politics of Contemporary Mobile Borders*, Baskingstoke and New York, Palgrave, pp. 1–19.

Šalamon N 2016 Asylum Systems in the Western Balkan Countries: Current Issues, *International Migration*, vol. 54, no. 6, pp. 151–163.

Tashman B 2015 Trump: Why Do Refugees Have Cell Phones? RightWingWatch.org, available at www.rightwingwatch.org/post/trump-why-do-refugees-have-cell-phones/, accessed 20 October 2017.

Telegraf 2015 PRETI NAM HUMANITARNA KATASTROFA: 50,000 izbeglica NADIRE u Srbiju. Ponestaju ZALIHE HRANE I VODE, 24 August, available at www.telegraf.rs/vesti/1716626-preti-nam-humanitarna-katastrofa-50-000-izbeglica-nadire-u-srbiju-ponestaju-zalihe-hrane-i-vode, accessed 8 March 2018.

Telegraf 2015 SRBIJA NA UDARU MIGRANATA: 7,000 izbeglica za noć stigne iz Makedonije. Sledi još VEĆI TALAS, 24 August, available at www.telegraf.rs/vesti/1716623-srbija-na-udaru-migranata-7-000-izbeglica-za-noc-stigne-iz-makedonije-sledi-jos-veci-talas, accessed 9 April 2018.

Telegraf 2015 TERORISTI SE KRIJU MEĐU MIGRANTIMA: Na stotine njih prošlo kroz Srbiju, sumnja se da su neki još uvek u našoj zemlji! (FOTO), 22

August, available at www.telegraf.rs/vesti/1714215-teroristi-se-kriju-medju-migrantima-na-stotine-njih-proslo-kroz-srbiju-sumnja-se-da-su-neki-jos-uvek-u-nasoj-zemlji-foto, accessed 9 April 2018.

Teokarević J 2016 Skroman napredak ka sve manje poželjnoj Evropskoj Uniji: Zapadni Balkan u evropskim integracijama 2015–2016. godine, in Simurdić M, Teokarević J, Minić J and Đukanović D (eds) *Zapadni Balkan: Između geografije i geopolitike*, Fondacija Fridriech Ebert i Evropski pokret u Srbiji, available at http://library.fes.de/pdf-files/bueros/belgrad/12678.pdf, accessed 10 October 2016.

The Delegation of the EU to the Republic of Serbia 2014 VIS Start of Operations in Serbia: Collection of Fingerprints for Schengen Visas, available at http://europa.rs/vis-start-of-operations-in-serbia-collection-of-fingerprints-for-schengen-visas/?lang=en, accessed 27 February 2018.

The Economist 2013 Asylum System Abuse: The EU and the Balkans, 5 January 2013, pp. 38–39.

The Economist 2017 Phones Are Now Indispensable for Refugees, 11 February, available at www.economist.com/news/international/21716637-technology-has-made-migrating-europe-easier-over-time-it-will-also-make-migration, accessed 10 July 2017.

The Guardian 2015 Macedonia Declares State of Emergency to Tackle Migrant Crisis, 20 August, available at www.theguardian.com/world/2015/aug/20/macedonia-state-of-emergency-migrant-crisis, accessed 15 July 2018.

Todorović M 2011 Putnici niotkuda za nigde, *Vreme*, 3 February 2011.

Trauner F 2011 *The Europeanisation of the Western Balkans: EU justice and home affairs in Croatia and Macedonia*, Manchester University Press, Manchester and New York.

Trauner F and Manigrassi E 2014 When Visa-Free Travel Becomes Difficult to Achieve and Easy to Lose: The EU Visa Free Dialogues after the EU's Experience with the Western Balkans, *European Journal of Migration and Law*, vol. 16, no. 1, pp. 125–145.

TV N1 2015 Srpsko-mađarsku granicu čuvaju i nemački policajci, 12 February, available at http://rs.n1info.com/a34963/Vesti/Srpsko-madjarsku-granicu-cuvaju-i-nemacki-policajci.html, accessed 1 March 2018.

Turak N 2018 The Future of Europe's Elections Will be All about Migration, Foreign Minister Says, available at www.cnbc.com/2018/06/01/the-future-of-europes-elections-will-be-all-about-migration.html, accessed 30 July 2018.

Turek J 2013 Human Security and Development Issues in Human Trafficking, in Bourke M (ed) *Human Trafficking: Interdisciplinary Perspectives*, Routledge, New York, pp. 73–87.

UN 2000 *Protocol to Prevent, Surpress and Punish Trafficking in Persons, Especially Women and Children*, Supplementing the UN Convention Against Transnational Organized Crime, UN, New York.

UN Department of Economic and Social Affairs 2015 International Migration Report 2015, United Nations, New York, available at www.un.org/en/development/desa/population/migration/publications/migrationreport/docs/Migration Report2015_Highlights.pdf accessed 23 January 2018.

UN General Assembly Human Rights Council 2018 Report of the Special Rapporteur on trafficking in persons, especially women and children, 18 June–6 July, Agenda item 3.

UNDP 2016 Kosovo Human Development Report 2016, UNDP, available at http:// hdr.undp.org/en/content/kosovo-human-development-report-2016, accessed 9 March 2018.

UNFPA 2013 *Linking Population, Poverty and Development,* available at www.unfpa. org/pds/migration.html, accessed 18 January 2018.

UNHCR 2006 Guidelines on International Protection: The Application of Article 1A(2) of the 1951 Convention and/or 1967 Protocol Relating to the Status of Refugees to Victims of Trafficking and Persons at Risk of Being Trafficked, *HCR/ GIP/06/07, 7 April,* UN Refugee Agency.

UNHCR 2016 *Connecting Refugees: How Internet and Mobile Connectivity Can Improve Refugee Well-Being and Transform Humanitarian Action,* UNHCR, Geneva.

UN Women 2018 Women, available at www.unhcr.org/uk/women.html, accessed 25 June 2018.

U.S. Customs and Border Protection 2015 Trusted Traveller Programs, available at www.cbp.gov/travel/trusted-traveler-programs, accessed 22 November 2016.

Valverde M 2001 Governing Security, Governing through Security, in Daniels R, Macklem P and Roach K (eds) *The Security of Freedom: Essays on Canada's Anti-Terrorism Bill,* Toronto University Press, Toronto, pp. 83–92.

Van der Ploeg I 1999 'EURODAC' and the Illegal Body as Information: Normative Issues in the Socio-Technical Coding of the Body, in Lyon D (ed) *Surveillance as Social Sorting: Privacy, Risk, and Automated Discrimination,* Routledge, New York, pp. 57–73.

Van der Ploeg I 2006 Borderline Identities: The Enrolment of Bodies in the Technological Reconstruction of Borders, in Monahan T (ed) *Surveillance and Society: Technological Politics and Everyday Life,* Routledge, New York, pp. 177–193.

Van der Ploeg I and Sprenkels I 2011 Migration and the Machine-Readable Body: Identification and Biometrics, in Dijstelbloem H and Meijer A (eds) *Migration and the New Technological Borders of Europe,* Palgrave Macmillan, Basingstoke and New York, pp. 68–104.

Vasilev G 2015 Open Borders and the Survival of National Cultures, in Weber L (ed) *Rethinking Border Control for a Globalizing World,* Routledge, London and New York, pp. 98–115.

Vaughan-Williams N 2010 The UK Border Security Continuum: Virtual Biopolitics and the Simulation of the Sovereign Ban, *Environment and Planning,* vol. 28, pp. 1071–1083.

Vaughan-Williams N 2011 Off-Shore Biopolitical Border Security: The EU's Global Response to Migration, Piracy and 'Risky' Subjects, in Bialasiewicz L (ed) *Europe in the World: EU Geopolitics and the Making of the European Space,* Ashgate, Surrey and Burlington, pp. 185–200.

Vaughan-Williams N 2015 *Europe's Border Crisis: Biopolitical Security and Beyond,* Oxford University Press, Oxford.

Večernje Novosti 2011 Sa aerodroma Nikola Tesla vraćeni Romi, 1 December, available at www.novosti.rs/vesti/beograd.74.html:355921-Sa-aerodroma-Nikola-Tesla-vraceni-Romi, accessed 20 June 2018.

Večernje Novosti 2012 Lažni azilanti: Oskudica vraća begunce kući, 18 October, available at www.novosti.rs/vesti/naslovna/drustvo/aktuelno.290.html:401908-Lazni-azilanti-Oskudica-vraca-begunce-kuci, accessed 22 March 2018.

Večernje Novosti 2013 Azilanti: Romi će nam vratiti vize, 28 January, available at http://91.222.5.72/vesti/naslovna/drustvo/aktuelno.290.html:417091-Azilanti-Romi-ce-nam-vratiti-vize, accessed 18 June 2018.

Vullnetari J and King R 2014 'Women Here Are Like at the Time of Enver [Hoxha]…': Socialist and Post-Socialist Gendered Mobility in Albanian Society, in Burrell K and Horschelman K (eds) *Mobility in Socialist and Post-Socialist States: Societies on the Move*, Palgrave, Basingstoke, pp. 122–147.

Vujadinović S, Šabić D, Joksimović D, Golić R, Živković L J and Gatarić D 2013 Asylum Seekers from Serbia and the Problem of Returnees: Why Serbia is among the World's Leading Countries in Number of Asylum Seekers, *Dve Domovini*, no. 37, pp. 53–68.

Vujić T 2015 Evropa nemoćna pred bujicom migranata, 1 September, available at www.politika.rs/rubrike/Svet/Evropa-nemocna-pred-bujicom-migranata.lt. html, accessed 8 March 2018.

Vukelić T 2013 Immigration of Roma from Republic of Serbia, *Sfera Politicii*, Cuprins 173, available at www.sferapoliticii.ro/sfera/173/art22-Vukelic.php, accessed 8 March 2018.

Vukosavljević D 2011 Broj laznih azilanata drastično smanjen, Politika, 22 December, available at www.politika.rs/sr/clanak/202041/Број-лажних-азиланата-драст ично-смањен, accessed 2 March 2018.

Vukov T and Sheller M 2013 Border Work: Surveillant Assemblages, Virtual Fences, and Tactical Counter-Media, *Social Semiotics*, vol. 23, no. 2, pp. 225–241.

Walker R 2006 The Double Outside of the Modern International, *Ephemera: Theory and Politics in Organization*, vol. 6, no. 1, pp. 56–69.

Wall T and Monahan T 2011 Surveillance and Violence from Afar: The Politics of Drones and Liminal Security-Scapes, *Theoretical Criminology*, vol. 15, no. 3, pp. 239–254.

Walters W 2011 Foucault and Frontiers: Notes on the Birth of the Humanitarian Border, in Bröckling U, Krasmann S and Lemke T (eds) *Governmentality: Current Issues and Future Challenges*, Routledge, London and New York, pp. 138–164.

Weber L 2003 Down that Wrong Road: Discretion in Decision to Detain Asylum Seekers Arriving at UK Ports, *The Howard Journal*, vol. 42, no. 3, pp. 248–262.

Weber L 2006 The Shifting Frontiers of Migration Control, in Pickering S and Weber L (eds) *Borders, Mobility and Technologies of Control*, Springer, Dordrecht, pp. 21–44.

Weber L 2013 *Policing Non-Citizens*, Routledge, London and New York.

Weber L 2015a *Rethinking Border Control for a Globalizing World*, Routledge, London and New York.

Weber L 2015b Peace at the Border: A Thought Experiment, in Weber L (ed) *Rethinking Border Control for a Globalizing World*, Routledge, London and New York, pp. 1–14.

Weber L and Lee M 2009 Preventing Indeterminate Threats: Fear, Terror and the Politics of Preemption, in Lee M and Farrall S (eds) *Fear of Crime: Critical Voices in An Age of Anxiety*, Routledge-Cavendish, New York, pp. 59–81.

Weber L and Pickering S 2011 *Globalization and Borders: Death at the Global Frontier*, Palgrave Macmillan, Hampshire.

Weitzer R 2007 The Social Construction of Sex Trafficking: Ideology and Institutionalization of a Moral Crusade, *Politics & Society*, vol. 35, no. 3, pp. 447–475.

Wendling M 2015 Laith Al Saleh: This Viral Photo Falsely Claims to Show an IS Fighter Posing as a Refugee, available at www.bbc.com/news/blogs-trending-34176631, accessed 6 September 2018.

Wilson D 2006 Biometrics, Borders and the Ideal Suspect, in Pickering S and Weber L (eds) *Borders, Mobilities and Technologies of Control*, Springer, Dordrecht, pp. 87–109.

Wilson D 2013 Border Militarization, Technology and Crime Control, in Pickering S and Ham J (eds) *The Routledge Handbook on Crime and International Migration*, Routledge, Abingdon and New York, pp. 141–154.

Wilson D and Weber L 2008 Surveillance, Risk and Preemption on the Australian Border, *Surveillance & Society*, vol. 5, no. 2, pp. 124–141.

Wilson T and Donnan H 2012 Borders and Border Studies, in Wilson and Donnan (eds) *A Companion to Border Studies*, Wiley-Blackwell, Chichester, pp. 1–26.

Wolff J 1993 On the Road Again: Metaphors of Travel in Cultural Criticism, *Cultural Studies*, vol. 7, no. 2, pp. 224–239.

Women's Refugee Commission 2016 No Safety for Refugee Women on the European Route: Report from the Balkans, available at www.eldis.org/document/A100294, accessed 25 June 2018.

Wonders N 2006 Global Flows, Semi-Permeable Borders and New Channels of Inequality: Border Crossers and Border Performativity, in Pickering S and Weber L (eds) *Borders, Mobility, and Technologies of Control*, Springer, Dordrecht, pp. 63–86.

Wonders B, Solop F and Wonders N 2012 Information Sampling and Linking: Reality Hunger and the Digital Knowledge Commons, *Contemporary Social Sciences: Journal of the Academy of Social Sciences*, iFirst, pp. 1–16.

Young J 2007 *The Vertigo of Late Modernity*, Sage, London.

Zaragoza-Christiani J 2017 Containing the Refugee Crisis: How the EU Turned the Balkans and Turkey into an EU Borderland, *The International Spectator*, vol. 52, no. 4, pp. 59–75.

Zedner L 2007 Pre-Crime and Post-Criminology, *Theoretical Criminology*, vol. 11, no. 2, pp. 261–281.

Zedner L 2009 *Security*, Routledge, London and New York.

Zijlstra J and van Liempt I 2017 Smart(phone) Travelling: Understanding the Use and Impact of Mobile Technology on Irregular Migration Journeys, *International Journal of Migration and Border Studies*, vol. 3, no. 2–3, pp. 174–191.

Zimmerman T and Jakir A 2015 Introduction, in Zimmerman T and Jakir A (eds) Europe and the Balkans: Decades of "Europeanization"? Königshausen and Neumann, Magdeburg, pp. 9–30.

Index

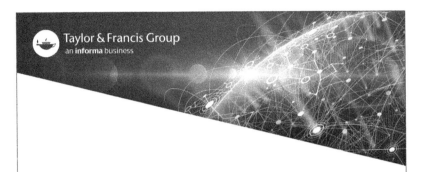